INSTRUCTIONAL CONSULTATION

SCHOOL PSYCHOLOGY

A series of volumes edited by
Thomas R. Kratochwill and James E. Ysseldyke

Stark, McGee, and Menolascino • International Handbook of Community
Services for the Mentally Retarded

Horne • Attitudes Toward Handicapped Students:
Professional, Peer, and Parent Reactions

Thaw and Cuvo • Developing Responsive Human Services:
New Perspectives About Residential Treatment Organizations

Elliott and Witt • The Delivery of Psychological Services in Schools:
Concepts, Processes, and Issues

Maher and Forman • A Behavioral Approach to Education of
Children and Youth

Rosenfield • Instructional Consultation

Sandoval • Crisis Counseling, Intervention, and Prevention in the Schools

INSTRUCTIONAL CONSULTATION

Sylvia A. Rosenfield
Temple University

1987

LAWRENCE ERLBAUM ASSOCIATES, PUBLISHERS
Hillsdale, New Jersey   Hove and London

To my beloved parents,
Leah Eisenberg Schulman and Morris Schulman,
who first modeled for me the concepts of caring and support
upon which consultation thrives

Lawrence Erlbaum Associates, Inc., Publishers
365 Broadway
Hillsdale, New Jersey 07642

Library of Congress Cataloging-in-Publication Data

Rosenfield, Sylvia A.
    Instructional consultation.

    (School psychology)
    Bibliography: p.
    Includes index.
    1. Teaching.   2. Teacher-counselor relationships.
3. School psychologists.   I. Title.   II. Series.

    LB1027.R655   1987   371.1′02   86-29073
    ISBN 0-8058-0014-X

Printed in the United States of America
10 9   8   7   6

CONTENTS

Section III

Instructional Intervention—Planning and Implementation

PREFACE

The concept of instructional consultation is beginning to surface in the literature of school psychology and special education. At the National Conference on Consultation Training (Alpert & Meyers, 1983), held in Montreal in 1980, Bergan and Schnaps (1983) presented a paper entitled, "A Model for Instructional Consultation." They described instructional consultation as an extension of behavioral consultation techniques, to be "applied in situations in which the purpose of consultation is to modify teacher behavior to enhance the learning of all students in a class" (p. 105). Their use of the concept was largely limited in perspective to a combination of academic learning time variables and behavioral consultation, and the focus of their paper was on research examining verbal interactions between consultant and consultee. However, they underlined the potential for using consultation around instructional issues to modify teacher behavior for the purpose of enhancing the learning of all children, including those with academic learning problems.

The importance of a role in the instructional process for school psychologists has been defined in *School Psychology: A Blueprint for Training and Practice* (Ysseldyke et al., 1984), a document created to "help in the necessary redefinition of the role, functions, and training needs of school psychologists" (p. 2). As part of the necessary transformation of the role of the school psychologist envisioned in this futures document, several domains of knowledge were delineated. Among the domains presented were those related to instruction: "The school psychologist should be prepared to advise and consult on matters relating to the general improvement of instruction" (p. 11); and basic academic skills: "School psychologists should be able to help teachers help students master basic skills in reading, writing, mathematics, speaking, and listening" (p. 10). Conducting these roles effectively requires expertise in several content areas and in the techniques of consultation.

The purpose of this book is to present a synthesis of consultation techniques with the knowledge base about instruction to enable school psychologists and other educational consultants to improve their effectiveness in working with teachers in the classroom around instructional issues. This book is the outcome of 13 years of teaching a course, "Psychology of School Subject Disabilities"; the model of instructional consultation developed in that course forms the underlying structure for the book. It is the author's hope that the book will provide a format for training and for research for working with the model of instructional consultation.

This book is divided into four sections. Section I provides an introduction. The first chapter describes the model of instructional consultation and sets forth the underlying assumptions and theoretical base.

Section II contains four chapters, each of which is devoted to assessment concerns. However, the assessment process is presented from a consultation perspective. Thus, the first chapter in this section, chapter 2, explores the development of the consultation relationship prior to beginning the assessment process. Teacher interviewing to explore problem definition is the focus of chapter 3. Chapter 4 considers observation as a tool for gathering data related to academic problems. Chapter 5 is built around curriculum-based assessment, including error-analysis methods.

Section III is devoted to the process of intervention in the classroom. Chapters 6 and 7 develop in detail how the instructional psychology knowledge domain can be translated into the instructional interaction between teacher and child. Chapter 6 describes management of the learner, while chapter 7 is devoted to management of learning. Chapter 8 considers some of the issues around enabling school personnel to change the process of instruction. In chapter 9, the end game is considered, as the termination of the consultation relationship between teacher and consultant is described, both in terms of interpersonal contact and written record.

Section IV consists of a concluding chapter, chapter 10, in which a research agenda and future directions are considered.

No single text can present everything related to a given topic. This text focuses on one aspect of the work of the school psychologist as a consultant, that related to instructional concerns. The author is certainly aware of other issues relating to children's progress in school and academic achievement. Many of these have been extensively treated elsewhere in the literature. However, less comprehensive treatment has been devoted to the role of the school psychologist as an instructional consultant, and it is that role that is the theme of this book.

ACKNOWLEDGMENTS

The process of developing this model has been supported by several sources. First, I would like to thank Fordham University for the faculty fellowship that allowed me the time to complete writing the book. Second, I owe an enormous debt to the Fordham school psychology students, many of whom were certified school psychologists continuing to practice in the schools during their doctoral studies, who encouraged and questioned me. They conducted the process described here in spite of, on occasion, their confusion and questions about the process as it was being developed, and later came back to give me feedback about the usefulness of the model to them in their practice as school psychologists. Their work is included in the book in many places. In particular, the case presentations in the observation chapter and the examples of final reports are the work of: Lillian Garcia, Teresa Hernandez, Sarah Kuralt, Talia Matalon, Milagros Mendez, Florence Rubinson, Joseph Schippa, Diana Shahpazian, and Ilene Weinerman. Finally, I want to acknowledge the support and love of my three children, Alison, Andrew and Hilary, who have grown to maturity concurrent in time with the development of the model of instructional consultation.

I would also like to thank the following publishers and authors for the use of their material:

Figure 4-3 from TIES Instructional Environment Scale. Copyright © 1987 by James E. Ysseldyke and Sandra L. Christenson. Reprinted by permission. Edward S. Shapiro and Francis E. Lentz, Jr. Figure 4-5 from "Behavorial Assessment of Academic Skills." In Thomas R. Kratochwill (Ed.) *Advances in School Psychology*, Vol. V. Copyright 1986 by Lawrence Erlbaum

Section I

INTRODUCTION

Chapter 1

INSTRUCTIONAL CONSULTATION
A Model for Service Delivery
in the Schools

Instead of diagnosing the learner, we begin by diagnosing the instruction. We identify flaws in the instruction and correct them, with the assumption that the learner's problems were caused by flaws in the instruction.

—Engelmann & Carnine, 1982, p. 18

Instructional consultation represents a joining of two major strands in the field of school psychology and educational consultation: the process of collaborative consultation and the knowledge domain of instructional psychology. It has been suggested that skill in consultation as a collaborative process along with expertise in a specific area of content are both essential for effective consultation (Meyers & Alpert, 1983). The purpose of this book is to coordinate the growing expertise of school consultants (e.g., Alpert and Associates, 1982; Conoley & Conoley, 1982; Idol-Maestas, 1983; Parsons & Meyers, 1984) with the explosion in knowledge around instruction (e.g., Becker, 1986; Gagné & Dick, 1983; Resnick, 1981; Rosenfield, 1985a) and classroom management (Bents, Lakin, & Reynolds, 1980; Paine, Radicchi, Rosellini, Deutchman, & Darch, 1983).

Over the past 20 years the nature of our understanding of the effect of instructional variables on learning outcomes has blossomed. As a result, educators have gone from believing that schooling does not make much of a difference (e.g., Jencks and Others, 1972) to a substantial body of literature that asserts that teacher behavior does make a crucial difference to children's achievement. In the foreword to *Becoming a nation of readers*, Glaser (1985a) asserts: "The accumulation of findings on certain essential aspects of schooling has reached a critical mass and deserves close attention" (p. *v*). Further, the report itself states that:

> the last decade has witnessed unprecedented advances in knowledge about the basic processes involved in reading, teaching, and learning. The knowledge is now available to make worthwhile improvement in reading throughout the United States. If the practices seen in the classrooms of the best teachers in the best schools could be introduced everywhere, the improvements would be dramatic. (Anderson, Hiebert, Scott, & Wilkinson, 1985, p. 3)

Without question, learning outcomes are the result of a large number of variables, of which instructional factors are only one aspect. Walberg (1984), in a massive analysis of the causal influences on student learning, involving 43 quantitative syntheses of 2,575 studies, found three major causal influences on student learning: aptitude, including ability, development, and motivation; instruction, including amount and quality; and environment, including home, classroom, peers, and television. Walberg (1985) concluded that classroom learning is a:

> multiplicative, diminishing-returns function of four essential factors (student ability and motivation, and quality and quantity of instruction) and possibly four supplementary or supportive factors (the morale or social-psychological environment of the classroom, education-stimulating conditions in the home and in the peer group, and exposure to mass media, particularly television). . . . Within this theoretical perspective, . . . educators seek to modify the amount and quality of instruction to make it more suitable to the ability and motivation of each student to (a) raise the average class achievement, (b) bring each student to at least a minimum, (c) diminish the variability of outcomes, or (d) optimize a combination of these three goals. (p. 7)

Thus, without minimizing the strong causal impact of environment and aptitude, the results of Walberg's research demonstrate the powerful influence of instructional quality and time on learning. However, much of the literature on learning disabilities and on the academic achievement of disadvantaged children continues to focus on the other two sets of variables. The intention of this book is to call the reader's attention to the instructional variables and to provide a method of service delivery for school psychologists to assist the classroom teacher in improving instructional quality.

In sum, it is now apparent that the quality and quantity of instruction are critical variables. Additional data imply that this impact may be most crucial during the early grades (Chall, 1983) and on low-achieving children. It has been suggested that as many as 25% to 40% of all children display sufficient variations in learning or behavioral style to warrant specially designed educational programs for at least short intervals during their school years

(Gickling & Havertape, 1983). The teacher's ability to supply such programs is critical.

PROVIDING QUALITY INSTRUCTION:
CURRENT STATE OF THE ART

How successfully do teachers provide quality instructional programs? While the research literature has begun to define the characteristics of quality instruction, relatively little is known about the quality of learning experiences provided for children in schools. However, there is concern that many children do not receive adequate instruction (e.g., Anderson, et al., 1985; Bennett, Desforges, Cockburn, & Wilkinson, 1984; Donaldson, 1978).

The concern about the classroom teacher's ability to deliver quality instruction takes several forms. At one level is the wider issue that research on instruction and cognition is not widely accepted by teachers (e.g., Amabile & Stubbs, 1982; Floden, 1985; Huberman, 1983; Rosenfield & Rubinson, 1985). Huberman (1983) drew a portrait of the classroom practitioner as a practically oriented professional, drawing chiefly on individual and peer experience to resolve problems or otherwise modify instructional practices:

> Recourse to more scientific, distant, or noneducational sources is infrequent, with the exception of magazine and reference materials to which teachers have easy access. . . . Both teachers and administrators may be caught up in the immediacy and diversity of daily classroom and building-level demands while being isolated from other classrooms and buildings, such that problem solving becomes an essentially private process of trial and error, recourse to personal experience, and, when appropriate, retrieval of fragments of preservice training. (pp. 483-484)

But there is a growing awareness that research does not so easily translate directly into practice. Stubbs (1982), commenting from this perspective, suggested that teachers are interested in collecting additional information to improve their own decision making in their classrooms, but that:

> their desire for more information is thwarted by the fact that practitioners often regard the research literature as inaccessible, either because they have little time to locate academic journals, or because when they do collect scientific reports on a topic the reports are often too technical or too poorly written to be of use. Even when practitioners are able to translate the research reports into comprehensible prose, they often discover that the research findings fail to substantiate conclusions they've drawn from their own experience. (p. 34)

The translation of research into practice in individual cases requires another particular kind of knowledge and skill that does not seem to be readily available to teachers in their practice.

The reluctance of teachers to use research findings would be less troublesome if there was some evidence that most teachers intuitively used high-quality instructional strategies. However, that does not seem to be verified (see, e.g., Anderson et al., 1985; Bennett et al., 1984). For example, there is evidence that a large percentage of the tasks assigned to children are not well matched to their instructional level. The result is that high-achieving children are not introduced to new material that would stretch them, whereas low-achieving children are "mystified" (Anderson, 1981; Bennett et al., 1984). In addition is the growing issue of whether teachers actually provide instruction; that is, that they demonstrate in small steps what is to be learned, use appropriate and specific examples, and evaluate whether students actually have mastered the material (Becker, 1986). Stated another way, do teachers forster academic-engaged time and mastery learning through their teaching behaviors? A number of studies indicate clearly that they do not.

Two of those studies are in the area of reading comprehension, which has become a focal interest in the area of basic skills today. Durkin (1978-79) observed 24 fourth grade teachers during reading period, and found that instruction occurred less than 1% of the time. Steely and Englemann (1979) analyzed the instructional programs for teaching reading comprehension in four of the most widely used basal reading programs at the fourth-to-sixth grade levels, as well as use of these programs by teachers. Not only did the programs have limited instructional examples, but the material provided the possibility for misinformation to be communicated to the children. The teachers relied heavily on the programs but required few student responses and corrected errors only 37% of the time. Anderson et al. (1985), in their review of the literature on reading, provided additional evidence demonstrating that the level of instruction in many classrooms is not matched to the knowledge base on teaching effectiveness that has developed in the last 20 years.

Experience in doing instructional consultation with teachers confirms the research evidence. An example from a teacher-consultant discussion might add meaning to the research evidence itself. In this case the teacher was concerned about Alex's inability to associate sounds and graphemes. The consultant was attempting to elicit the teacher's alternative teaching strategies when the child was experiencing difficulty.

T: I say, this is the letter *M*, Alex. It says, *MMM*. Alex, this is the word "*Mother*." Does *MMMother* say MMM? Sometimes he would say yes, sometimes he would say no, because he does not understand the transfer, the MMM to Mother. He does not understand what I want to know.

C: Have you tried other ways, other instructional strategies, when he cannot do that?

T: Well, there are very little ways, besides showing the letters, showing words, showing pictures. I don't know of other ways of showing him what to do with this. I don't know of other ways myself.

It is clear from the data that there is a need for working with teachers on instructional programs, to help them provide quality instruction to vulnerable learners, if not to all children.

While there is a massive literature on teacher training and professional development, Anderson et al. (1985) cast doubt on the effectiveness of traditional approaches for in-service training of teachers. They conclude that:

> Specialists in the continuing professional development of teachers believe that brief workshops introducing new ideas about teaching seldom lead to enduring changes in classroom practice. Better results are seen when a consultant works with teachers on a number of occasions over a period of time and visits their classrooms in order to assist them in making agreed-upon changes. (p. 111).

Thus, the role of instructional consultant can be conceptualized not only as an indirect service delivery method for working with children with academic problems, but also as a potentially powerful in-service training process for school psychologists and other resource personnel in schools.

INSTRUCTIONAL CONSULTATION

Underlying Assumptions

Working as a consultant to the teacher in the classroom requires that we examine some of the assumptions that we hold about children who are experiencing learning difficulties in the classroom. The traditional psycho-diagnostic model or medical model assumes that the learner is at fault for any learning inadequacies, whereas an alternative hypothesis might be that the instructional program in the classroom is the cause of the learner's "failure." Bloom (1976) was an early proponent of examining alterable variables rather than examining stable ones such as IQ. (Current perspectives on intelligence focus upon cognitive modifiability and learning potential, e.g., Feuerstein, 1979. Often overlooked in Feuerstein's approach is that the critical element is in the mediation role played by the adult. While some psychologists seek to determine how they can use Feuerstein's assessment procedures for psycho-educational evaluations, there does not seem to be equal emphasis reflecting his focus on the role of the "teacher" [whether it be parent or instrumental enrichment instructor] in the modification of the student. Equally extensive training is required of those who wish to teach instrumental enrichment techniques).

Descriptions of the misuse of school psychologists in working with children who are having difficulty in meeting the academic demands of their school setting have been provided elsewhere (see, e.g., Ysseldyke & Others, 1984). Although the current zeitgeist in special education has been on the search for causality in the defective child, it is apparent that we could as easily look for the violation of instructional principles and assess the quality of instruction. Even within the mandate of P.L. 94-142, an instructional consultation role for the psychologist is evident. In fact, Alpert and Trachtman (1980) contended that P.L. 94-142 could involve an increased role for consultation:

> In sum, the Act (P.L. 94-142) requires the placing of handicapped children in the least restrictive educational environment appropriate to their needs. In order to select placements, information about both child and environment is needed. The placement is more likely appropriate if the environment is accurately described, if there is preparation for the environment, and if attempts are made to improve the environment's ability to provide individualized responses to its members. . . . What is clear is that psycho-educational assessment alone will not enable the realization of the "Bill of Rights" for the handicapped. Adding various types of consultation to psycho-educational assessment will enable better the intent of the law. (p. 237)

Wang and Walberg (1985) agreed that P.L. 94-142 has, in fact, "mandated support systems to accommodate the diverse needs of individual students in regular classrooms" (*xiv*), and find the schools more supportive of individualizing instruction, of combining "direct assessment of student capabilities with direct instruction that builds each student's competence in the basic skills" (p. *xiv*). They concluded that the "opportunities seem better now than ever before to respond constructively to individual differences in learning and to increase the effectiveness of instructional practices" (p. *xiv*).

But even more directly, the definition of learning disabilities assumes that the child is to be considered learning disabled only if, *after receiving adequate instruction*, the child fails to learn. Section 121a.541 of P.L. 94-142 (DHEW, 1977) specifies, for the diagnosis of a specific learning disability, that the child does not achieve when provided with appropriate learning experiences for the child's ability and age. Without a strong base in understanding the nature of quality instruction, the evaluation team is at a disadvantage in the assessment process to determine if the criterion of an appropriate educational experience has been met. However, when the members of the multidisciplinary team are school based, they are uniquely able to evaluate the dysfunctional system in which a child may be placed, and in fact, bring to bear expertise in consultation and instruction prior to a referral for special educational placement.

It is not news to most readers that special education has become overburdened with mildly handicapped children (Algozzine, Ysseldyke &

Christenson, 1983) nor that issues of bias have raised strong concern and outrage (Galagan, 1985). National surveys by the Office for Civil Rights (OCR) of the U.S. Department of Education have consistently documented the overrepresentation of minority children and males in special education programs for the mentally retarded. The National Research Council, which OCR asked to explore the nature of the observed disproportionate placement and to formulate policy, appointed the 15-member Panel on Selection and Placement of Students in Programs for the Mentally Retarded. According to Messick (1984):

> When confronted with this problem of overrepresentation . . . in special education programs . . ., the panel responded not with solutions focusing on the direct reduction of disproportion per se, but rather with solutions focusing on the functional needs of children and on the quality of services that should be provided. . . . In its deliberations the panel came to view the statistics of disproportionality as symptomatic of a deeper educational problem: The key issue is not disproportionality itself, but rather the two issues of the *validity* of referral and assessment procedures and of the *quality* of instruction received, whether in the regular classroom or in special educational settings. (pp. 3-4)

Further, the search for alternatives to traditional practice has gained momentum (Graden, Casey & Christenson, 1985; Ysseldyke & Others, 1984; Ysseldyke, Thurlow, Graden, Wesson, Algozzine, & Deno, 1983). There is an increasing move toward prereferral models, toward helping regular education serve more children. According to Reschly and Genshaft (1986, April), 90% of school psychologists agree that "better regular classroom instruction would prevent many students from being classified as LD" (Learning Disabled) and 98% agree that "school psychologists should assist teachers in designing, implementing, and evaluating pre-referral interventions before students are considered for LD classification" (p. 44). Indirect special services through consultation might provide a reconceptualization and reallocation of services to children, such that "resources traditionally used to test and place large numbers of students are redirected toward providing assistance for students and their teachers in the regular classroom, where the problems first arise" (Graden et al., 1985, pp. 377-378).

However, even where children are referred for special services, there is a need for assistance to teachers to help them provide quality and adequate instructional programs. While there is some evidence that effective prereferral interventions reduce the number of special education children (e.g., in New York City, the school-based support teams in one school reported a 67% reduction in referral for formal assessment based on a prereferral intervention model, Weybright & Avigad, 1984), it is also important to focus on the improvement in academic functioning of two other groups of children: those with problems not severe enough (in some cases, not severe enough *yet*) to have led to their teacher making a referral for special education services and those who were actually placed but whose teachers need additional assistance in developing academic programs.

THE INSTRUCTIONAL SYSTEM

The model of instructional consultation proposed here views the learner as part of an instructional system:

> Learners do not bring their unique characteristics singly to bear on teaching and learning transactions. Rather, they bring these characteristics to bear on learning behavior in dynamically orchestrated patterns or clusters. . . . Thus, it may be important that the teacher know the dominant features of each pupil's cognitive style, temperament, and so forth, but even more important that the teacher be sensitive to the stimulus conditions and situational constraints under which aspects of each of these domains change (Gordon, DeStefano, & Shipman, 1985, p. 60).

Taking this transactional perspective forces us to shift the focus from the defective learner to viewing the learner as part of an instructional system. The major components of the system include three sets of variables: the task, or what is to be learned; the learner, in terms of his or her readiness to undertake the learning task; and the treatment, or the instructional and management strategies (Rosenfield, 1984).

Currently, too often when children are referred for academic problems, the assumption is made that the child has a problem and that the instruction has been at least minimally adequate; the task at which the child is having difficulty is often globally conceptualized as learning to read, doing math problems, or spelling on grade level. However, the process of instructional consultation, as defined here, begins with a different set of assumptions. The focus is on the quality and nature of the interaction, which usually is an instructional mismatch, between an often vulnerable learner, inadequate instruction, and a muddled conception of the task. It is the goal of the collaborative consultation process to analyze the mismatch and facilitate a more productive interaction. Assessment is not for the purpose of classification and/or placement, but for classroom instructional decision making.

The heart of instructional consultation is not the referred child in isolation from the task and the instruction. Even when the child is the focus, the child is viewed as a learner—a potential learner rather than a disabled one—and assessment is concerned with alterable variables directly related to the learning situation rather than more global and static constructs such as intelligence. In addition, there is a differentiation between the task that needs to be learned and the treatment (i.e., the instructional/management strategies). We need to know both what the task is and how the task is being taught. Recommendations to change the task, such as to teach sight words rather than phonics, without attention to the instructional principles used to teach the task, are avoided. All specific recommendations about instruction are worked through together with the teacher. Finally, there is a continuous focus on the relationship between the teacher and the consultant, based on the nature of the change process involved in consultation.

THE PROCESS OF INSTRUCTIONAL CONSULTATION

The process of instructional consultation is not different in basic underlying structure from other forms of consultation that have been described in the literature (e.g., Conoley & Conoley, 1982). A useful definition of consultation, one that incorporates the essential features usually considered in the tradition of school consultation developed from Caplan's (1970) work, has been widely accepted: "Consultation is a voluntary, nonsupervisory relationship between professionals from differing fields established to aid one in his or her professional functioning" (Conoley & Conoley, 1982, p. 1). In addition, instructional consultation may function at all of the four levels of consultation defined by Meyers, Parsons, and Martin (1979). At times it may be necessary to engage in (1) direct service to the client by gathering data about the child directly through assessment, interviewing, or observation; however, (2) indirect service to the client through the consultee may be the level most used by instructional consultants—at this level, the consultee works with the consultant, but remains responsible for most of the data gathering and intervention implementation; the third level (3) service to the consultee, may be the focus when the primary goal is change in the consultee, with the assumption that this change will eventually result in changes for the pupil clients as well; and finally, instructional consultation may provide (4) service to the system when changes in the structure of the instructional system in the school lead to improved organizational functioning of the whole system.

The model of instructional consultation developed in this book focuses primarily on level 2, indirect service to the client, a child referred for a learning problem, through the consultee, the child's teacher. However, sometimes it is necessary for the consultant to gather data on the child (as in level 1). Teachers sometimes lack the skill or the resources to be able to do the assessment needed to plan for the child's instruction. A consultant may decide to model the process or find it necessary for other reasons actually to collect the data. At other times, the initial referral of the child becomes an entry point for the consultant to work with teachers around issues of primary concern to them (level 3), which eventually results in improved instruction to children. For example, one school psychologist began working with a bilingual teacher, in her first year in the field, who was concerned about a child who was having difficulty in an academic area. It became clear to the psychologist that the teacher's classroom management strategies were almost nonexistent; the classroom teacher was equally concerned about her management techniques and they began a program to improve her functioning in that area.

At other times, the instructional consultant has been utilized to do more organizational interventions (level 4), as in the case of a school psychologist whose expressed interest in instructional matters led to his being asked to assist a school in improving the social studies curriculum, which most of the students were finding too difficult. His articulation of the concept of instructional matching led to a reconsideration of the social studies textbook in light of the known reading level of the students.

Another way in which instructional consultation fits the consultation paradigm is that it follows the usual stages of consultation. Within the consultation literature, there is considerable agreement about the stages of the consultation process. In whatever model of consultation, whether it be mental health, behavioral, organizational, or instructional, it is generally assumed that there is an entry and contracting stage, a problem identification and analysis stage, an intervention or implementation stage, and an evaluation/termination stage.

Moreover, the interpersonal skills of good consultation are incorporated as an underpinning to instructional consultation. Parsons and Meyers (1984) elaborated some of the basic skills required for collaborative consultation, the form of consultation required here. They present two types of techniques to implement collaborative consultation: techniques that emphasize the consultee's role and those that stimulate behavior change.

The remainder of this chapter provides an overview of how the stages are conceptualized in the process of instructional consultation.

Entry and Contracting

In order for a collaborative relationship to be established between the consultant and the teacher around instructional issues or problems, it is necessary for the teacher to understand and accept the role of consultee. The teacher has to be prepared for the process of consultation, to have an overview of what the purpose of the consultation is, and how it may differ from previous experiences with school psychologists and other educational consultants/resource people.

When school psychologists take on the role of instructional consultant, it is often necessary to confront the teacher's expectations for the interaction. In the current referral process in many schools, particularly since the passage of P.L. 94-142, teachers usually assume that if they are referring a child for services, the psychologist will help them to figure out what is wrong with the child. This medical model approach to etiology for learning problems is not only the most common philosophy, but one that is comfortable for teachers, in that it relieves them of responsibility for causing or curing the problem. As a result, the shift to a collaborative, classroom-centered, problem-solving approach to learning problems is not easily made by the teacher (or, in many cases, by the members of the multidisciplinary team).

Second, teachers (and many school psychologists themselves) will often not consider a psychologist an appropriate professional to solve instructional problems, because many school psychologists have received relatively little training in this area. A communication process must occur in which the teacher is helped to understand that the psychologist will not begin by testing the child. The teacher needs to move toward a commitment (perhaps tentative at first) to a problem-solving relationship, to determine if the child's learning problem or the teacher's instructional question can be resolved. The skills for entry and contracting will be considered in chapter 2.

Problem Identification and Analysis

The Referral Process.   The literature on consultation stresses the importance of problem identification, a process often minimized in practice. Since the problem-identification-and-analysis stage usually begins with the teacher's referral of the child, an initial referral interview, or a series of such interviews, is the place to initiate this phase of the process. Once the nature of the working relationship has been clarified and the teacher understands the purpose of the interview (through the process of entry and contracting), the psychologist can focus on obtaining the information necessary to help identify the problem itself.

Several authors have focused on the importance of the language used in this initial interview. Tombari and Bergan (1978) described the effect of using specific behavorial cues, such as "Tell me about Johnny's behavior in your class" as opposed to more general ones such as "Tell me about Johnny's problems" in terms of influencing the teacher's beliefs about the likelihood of solving the child's problems within the classroom, a particularly important perspective for instructional problems. According to their research, teachers are more apt to express optimism about solving the problems in the classroom setting if given the more behavioral type of verbal cue.

In every respect, good communication skills are essential. In analyzing teacher-consultant initial-interview transcripts in which teachers were referring children for academic problems, one quickly becomes aware of how confused the dialogue is, how often teachers say things that are unclear or have multiple interpretations. Yet the consultants interviewing the teachers do not ask for clarification. Some assume they understand, and only upon questioning begin to reflect on the possibility that they might have interpreted the teacher within their own framework rather than heard what the teacher was trying to communicate. Others, particularly school psychologists with little background in instruction or teaching, report with startling honesty that they do not wish to show their ignorance about classroom instructional procedures. Techniques for establishing clear communication, such as the use of paraphrasing and clarifying questions, will be considered in chapter 4.

Before the end of the interview, the psychologist and teacher might have begun to see more clearly what the problem is that underlies the teacher's decision to make a referral and have clarified what additional information needs to be gathered to determine the nature of the discrepancy between the desired performance for the pupil and the child's actual current level of functioning. Dimensions such as problem frequency, duration, intensity, and antecedent conditions are identified, as is typical of behavioral consultation. However, the problem definition must include specific data on the instructional strategies used by the teacher and the types of tasks with which the child has difficulty. Questions that need to be considered include:

What are the particular objectives that the child is expected to master?
What skills must the child have in order to meet those objectives?
Does the child have the prerequisite skills?
What strategies have been tried in terms of modification of instruction and/or instructional materials?

Thus, the analysis and identification of the problem focuses on the entire system in great detail, not just upon the child's performance and behavior. The assessment process that follows and is a part of problem identification arises from these issues.

Observation.   Classroom observation can play a useful role in instructional consultation. Gathering data using structured observations is a valuable adjunct to the process. Sometimes unexpected factors are discovered. In one consultation situation, a teacher was confused about a child who did his seat work well and yet did poorly on tests. A school psychology student observing the child's on-task behavior in the classroom discovered the more important fact that the child was simply copying his seat work from other children. The teacher, occupied with her small groups, had not noticed the covert copying. Moreover, teachers are sometimes unaware of their own behavior or teaching styles, and with appropriate support, can welcome feedback on their teaching. One school psychologist introduced a teaching-observation checklist to a group of teachers, who became interested in knowing how they were performing. Observation techniques centering on instruction will be discussed in chapter 4.

Curriculum-Based Assessment.   Answers to some of the central questions just raised about a child's academic problems begin with a curriculum-based assessment (Deno & Mirkin, 1977; Gickling & Havertape, 1982; Shapiro & Lentz, 1985b; Tucker, 1985). For example, the teacher may state that the child has a problem in learning phonics. First, it is necessary to determine what the child is expected to be able to do in the domain of phonics in that classroom setting, that is, what is the scope and sequence of the reading program used by that teacher? What are the child's skills in that scope and sequence compared to where the teacher expects the child to be in the area of phonics?

The concept of grade level, as measured by a standardized test, is useless for these purposes. There is not a one-to-one correspondence between one standardized test and another, nor between standardized tests and basal reading series, nor between basal reading series themselves. A study by Jenkins and Pany (1978), for example, illustrates the lack of congruence between five basal reading series and four commonly used standardized achievement tests, including the WRAT, PIAT, Metropolitan Achievement Test, and Slosson Oral Reading Test. Given that norm-referenced tests are inadequate for making curriculum-intervention decisions, the critical feature of curriculum-based assessment is the evaluation of the child's skill level within the classroom curriculum itself. Once this evaluation is completed, it is frequently found that the child is working at frustration level rather than instructional level, that is to say, the child is on a daily basis confronted with material that is too hard, rather than material that the child could master. For some cases, this knowledge is where the intervention begins—the first step in the intervention consists of placing the child in materials at instructional level.

While the classroom teacher might be expected to provide data about the child's skill level, often he or she cannot. It is then sometimes necessary for the instructional consultant to model the procedures or to instruct the teacher in how to conduct a curriculum-based assessment. The teacher may more accurately be able to answer the question of what skills have been covered rather than what the child has actually mastered. Further, we have experienced in a considerable number of cases that the teacher is incorrect in assessing the child's level of functioning, either over- or underestimating what the child has mastered. The research of Bennett et al. (1984) confirms that teachers have difficulty in instructional matching. Thus, gathering data here is required for an accurate picture of the child's level of functioning. Chapter 5 will detail the procedures for doing so.

Another important feature of curriculum-based assessment is error analysis (Englemann & Carnine, 1982; Gickling & Havertape, 1982; Meyers, 1985). By careful analysis of the child's actual performance on the curriculum materials and/or by discussion with the child about how the task was approached, it is often possible to locate the type of error. Usually there is a logic to the child's error pattern that either reflects a consistent but incorrect underlying error in strategy or one that reflects a deficiency in the instruction itself. For example, Russell and Ginsburg (1984) provided evidence that children with math difficulties are not seriously deficient in knowledge of basic mathematical concepts and procedures, nor do they show unusual bugs in math problem solving. Their strategies in solving problems are not unlike those of their better-achieving peers. However, they have considerable difficulty in rote mastery of math facts. Determining the type of error the child makes in individual cases is prerequisite to planning appropriate interventions.

Implementation of Interventions

In most cases, instructional interventions take place within the classroom and are managed, if not directly implemented, by the classroom teacher. Thus, at this point the consultation process involves working with the teacher to modify and manage classroom instructional procedures. The instructional descisions that need to be implemented for vulnerable children are often at variance with the "normal" way of doing things in many schools and must be integrated into the daily activities of the teacher. For example, finding that the child is working at frustration level requires that the child be provided with material that is less difficult. Resistance often occurs at this point in implementing an intervention because the teacher feels caught between "getting through the material" and moving the child to mastery at the slower pace that may be required. It is difficult for many teachers to accept that slower is faster in the long run (Rosenfield & Rubinson, 1985), that children make more progress when placed in material that is at their instructional level, even if it is at a point lower in the sequence, in spite of research evidence validating that strategy.

But the critical importance of ongoing consultation in the intervention stage is related to the consultant's accepting that new knowledge is not transmitted like a coin; it is not passed from one hand to another without modification. Adaption not adoption is the key to understanding what happens in the process by which interventions are implemented. As new information is integrated into the working knowledge of practitioners, including both teachers and psychologists, it is modified, interpreted, translated, and transformed (Kennedy, 1983). Consultants need to assist teachers during this process, not only by supporting them in attempting new behaviors, but in making sure that the strategies discussed and agreed upon are implemented appropriately (Rosenfield & Rubinson, 1985). These issues will be discussed in chapter 8.

However, in order to be an effective consultant at this stage, the instructional consultant needs to have acquired a knowledge base about quality instruction. This is particularly important because we know that teachers have difficulty in accessing this literature. For example, there is evidence that a large percentage of tasks assigned to children are not well matched to their instructional level; skills in instructional matching are therefore critical. A second concern is based on the evidence that teachers have difficulty providing instruction, that is, in actually demonstrating what is to be learned in small steps, using appropriate and specific examples, and evaluating whether students actually have mastered the material. The consultant must be able to design or at least be able to evaluate a quality instructional sequence. Stated another way, skills in helping teachers foster useful academic engaged time and mastery learning through their teaching behaviors are necessary.

In terms of types of instructional interventions, the instructional consultant can collaborate with the teacher in manipulating relatively few categories: the child's work setting, the arrangement of consequences based upon the learner's performance, the curricular materials, and instructional procedures (Haring & Gentry, 1976). The first two are considered in chapter 6, in which management of the learner is dicussed. Good instruction takes place most easily in well-managed classrooms, which facilitate not only productive engaged time, but also release teacher time and energy to concentrate upon instruction. Skills in using resources that teachers have available will also be considered in this chapter. Often aides, paraprofessionals, parents, and peers can act as facilitators for part of an implementation plan; helping teachers to use their resources effectively needs specific attention. The second two categories that the teacher can manipulate will be developed further in chapter 7, which focuses upon the management of learning. How to manipulate curriculum materials and to provide effective instruction in a skill will be included in the chapter.

Not all of the knowledge base related to working with children with learning problems can be considered in these chapters. Relatively little attention will be paid to behavioral techniques directly, as these have been considered extensively elsewhere in the numerous texts devoted to behavior modification in the classroom. Social skills, family issues, and other mental health interventions, which certainly have a relationship to the achievement level of children, also will receive scant attention here, not a reflection on their value but on the central concern of this text, which is to focus on the instructional interactions in the classroom setting between teacher and child.

The purpose of these chapters is to provide the consultant with some strategies for working with teachers to implement high-quality instruction in specific instances. But there are no simple rules, no cookbook prescriptions; there are good principles which have resulted from research and practice. Implementing them in a particular situation with a given child and teacher usually requires collaborative consultation in a problem-solving framework, in which a skilled consultant has an important role to play.

Ongoing evaluation is a necessary ingredient of quality instruction. All instructional strategies are formulated as hypotheses to be tested for effectiveness in achieving desired outcomes rather than as carved-in-stone recommendations to be carried out by the teacher until the academic year ends or the triennial evaluation comes along. We have not as yet reached the point at which our knowledge of aptitude-treatment-interactions is so refined that we can be sure which intervention will be effective with a given child on a given task in a given classroom, although we are at a point where we can have some fairly sophisticated hunches (more formally termed *hypotheses*) (Cronbach, 1975) based on sound principles. To rely on social science findings in a particular situation is not yet possible, and may never be so (Cronbach, 1975). As Berliner (1985) reminded us, clinical work is always idiographic! Without ongoing evaluation, we are at a loss to determine in an individual case how effective we have been in reaching the goals of an instructional intervention, that of moving the child as *efficiently* and *effectively* through the curriculum as possible. A number of strategies for evaluation to assist in the process of collecting this information will be presented.

Termination/Leaving a Written Record

A final section needs to confront the issue of terminating the consultation relationship, at least in respect to a particular problem or client, as well as the appropriate form for leaving written documentation about the instructional consultation. The emphasis will be on clear communication regarding the end of the consultation process, the report is seen as a written record of agreed-upon findings and programs.

SUMMARY

The process of instructional consultation moves the assessment and intervention components more closely together and in the direction of the educational agenda. Further, it facilitates a least-restrictive-environment solution for a number of children who might otherwise receive a label of mildly handicapped. The remainder of this book will be devoted to exploring in detail the procedures needed to conduct the stages of instructional consultation, which depends upon professionals having training in both collaborative consultation methods and knowledge of quality instruction.

Section II

PROBLEM IDENTIFICATION AND ANALYSIS

"Once consultative problem solving . . . was carried through problem identification, problem solution almost invariably resulted."
—Bergan & Tombari, 1976, p.12

Collaborative consultation around instructional issues is conceptualized as a problem-solving process. The first stage of the collaborative problem-solving process, once a teacher becomes concerned enough about a child to seek help, is problem identification and analysis. The four chapters of this section of the book are devoted to the problem-identification process.

We begin by examining briefly the collaborative consultation relationship, and then discuss three sets of skills that will facilitate a successful resolution of the problem-identification-and-analysis stage. First, the use of good interviewing techniques by the consultant will help the collaborative team to identify the problem. The interview process typically leads to the development of specific referral questions. Since further information usually is required as a result of the questions developed during the referral interview, two types of assessment skills will be introduced: classroom observation and curriculum-based assessment techniques. Each assessment method is responsive to different types of questions, and the connection between referral questions and assessment techniques will be developed.

Chapter 2

ESTABLISHING THE COLLABORATIVE RELATIONSHIP

Helping

And some kind of help
Is the kind of help
That helping's all about.
And some kind of help
Is the kind of help
We all can do without.
—S. Silverstein, Where The Sidewalk Ends (p. 101)

Development of the consultation relationship is a critical element in consultation, and has been elaborated upon in most texts in the field (e.g., Conoley & Conoley, 1982; Parsons & Meyers, 1984). The type of generic consultative relationship involved in instructional consultation is a collaborative one, and in this chapter, some aspects of the relationship essential to instructional consultation will be presented.

COLLABORATIVE CONSULTATION

The current literature on collaborative consultation defines the essence of collaboration as involving two professionals, each having his or her own areas of expertise (Parsons & Meyers, 1984). It is seen as an interchange between two or more professional colleagues, in a nonhierarchal relationship, working together to resolve a problem. After reviewing the sociopsychological underpinnings of collaborative consultation, Parsons and Meyers (1984) concluded

21

that the emphasis is on mutual power to influence rather than unidirectional influence of the consultant on the consultee; the nature of the relationship is egalitarian and trusting; empathy respect and genuineness are collaborative attitudes; and the focus is on "open, honest communication that is persuasive rather than coercive" (p. 38). Parsons and Meyers (1984) summarized their brief review of the research on collaborative consultation by suggesting that "collaborative conditions facilitate implementation of recommendations and consultee satisfaction" (p. 17).

PROBLEMS IN ESTABLISHING
COLLABORATIVE RELATIONSHIPS

Establishing a collaborative consultation relationship, however, is not an easy goal to achieve. Consultation is both an influence process by the consultant and a collegial process in which both parties exercise influence. The consultation literature refers to the problems that consultants have in downplaying the "expert" role and their difficulty in achieving the collegial relationship because of the consultee's need to establish the consultant as expert. In fact, many school professionals view the title of consultant as inherently reflecting an expert role. (It has been suggested by some that the use of the title "consultant" be changed!)

In attempting to understand the problems of establishing a collaborative relationship, relatively little attention seems to have been paid to the process of help-seeking itself. After all, the consultant is only there aiming to establish a collegial relationship because the consultee has a problem. The teacher who refers a child is a professional person who has tried to cope with his or her work problem. Despite training, intentions, and effort, the teacher has been unable to solve the problem. When teachers request help, their self-esteem is lowered, and, depending upon their attribution for the problem, teachers will be blaming either the child or themselves for what is often perceived as a failure. The consultant, however, is sought as the expert who will facilitate the problem-solving process. The consultant's self-esteem is boosted, as the teacher seeks relief in the consultant's expertise.

There have been several studies on the relationship between helper and helpee (e.g., DePaulo & Fisher, 1980; Tessler & Schwartz, 1972). The research has established that psychological costs associate with seeking help. Some of the research helps to explain why collaborative consultation models are so difficult to effect in the school culture.

For example, subjects are reluctant to seek help from a busy benefactor (DePaulo & Fisher, 1980). The overwhelmed school psychologist, who makes it clear that there are only a few minutes to spare for a teacher conference interspersed with the "real" business of assessing children, is unlikely to receive multiple requests for consultation. Careful attention needs to be paid to the unintended message of franticness that busy school psychologists sometimes display.

There are other aspects to consider. When rewards are less attractive for work done with the aid of another than for work performed by oneself, help-seeking diminishes (DePaulo & Fisher, 1980). Teachers work in relative isolation from adult surveillance and the norm of autonomy operates among teachers to minimize effectively the impact of outside influences (Doyle & Ponder, 1977-78; Huberman, 1983). It is part of the culture of the schools for teachers to close their doors and solve their own problems. Simply asking teachers to share their problems in a consultative relationship mode will not be easily heard by a large number of teachers, nor will it be viewed as a teacher behavior likely to receive approval from peers or administrators. In most other professions, it is accepted practice for professionals to seek consultation on difficult problems, and this orientation needs to be encouraged among those involved in schooling.

Moreover, there is a literature suggesting that subjects who asked for more help believed that the helper would perceive them as generally incompetent. Indeed, there is some evidence that helpers tend to denigrate those whom they have helped. Frequent help-seekers approach potential helpers with a justifiable degree of nervousness and discomfort. Exploring our own attitudes towards teachers and their ability to be collaborators with us requires a degree of honesty that we are holding up our part of the collaborative bargain. Many consultants may have negative attitudes toward teachers, particularly those whose classroom skills are perceived by them as not up to par, and authenticity in maintaining a collegial relationship may be difficult unless these attitudes are changed. It is probably genuinely necessary to view teaching as a difficult task and understand that many teachers received training that was not adequate for professional functioning in the classroom.

It is also known that subjects ask for help more frequently on difficult problems, rather than milder ones (Tessler & Schwartz, 1972). One problem for instructional consultants is that the teacher may not be willing to request assistance until the crisis stage has been reached. At that point it may be more difficult for the teacher to believe that the problem can be resolved in the classroom.

Finally, individuals are especially resistant toward accepting or seeking help on tasks that reflect on characteristics central to their self-concept (Tessler & Schwartz, 1972); teachers with high investment in their professional competence may be reluctant to view their classroom behavior as the source of the child's difficulty. The fundamental assumption of instructional consultation, that the quality of the instruction is the source of most children's classroom problems, places responsibility for resolving a learning problem squarely on the teacher. It is no wonder that pupil-services personnel and teachers have found it more appealing to look for the defect within the child.

STRATEGIES TO FACILITATE
ESTABLISHING COLLABORATIVE RELATIONSHIPS

In sum, the consultation process is not without cost to the consultee. Parsons and Meyers (1984) articulated the concept of generic forms of cost that must be taken into consideration in the initial stages of consultation, that is, entering the system and establishing a working contract with the consultee. They noted that there is time and energy expenditure, a tangible cost for the consultee. Awareness of the limited time and energy that teachers have available to take on new projects is imperative. In one instructional consultation situation, an exhausted and overwhelmed teacher requested that the consultant phone her at home at night. It was a mark of the success of the consultation as it proceeded that the teacher was able to see the consultant during the school day (Ford & Rosenfield, 1980). In addition, it is often an essential supportive strategy for the consultant to obtain the cooperation of the principal in either allowing time for consultation or acknowledging the teacher for giving of his or her time to the process.

Another major cost described by Parsons and Meyers (1984) is the psychic cost of fear of the unknown. Consultees in the process of learning to undertake that role express a number of specific anxieties about what might be required of them, personally and professionally. The ground rules for the consultation process must be established. But even more so, it is essential to provide the consultee with a conceptual understanding of the process. This does not mean providing a review of the sociopsychological constructs supporting consultation. It does mean informing the teachers clearly about the nature of consultation and the roles that both participants (or more, if other members of the team are to be involved) will play.

An additional consideration is the comfort level of the beginning consultant. Many school psychologists are reluctant to give up their assessment role and move into consultation, and for very similar reasons, for instance, time and energy expenditures and fear of the unknown. How to begin consultation when there is so much testing to be done? How to begin developing skills in consultation when assessment skills are so well honed? Teachers' reluctance to become consultees can reflect the insecurity and ambivalence of the fledgling consultant who is leading them into the new role.

Conoley and Conoley (1982) described some of the techniques for introducing consultation into a school from either an internal or external base. They described the entry process as "both the physical entry of a consultant into a system and to the expansion of services within a system" (p. 106). There is, in fact, research (Chandy, 1974) to indicate that more, and more appropriate, requests for consultation services are likely when consultants include in their introduction the information in Figure 2-1.

1. The consultant(s) is there to help with problems related to children experiencing classroom difficulties.
2. The process will be a collaborative effort between colleagues.
3. The consultant will clarify the nature of his or her role in the school.
4. The consultant will stress his or her value as an objective outsider with respect to the problem.
5. Confidentiality will be assured (this must be cleared in advance with supervisor/principal).
6. There are no cookbooks or quick solutions in most cases to resolve problems.
7. The consultant will communicate his or her respect for and interest in the consultee.
8. The consultant will place a low priority on direct work with the child.
9. The process will not begin with special education placement procedures. (That is, the school psychologists will not begin the test-and-place process until other options have been explored.)
10. The teacher is free to initiate, accept, or reject consultation, and to renegotiate the contract.
11. The purpose of the consultation is to increase the skills and knowledge of the teacher in order to facilitate problem solving in this case.
12. The consultant will want to visit the classroom.
13. It should be clear what each party is expected to give and receive in terms of number and length of visits, limits of service, etc.
14. The consultant should provide some explanation about the expected course of the consultation process.

Adapted from Conoley and Conoley (1982) and Parsons and Meyers (1984).

FIGURE 2-1. Entry Introduction Checklist. When consultants introduce the process of instructional consultation, they should include the information shown.

One useful strategy is to introduce the consultant (in some cases, a consultant team) model to the faculty of the school at a school faculty meeting, with the full support of the school principal. A classic introduction is Sarason's Port of Entry speech (Sarason, Levine, Goldenberg, Cherlin, & Bennett, 1960, pp. 58-62), which is developed for an external consultant to use on entering a school. However, several aspects of the presentation could be modified for explaining the role of the internally based instructional consultant. Prior to presenting the new service-delivery system to a school faculty, the staff involved need to carefully script the presentation to cover the items specified in Figure 2-1, and leave time for questions. While this process does not ensure that teachers will flock to the consultant, it does lay a framework for informed use of services.

It is not recommended that new consultants introduce this service to the full faculty until they are comfortable with it themselves. For school psychologists who are considering beginning to move into this type of service delivery, but who have had relatively little experience with it, a more·modest beginning is recommended. In several schools that have adopted a prereferral model incorporating instructional consultation, a brief introduction by the principal or team members about the process has been followed by a more expanded presentation later in the year. This follow-up session is conducted when the team has become more comfortable with the model and some teachers who have indicated their appreciation for the services are sitting in the audience.

In fact, experience in introducing instructional consultation to school personnel has demonstrated the difficulty in shifting from an evaluation to a consultation perspective. Even after careful explanation, many principals and teachers remain unclear about what is involved. Often, it is only after having gone through the process with a few children that a clear conception of what is involved emerges. When a teacher in the school can be part of the introduction to the full faculty, the process of acceptance seems to be facilitated.

DIFFERENCES IN UNDERLYING ASSUMPTIONS

One more barrier to developing a collaborative consultation relationship needs to be considered. Before undertaking instructional consultation, it is necessary for instructional consultants to understand how their points of view predispose them to seeing problems in ways that might be different from, and in conflict with, those of teachers:

> Our data suggest that differences in point of view and in basic premises about clinical concepts are more the rule than the exception. . . . For example, when making judgments about severity of disturbance, nurses focus on disruptive and explosive behavior, social workers on social skills and social attractiveness, and . . . psychiatrists on peculiarity and alienation. . . . Thus, what may at first be seen as differences in opinion should in fact be appreciated as differences in conceptualization and point of view. . . . The research supports the conjecture that division and disruption in . . . [collaboration] will most likely occur when differences in perspective are ignored or suppressed. (Colson & Coyne, 1978, pp. 420-421).

Differences in perspective are particularly likely when the consultant is not a teacher, or has not been a teacher, as may be true in the case of many school psychologists. Even consultants who were teachers, however, may lose their teacher-orientation when they move out of the classroom. According to Shectman (1979), the consultant who responds to the referral issues alone and not to the person making the referral is making a serious error. The true consultative alliance is formed only when the consultant can sense from the inside what life is like for the consultees, when the consultant can view the problem "from a mutually shared inside while simultaneously keeping a sense of separateness and maintaining one's own frame of reference against which the other person's viewpoint and experience are contrasted" (Shectman, 1979, p. 787). Since, as Bergin (1980) made clear, our work as professionals is rarely value-free, we need to focus on being explicit about our own belief system as well as understanding and respecting the value systems of our consultees (Rosenfield, 1985b).

Several sources of such potential conflict in the relationship between a consultant and a teacher-consultee have been identified (Berkowitz, 1975). Some of these are specifically related to instructional consultation. For example, a crucial conflict can occur if the consultant fails to realize the distinction between the teacher's focus on teaching and the consultant's focus on learning. As Berkowitz (1975) acknowledged, "Through teacher training, and also under pressures of lesson plans, achievement tests, and material to be covered, the teacher is primarily concerned with the teaching process and what is being taught" (p. 30). The curriculum-driven value system of teachers is reinforced often by their peers and administrators, and instructional consultants need to be aware of the powerful pressure exerted by this value system, in contrast to the one recommended by instructional experts, that of mastery of the material by the child. In fact, the pressure in this area may be growing more powerful under the force exerted by the current drive towards excellence in education, minimum-competency exams, and the like. It is necessary to help teachers see that children's achievement is not facilitated by pushing through the curriculum (followed by referral to special education for those that falter), but would be more likely if mastery of each skill is achieved by the children. In any case, it is crucial to evaluate how learning-oriented versus curriculum-driven a teacher-consultee is; to know which is perceived as more important—what is being learned or what is covered in the class—in order to understand where resistance might occur.

There is a need to respect the teacher's concern for getting through the curriculum, not because it is necessarily in the best interest of the child (it may, in fact, be a prime source of curriculum casualties who end up in special education), but because it reflects a school culture regularity. Irritation with the teacher for responding to the norms of the school is not a productive response. It is more productive to provide assurance that teachers will not be punished for slowing down the curriculum express, and to be supportive of their willingness to match the level of the curriculum to the child's level of

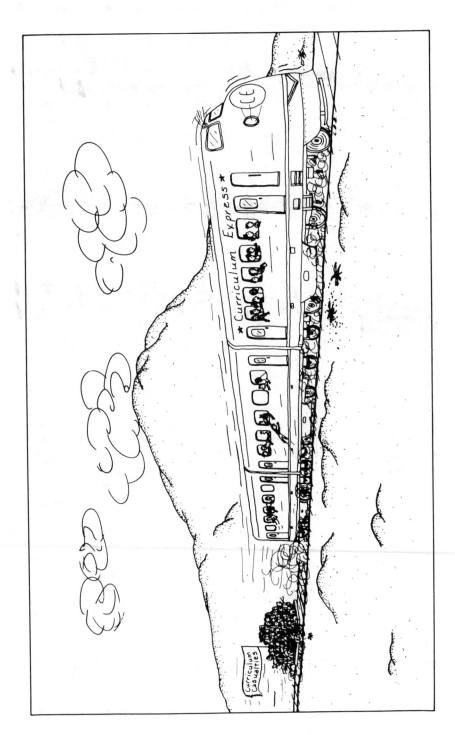

28

functioning. The need for support from the consultant and from the teacher's supervisor or principal cannot be underestimated in some settings (Rosenfeld & Rubinson, 1985). Berkowitz (1975) reminded us that most teachers need to be well thought of by other teachers and the principal. When we ask teachers to violate school norms, we need to be aware of the price they may pay for doing so.

Often teachers are aware that children are working at frustration level, but still feel pressed to move forward. Sometimes it is because they genuinely do not know what else to do. In fact, Bennett et al. (1984) confirmed this; when the teachers in their study were aware that the child was in difficulty, their response in about one-half of the cases would be to do more of the same or to move on. In one instance in our experience, a teacher articulated a similar philosophy: "I had children like that before, but I had them in the first grade. . . . What I had done was to constantly repeat, repeat, repeat; eventually they remember . . . but in this setting where I have just an afternoon, I can't afford to do that."

The instructional consultant, in order to avoid a "yes, but" response to the suggestion of moving the child to the instructional level in the classroom curriculum rather than continuing to have the child work at frustration level, will need to be ready to help the teacher develop an acceptable and demonstrably effective learning plan for the child, before the teacher may be willing to move the child back in the sequence.

Related to the first concern is the teacher's conflict between concern for an individual student versus concern for the whole class. It does not seem to matter particularly what size the class, because one can hear the same comment: "I can't do it with 10 other children in the class," from a special education teacher asked to individualize a reading program, to the more anticipated, "I can't do it with 35 other children in the class," from a regular classroom teacher. It has become clear over the years to the author that the classroom is perceived by most teachers as a group of individuals, rather than individuals in a group. Size is a related, but not a critical factor. The teacher's management skills and style, as well as orientation toward the classroom, are the essential factors.

In fact, there is some evidence that teachers find it very difficult to concentrate on individual children. Abidin (1975) described the negative feelings teachers have when asked to concentrate on a particular child in a behavior-modification program. One teacher's response dramatically exemplifies how others might feel:

Teacher: It's funny. I feel like I am in a bubble. . . . I can't explain it. It's like I am in a small cloud. It's like I don't feel that I know what's happening in the rest of the class. I don't like the feelings, it's like—well, it's like—it's like I am trapped in that cloud with Mark. I just don't like it (p. 54).

Teachers with serious classroom-management problems are often unable to successfully handle the individual needs of children. The following dialogue illustrates this point, as well as the general issue of group orientation and the curriculum-driven philosophy of the schools.

T: I have taught other letters, but she can't learn them. It is almost impossible to work independently with one child. I have heavy pressure from the rest of the class and from my supervisor, who wants the curriculum finished by the end of May.

C: When you mention "a lot of pressure," what do you mean?

T: I refer to having 32 children who need attention, who are very active and, overall, without a paraprofessional, it is very hard for me to individualize the instruction. When I try to put more attention on one or two, the rest start playing around or want to leave the classroom.

This dialogue, between a school psychologist and a first-year, bilingual-class teacher, reflects well the teacher's dilemma. It also exemplifies a productive interchange, as it alerted the consultant psychologist to the teacher's frustration in classroom management and eventually led to his assisting her in improving her classroom-management techniques.

Sometimes, however, it is the case that the teacher will be so stressed and hassled that even the most minimal expenditure of effort in adapting the classroom to the child is perceived as impossible. Sometimes consultants need to help the teacher find another resource person to undertake the adaptation, or to do it themselves (this process will be discussed in more detail in the intervention section). But, given the stress on teachers, support is often helpful, even in the earliest stages when building the relationship and it is useful to communicate to teachers that their perspectives and concerns are appreciated and that ways will be found to help them work individually with specific children in the classroom.

The concerns discussed so far may in combination underlie a teacher's desire for disposition rather than recommendations (Berkowitz, 1975). Given a child with problems in a large and/or difficult class, with pressure to get through the curriculum, the teacher is often seeking some disposition of the problem to alleviate the pressure. The importance, stressed earlier, of communicating about the nature of the consultation process cannot be underestimated in dealing with this concern. Assisting a school, genuinely, to embrace a prereferral model, rather than paying lip service to it ("We did that consultation stuff, now please get the child evaluated and placed!"), is an ongoing process in most schools.

A third issue in the values category involves how the teacher relates to a child in trouble—sometimes it is as teacher as therapist or teacher as savior (Berkowitz, 1985). But the important stance for the consultant to help the teacher assume is teacher as teacher. Children in trouble sometimes bring out the need in us to do good, luring teachers into taking on roles and obligations beyond their competence or power. One of the most important ways for a teacher to help children is to enable them to succeed in school as learners. If both consultant and teacher can use the language of instruction and behavior in describing the problem, the teacher will feel more enabled in his/ or her role in the classroom (Tombari & Bergan, 1978).

On the other hand, we have encountered teachers who feel incapable of being able to help a child. Although full of sympathy for the broken home or impaired brain functioning, some teachers communicate hopelessness and/ or pity, rather than a positive sense that the student can achieve. For example, in the following dialogue, the teacher is concerned about a child's inability to copy:

T: There, you wanted concrete, there.

C: She is really not able to copy the letters correctly.

T: Not in sequence that makes a word.

C: You are right, look at that, it doesn't make sense.

T: This is why I have been saying for awhile that she needs to be tested. This is a child where there is something not right here.

At another point in their interview, the teacher commented:

T: "That's right, they [the multiplication facts] just don't come. I don't know what we are dealing with; we could be dealing with a real learning disability; we could be dealing with a brain injury.

In spite of the consultant's ability to demonstrate that the child made progress in learning her multiplication tables under structured learning conditions, the school staff referred the child out for a neurological exam and a psychological exam to a local hospital clinic. Months passed. No report was ever submitted to the school, and the teacher continued to feel unable to work with the child because of her "learning disability." Berkowitz (1975) reminded us of the importance of helping teachers not to confuse sympathy with empathy. It is also important that we understand that teachers can become unwilling to attempt intervention if we convince them of the importance of medical-model or family-model causation. While certainly factors outside the teacher's control are important, our continuing emphasis on those factors undervalues the importance of the quality of instruction.

On rare occasions, we have encountered teachers so angry at parents and/ or child that they have been unable to respond easily as consultees. One such teacher engaged in the following dialogue with the consultant:

T: No, he can't read. He just won't. He looks at it and nothing, and he looks smart but . . .

C: He's a bright child.

T: Oh, he's no dummy. Like when he was referred to the SBST (assessment team for placement in special education) or whatever. He probably was able to answer some of their key questions and their recommendation was to put him in a resource room one or two days and back to the classroom. What he needs is a lot of one-on-one.

C: You feel he needs special attention.

T: Yes, because he doesn't get it at home. The problem is from home.

This teacher proved to be extremely difficult to work with concerning this child. The verbal dialogue does not fully capture her anger at the child and his family. The consultant commented, "I feel that he is having very real difficulties, but how do you convince a teacher of this?"

Another perspective on this issue is the concern of some teachers with the shoulds rather than the coulds (Berkowitz, 1975): "No matter how much . . . the teacher should approach a student on the level at which he can function, the teacher has a preconceived idea of the level at which the student should function"(p. 82). The teacher in the dialogue demonstrates this point in terms of her expectations of what children should come to school knowing:

C: Can you tell me what it is that you think might be the problem?

T: I think . . . Well, Andy is having a problem with letter recognition. Being only the first few weeks of school, I've found most children have come knowing the alphabet, being able to recognize the letters, and Andy can't.

After a month of school, she had already labeled the child, in part based on his lack of early reading skills. She was not easily turned towards teaching him the skills either—after all, he should have come to school knowing them! Paskewicz (1984) found a relationship between the use of shoulds by teacher consultees and their inability to change thier classroom behavior.

These differences in underlying assumptions can short-circuit a collaborative relationship. The purpose of describing them in this chapter has been to alert the consultant to their presence, so that they can be anticipated and worked through with the consultee. Sometimes teachers are simply not interested in changing their behavior. Biklen (1985), for example, found that some teachers openly resisted opportunities to work with consulting teachers or to participate in in-service programs in order to become more skilled in working with the handicapped child. Their behavior reflected an underlying unwillingness and/or disinterest in changing their behavior to accommodate the handicapped child in their classroom. However, we have found many teachers willing to modify their classroom behaviors, usually in small steps at first, when they felt understood and supported throughout the process, and did not feel they were being asked to do what they were unable to do (a concern that will be dealt with in a later chapter). The consultant who is able to establish a collaborative relationship, to engage the teacher in the process of change, begins with understanding the underlying assumptions, values, and concerns that the teacher brings to the relationship.

SUMMARY

Establishing the collaborative relationship is related to the effectiveness of the beginning, middle, and end of the consultation process. The purpose here has been to alert the reader to some of the issues that need to be faced in creating an effective collaborative relationship. In some ways, as has been stated, this relationship has a built-in contradiction. The teacher, in difficulty, calls in an expert, who then becomes his or her collaborator in solving the problem. While on the surface that seems reasonable, underlying factors make it difficult for the teacher to accept help in solving the problem at the classroom level. The school culture is not structured to encourage open help-seeking, and the psychological costs of help-seeking make it difficult as well. However, careful preparation and discussion of the process with potential consultee teachers and administrators, along with awareness of our own agendas as consultant help-givers, are effective strategies.

The second issue to be faced here is that of the value differences between teachers and consultants, as well as some perceptions that teachers hold that make it difficult for them to examine how their own behavior might be contributing to the child's learning difficulties. Among those factors considered are the curriculum-driven pressure faced by teachers, the teacher's concern with the class as a whole, rather than with individuals, and specific teacher attitudes and perceptions about students with learning problems.

While some strategies have been suggested in this chapter, and others will become apparent as the reader continues, it is perhaps awareness of the complexity of the relationship and its many levels that should be highlighted here.

Chapter 3

THE PROBLEM-IDENTIFICATION INTERVIEW

> *Teacher: "Well, Danny is a great break dancer. He's not too bad in math. Sentence writing he's not too good in, neither is his grammar. Reading is his worst problem. His comprehension and phonic skills are very poor. Somedays he knows it. . . ."*

The importance of the referral process has been underscored in the recent research done by Ysseldyke et al. (1983). Apparently, once a teacher refers a child for evaluation, the child's chances are high for being labeled as handicapped and placed for services. They indicate that 3%-5% of the school-age population is being newly referred each year for psycho-educational evaluation. Of those who are referred, 92% are tested. Of those who are tested, 73% are declared eligible for and placed in special education. Without question, it is critical to begin at the point where the teacher refers the child, if the problem is to be resolved within the regular classroom setting.

Experience with the process also suggests that the child is often rushed into a routinized evaluation-and-placement process before the teacher and the evaluation team have a clear conception of what the problem is (Batsche, 1984). The problem-identification interview is part of the referral-oriented model described by Batsche, who states four purposes to this model: (1) to clarify reasons for referral so that evaluations and report writing are goal and intervention oriented; (2) to individualize assessment and report writing to the greatest extent possible; (3) to increase validity of assessment procedures utilized; and (4) to relate the report directly to the referring and intervention agents (p. 6). The outcome of the process is to answer questions in such a way that the responses lead to interventions specific to the problems posed by the questions, not to labels or placements.

34

In this chapter, the problem-identification stage for academic difficulties is described from the initial preparation for the referral interview through the follow-up. Given that teachers' number one referral reason is a reading problem, number two is classroom behavior, and number three is math problems (Dr. James A. Tucker, personal communication, Educational Directions, Inc.), it is clear that academic reasons for referral are the most common source. The focus of the process to be described in response to academic referrals, however, is not on the behaviors and traits of the child alone, but on the teacher's perception of the child's behavior in relationship to the situation, a psycho situational-assessment model: "Thus, the situation within which the person finds himself may lead a person to behave in a particular way with equal or greater force than some hypothetical set of internal predispositions. Behavior is seen, then, as a function of both prior learning (a behavioral repertoire) and the stimulus situation" (Bersoff & Grieger, 1971). The interview strategies to be considered include both the form of the interview and the content to be obtained.

THE REFERRAL PROCESS

A problem occurs when a teacher believes that a child in her classroom is having a problem. However, that is a far cry from the conclusion that the child is the source of the problem, or more specifically, that some trait or behavior of the child is at the root of the problem. Sarason (1985), in describing the clinical role of the teacher in problem identification, cautions against the unreflective tendency to assume an identity between the world view of the teacher and that of the child perceived as having a problem. A blind child reading braille is not experiencing a problem: the environment and the child are matched. But when one member of the teacher/child dyad is concerned, there is a problem. However, we do not yet know what the problem is or whose problem it is. Thus, the first step in problem solving is problem setting:

> the process by which we define the decisions to be made, the ends to be achieved, the means which may be chosen. In real-world practice, problems do not present themselves to the practitioners as givens. They must be constructed from the materials of problematic situations which are puzzling, troubling, and un-certain. (Schon, 1983, p. 40).

Our first goal is to identify the nature of the problem through a process to facilitate answering the following questions:

1. What is the concern, in terms of specific behaviors, that is the basis for the teacher's referral?

2. What is the discrepancy between the desired performance for the child and the child's actual performance? Is the discrepancy sufficient to warrant intervention?
3. What strategies is the teacher using to eliminate the discrepancy between the desired performance and the actual performance?
4. What additional information needs to be obtained, and who will be responsible for gathering it?

Only after these questions have been addressed can the referral questions be clearly articulated and the next stage, that of developing an intervention, entered.

Initiating an Instructional Consultation

The process of initiating an instructional consultation can be formal or informal. If the consultant has completed the entry phase into the school, teachers will know that they have consultation resources available to them, and know with whom and how to initiate a referral. If school psychologists have slipped into the role informally, teachers may contact them informally. Or, in some settings, the consultation may be mandated as the prereferral phase prior to or part of the referral process for special education. In all cases, however, teachers will need to have a clear idea of the process and what is expected of them, as suggested in the previous chapter.

Whether the initial contact is informal or formal, it is important to set the stage for the problem identification interview. The teacher needs to understand what will be expected and what can be anticipated in terms of the process. He or she needs to understand the critical role of problem identification as well as the importance of the teacher's role in it. Witt and Elliott (1983) suggested a specific opening statement by the consultant to set the tone for an initial interview.

C: I would like to talk with you a few minutes about John and the behaviors he has which bother you most. In order to help you, we will need to discuss his behaviors, when they occur, how often they occur, and what things in your classroom influence them. If we work together, we may be able to accomplish this in 20 to 30 minutes (p. 43).

This statement communicates that a problem-solving process is underway, clarifies what the interview will cover in terms of content, reduces the expectation that the school psychologist will immediately begin testing, and emphasizes that the focus is on the child's behavior (Rosenfield, Rubinson, Righi, LiPuma, & Yoshida, 1985).

However, for instructional consultation, some additional factors need to be considered. First, when the term "behaviors" is used, teachers are less apt to consider academic behaviors, particularly when talking to a psychologist. It is recommended that the term "academic behaviors" be included. Second, it is important to have the teacher prepared to go over the child's actual work with the consultant. Looking at the child's work together is often more fruitful than having the teacher describe it. As is apparent when one examines transcripts of teacher interviews, the difficulty teachers have in describing the tasks is often a barrier to clear communication. Thus, for instructional consultation, a variation of the following opening statement is useful:

> **C:** We need to arrange time to talk together about Herb and the academic behaviors he has which concern you the most in the classroom, when they occur, how often, and what influences them. We will be looking at the curriculum, what you are asking him to do, what he can do, and where he is not able to do it. It would be helpful if you have examples of his work available. We should be able to accomplish this in 20 to 30 minutes. Let's set up a time.

Communicating this information to the teacher prior to the interview sets the stage for what will happen and allows teachers some time to prepare themselves appropriately.

In many school systems, the process is set in motion with a referral form. Several types of referral forms, varying from more to less structured formats, are found in the literature and in practice. The first type of referral form (Figure 3-1) is familiar, easy for teachers to complete, and provides little specific information. It does, however, initiate the process. More structured referral forms (for example, see Alper & White, 1971) provides more information, but are hard for teachers to fill out, sometimes requires them to do assessments that they find difficult to do (either because they lack skill or time), and is often a route used to slow down the referral numbers in a school.

A useful referral form (Figure 3-2) for instructional consultation is provided by Deno and Mirkin (1977). It focuses on specific academic behaviors, but asks for information that the teacher might easily provide, makes it clear that the purpose is to initiate a conference about the child, and provides a format for setting up the conference. A similar but even simpler referral form was developed in another district (Figure 3-3).

Thus, in developing a referral format for a school, it is important to recognize that the form itself probably cannot provide more than an entry to the interview. It should be a call for contact, rather than be considered a major source of information about the problem itself. What information can be provided on the form will be a function of what the teachers in a particular school setting can provide comfortably, without feeling inadequate. As in-service training in a district or school is accomplished, what can be expected from the teacher on the referral form can be upgraded. As with children, asking teachers to perform above their skills level is not productive.

REFERRAL FOR EDUCATIONAL/BEHAVIORAL EVALUATION

NAME _Rick_ DATE OF BIRTH _9-3-71_

SEX _Male_ SCHOOL _*** Elementary_

GRADE _3_ TEACHER _Ms. Lewis_

REASON FOR REFERRAL _Rick is not performing grade level work in spelling and reading. He is starting to have temper outbursts in class, refusing to work and he wanders around the classroom._

DESCRIBE SPECIFIC EDUCATIONAL/BEHAVIORAL PROBLEMS: _Rick within the last month is having pouting episodes, refusing verbally and physically to complete his assignments even in small groups and one to one with the teacher aide. Other students read for him to help him finish his work._

LIST STRATEGIES USED TO ENHANCE STUDENT ACHIEVEMENT AND/OR CLASSROOM BEHAVIOR:

1) Given him additional time to complete assignments 2) Praised him when he tries. 3) Since October he has attended twice a week a "right to read" remedial class.

CURRENT EDUCATIONAL FUNCTIONING: _Below grade level and his potential is much higher than his present performance in both reading and spelling._

RESULTS OF GENERAL VISION, HEARING, AND MEDICAL SCREENING: _Vision and hearing screening normal._

PLEASE SIGN:

Linda Lewis , REFERRING TEACHER(S)

_____ , PRINCIPAL

S. Keith , COORDINATOR OF SCREENING COMMITTEE

DATE OF REFERRAL: _12-3-79_

I&O/W5

38

CHILD STUDY TEAM REFERRAL

NAME _Ralph_ _Jones_ GRADE _1_ DATE OF BIRTH _12/30/77_

SCHOOL _East Park_ TEACHER(S) _Jean Miller_

PARENT'S/(GUARDIAN'S) NAME (CIRCLE ONE) _Hazel Porter (grandmother)_

ADDRESS _Forest Drive_ PHONE _555-8725_

REFERRED BY _Jean Miller_ DATE OF REFERRAL _2/20/86_

RECEIVED BY BUILDING PRINCIPAL: DATE _2/20/86_ INITIAL _____

I. CLASSROOM TEACHER(S):

A. Reason for Referral: Please indicate the specific reasons and/or situations that make you feel that a referral to the CST is needed.

1. _retained in k gm 6/84 – will be 8 on 12/30/85 I feel he should be tested_

2. _short attention span (can't sit still – falls off chair, wanders around room, bothers peers)_

3. _not performing grade-level work in reading or math_

B. Attempts to Resolve: Please indicate all attempts to resolve each of the above listed reasons within the current education program. This should include what was done, for how long, and by whom. Attempts to resolve should follow the sequence of reasons listed above.

1. _praise_

2. _firmness_

3. _____

39

C. Current functioning levels:
   1. Academic

   short attention span & lack of motivation affecting performance

   2. Social

D. What are student's strong points? (e.g., academic and behavioral strengths, likes, interests, etc.)

   having difficulty with peers + adults (special area teachers have expressed concern)

E. Has parent been informed of student's problem?_____
   Of referral to CST?_____ Summarize parent contacts and any recommendations made.

II. MEDICAL INFORMATION

   A. Summarize findings including dates, impressions, and/or comments.

      1. Pre-School Screening

      9-19-83

      2. Vision

      10/85   20/30 each eye—normal results

      3. Hearing

      10/85 5/20 each ear—normal results

      4. Latest Physical

      2-4-86 Normal findings

FIGURE 3-1. Two typical referral forms.

40

REFERRAL FORM ①

Directions: Please complete all items on top half of the form. Additional
comments are welcomed but not required. Please leave in SERT's box. A
conference will be scheduled within 5 days of receipt of request.

Request for Program Modification

   To: Special Education Resource Team
   From: _Ms. B._   Date: _9-9-75_
   Re: _Ricky J._   Grade: _3_
   Age: _9_ Room #: _204_
   Parent, Name: _Harry J._
   Parent, Address: _14092 Lucky Lane_ Home Phone: _948-2735_
   Reason for Referral: (Describe child's problem in brief
                  but specific terms.)

Teacher's Comments

✓ Reading difficulty. If so, at what level does student
currently read with 85% accuracy? Series _Read_ Book _B_

At what level would student have to be reading by the
end of the year to not be considered a reading problem?
Book _D_

✓ Mathematics difficulty. If so, on what pages of the
math book can the student succeed? Book ___ Pages ___ _none used_

How far do you expect to go in that book by the end
of the year? Page ___

✓ Social difficulty. Please list those specific things
the student does, or doesn't do, which make the student _Makes a lot of_
different from classmates. _noise; fights a lot._

✓ Other areas of academic difficulty. (Be specific.) _Handwriting; spelling_

Request for Conference with Referrer

   Please list three alternative days and/or hours during the next school
week which would be convenient for you to meet with the Special Education
Resource Teacher (SERT).

	TIME	TIME
Monday	930 - 950	Lunch
Tuesday		
Wednesday	10¹⁵ - 10³⁵	
Thursday		
Friday		

COMMUNICATION WITH REFERRER ②

Your application for Special Education assistance for _Ricky_ was received on _9-9-75_.
                                             name of child   date

SERT will meet with you in _teacher's lounge_ on _9-12_ at _9³⁰_.
SERT's name   room #   date   time

Please bring any samples of work or materials which are appropriate.

FIGURE 3-2. Referral Form for Instructional Consultation. From Data-Based
Program Modification: A Manual, p. 59, by Stanley Deno and Phyliss Mirkin.
Published 1977 by the Leadership Training Institute/Special Education, University
of Minnesota.

```
┌─────────────────────────────────────────────────────────────────┐
│                                                                 │
│   Child's Name _____ │
│   Date of Birth _____         │
│   Age  _____        Grade _____   │
│   Teacher _____   │
│   PROBLEM: (check those that apply)                              │
│            Academic _____                 │
│            Behavior _____                 │
│            Speech/Language _____                   │
│            Other _____                  │
│   List three possible dates/times for initial meeting:           │
│   _____  │
│   _____  │
│   _____  │
│                                                                 │
└─────────────────────────────────────────────────────────────────┘
```

FIGURE 3-3. Consultation request form.

The Problem-Identification Interview

Witt and Elliott (1983) considered the initial interview "the most important and challenging component of the consultative process" (p. 42) and problem identification as "potentially the most difficult challenge encountered by a consultant" (p. 43). The purpose of the problem-identification interview is to collect information and develop assessment questions to "operationalize problem behaviors so they can be measured and modified" (Witt & Elliott, 1983, p. 42); but the process occurs in an interpersonal context. As has been stated earlier, problem operationalization has a critical relationship to the success of the consultation and problem solution (Witt & Elliot, 1983). Thus, there is a need for developing the skills for effective functioning in this process.

There are two sets of skills involved:

1. Using communication skills that facilitate the relationship and information gathering.
2. Obtaining the information to clarify the referral problem and to develop a plan for gathering additional data for problem identification and/or for intervention.

Communication Skills

Different types of skills need to be discussed here. First, there are basic listening and communication skills, found in much of the literature on helping (e.g., Egan, 1986). But there are also some particular language skills related to working with teachers in the classroom context that need to be considered. Bergan (1977) provides an additional framework, within the problems-identification-interview setting, for approaching communication skills.

Basic Communication Skills

One needs to begin with clear communication, simple skills that help to ensure that communication will be clear. Experts in communication theory understand how difficult it is for clear communication to occur, how often we fail to understand one another. In the larger sense, the importance of communication to our very being has been presented movingly by Luft (1969):

> Feeling understood appears then to be a necessary though perhaps not sufficient condition for man to come to terms with the world and with himself. Hypothetically, every man can offer the gift of really feeling understood to someone, provided he can relate with him in a way that makes it possible to co-experience what is going on within.
>
> Being understanding, when one is able to do so, is rewarding in its own right even though it is not the same as feeling understood. But when it is mutual, when you and I understand as well as feel understood simultaneously, then for that moment the world is home and bread is baking in the oven. (p. 145)

Interpersonal communication can be conceptualized as a "process of establishing and maintaining relationships"(Littlejohn, 1978, p. 251). We are always both functioning on the content, direct level and a meta level on which the relationship is maintained. The question of concern here is how the communication processes used by the consultant can be directed to effectively obtain the information needed and sustain the collaborative relationship.

Often in a referral interview, the school psychologist acts as if its sole function were to obtain information from the teacher about "the problem," after giving the teacher time to ventilate about the problem and/or student. The strategy most often used, therefore, would be a series of questions in which teachers tell psychologists what the latter want to know. This process of question and answer has several drawbacks. First, it destroys the possibility for emergence of a collaborative relationship, and places the psychologist squarely in the role of expert. Second, the process of questioning itself has its "dark side," according to Dillon (1979). In a thought-provoking article, Dillon explored the clinical and empirical evidence on questioning in interview situations, and finds a number of problems:

> Far from encouraging client expressiveness, questions are held to produce blocking, to reduce input, to cut off conversation, and to inhibit response. . . . Beyond reducing verbal response, moreover, the practitioner is said possibly to miss the point. In answering the questions, the client will reveal the information

requested, but expressions of problems, feelings, relevant facts, and other data pertinent to understanding the client's situation will not be forthcoming—indeed, will likely be derouted by further questions. . . . Questions are thought to have these effects because, generally, they are perceived negatively by the client. At best they cause him/her to settle into a passive, acquiescent role, or at worst they provoke a sense of threat, resistance, and defensiveness. (p. 76)

He concluded with a truth we know, that answering question after question is perceived as unpleasant for most of us:

We begin to wonder why the questions are being asked and to what uses our answers will be put—and with what consequences for us personally. . . . We become cautious about volunteering information and opinions that are not asked for, and about exposing our feelings or involvement in the matters discussed. We might object to being put in such a situation and leave it with relief, as soon as possible. . . . It is much better to be in the position of the one who asks the questions. . . . (p. 579)

Because the use of questions is so dominant in referral interviews, and appears so logical, it is difficult to avoid their use unless clear alternatives are available. There are alternative communication strategies to use in the interview situation, which will elicit the needed information *and* maintain the collaborative relationship.

Maintaining the relationship is a high priority. It is central for the consultant to be perceived as facilitative, to demonstrate characteristics such as empathy and positive regard (Schowengerdt, Fine & Poggio, 1976). It has been demonstrated that the teacher's perception of the facilitativeness of the consultant is related to teacher satisfaction with the consultation process.

But equally impressive is the view of these same communication skills as part of the influence process that the consultant exerts (Parsons & Meyers, 1984). In their responses to consultee statements, consultants are often selective about to what they choose to respond. Their selection of material to question, to paraphrase, to perception-check, in part influences the direction and focus of the interview interactions. The following provides a clear illustration:

T: Well, in phonics, for example, some days he could put all three sounds together, other days he knows the sounds and he can't put them together. He doesn't try.

C: What sounds does Danny get frequently?

Here the consultant chose to focus on the academic skill rather than moving into the child's motivation. School psychologists who have responded to this segment usually focus on the motivational component, avoiding the academic issue. In fact, this child did not know his vowels, as the consultant suspected. Focusing on how hard the child was trying would have led the interview away from the core problem, although it was the major issue for the teacher when the interview began.

The following set of communication strategies presents an array of options. Questions are not totally eliminated, but are presented as only one way to conduct the information-gathering process. Examples of how and when to use the strategies are included. However, it is critical to keep in mind that the essential goal is to hear and to understand, not to use these skills in some rote, mechanical way. In addition, knowing that the consultant using these skills remains in charge of the direction of the interview and of the relationship building is important as well.

Requesting Clarification

Perhaps the most consistent error made by interviewers is to assume that they have understood the speaker. Another, related error is to pretend they do. Often these errors arise from the need to maintain the expert stance. Yet many things that teachers say in referral interviews are unclear or have multiple interpretations. It is important to be able to respond by asking the teacher to clarify what has been said.

There are two simple ways to request clarification. One can say, "I'm not sure that I understand what you just said." That usually leads to the teacher elaborating on the message. Or it is possible to ask the teacher to define or illustrate a particular word or phase used, as "What do you mean when you use the word *immature*?" Here the consultant is asking for definitions, or, more typically, examples, which forces the teacher to be more precise.

The following is an example of a consultant using a clarifying question to define a particular phrase:

> **T:** I even gave him an extra drill book to help him. However, he doesn't always complete these tasks and I have to keep at him to get them done.
>
> **C:** How do you "keep at him"?
>
> **T:** I constantly tell him to finish his work. Sometimes I have him come up to my desk and do it with me but this takes too much time.

Here the teacher's ineffective strategy was clarified, and the consultant had a clearer picture of where an intervention might be useful. In another situation, the teacher's definition of attention span was clarified:

> **T:** He stares around. He has no discipline and a very poor attention span.
>
> **C:** Could you explain that to me: "poor attention span"?
>
> **T:** I call his name and he pays no attention. He stares out the window.

In another type of situation, the consultant needed to know more about the kindergarten curriculum. The following example demonstrates how informative a clarifying exchange can be:

C: Let me tell you, I'm not familiar with the activities that are usually done in kindergarten, so . . .

T: Everybody does their own.

C: Okay, so I don't even have to apologize . . .

T: No, no, I can tell you what I tend to do.

C: I'll tell you what I would like you to tell me, I would like you to tell me what exactly you do with the children, what are your goals for them, and of those goals, what are the goals that Yvonne is not achieving, accomplishing.

T: All right, I am academically oriented for a kindergarten teacher, because my own children went to this school, and when they came they knew so much more, they are bright children, but the amount of learning that my children had before they came into kindergarten was so far away, so much more than these children, that I feel that I have to do a lot, so that when they get into first grade they are not so far behind. . . . So I feel that in these few hours that they are in school I have to give them this, I have to give them culture, I have records like "Peter and the Wolf," which they would never have at home. I do a lot of writing, a lot of reading. I read a lot of stories to them. I was told not to use the pencil so much, I mean, that they do too much using their pencils. There is some validity that they have to learn how to describe pictures, to use language. We found that these children in our school are somewhat nonverbal, they tend to use their body rather than words, so we have to get them used to using words, so I'm changing the curriculum somewhat. . . .

The open request for clarification here brought forth invaluable information about this teacher's philosophy and intentions, that were extremely helpful to the consultant in understanding her consultee's classroom procedures and eventually in formulating an intervention that the teacher could accept.

Paraphrasing

The technique of paraphrasing also facilitates effective communication. Consultants often assume that they have understood the teacher, a dangerous assumption without verification. There are often problems when two persons "think" that they have understood one another. If a teacher says, "Mary is having trouble with her reading," the consultant may hear that the child can not decode words, while the teacher may mean that the child can not sit still during the reading class.

It is a good habit to use a paraphrase to test understanding of the teachers' responses by restating their statements into the consultant's own words. When responding with a paraphrase, the consultant does not merely repeat what was said. Instead, the message is reproduced in the consultant's own words, or an example is used to make it more specific than originally stated. It does not mean making statements such as, "What you are trying to say is . . ." or "What you mean to say. . ." or "What you really mean is. . . ." That gives the impression that the consultant is saying for the other person what he or she can best say for himself or herself. The purpose of paraphrasing is not to say it better, but to report the listener's level of understanding of the other person's message. Here's an example of a paraphrase:

T: In the beginning she wouldn't talk to me at all. But now she's more open about doing the reading and she's not worrying about sounding out words she doesn't know. She'll also ask me what a word means.

C: In other words she seems to be more relaxed with you and not hesitant about asking for help.

T: Not with me, she isn't. Of course, it's more of a one-on-one situation.

In another case, the consultant's use of paraphrasing enabled the teacher to restate her position:

T: Some days she's all right and . . . you know, it's very hard. Some days she does it without too much trouble. She never does it . . . and some, many days she does it with a great deal of trouble, a great deal of effort, a great deal of really having to make her hold those sounds.

C: So she forgets what she's learned the day before?

T: I don't know if she forgets or it's that she's so easily distracted. She can't cope. You know, I think it's in there (points to her head). I don't think it's that she forgot.

In the following case, the consultant almost lost the teacher with his use of jargon in the paraphrase. However, she managed to bring him back to behavior, and short-circuited an inappropriate hypothesis that he had begun formulating:

C: So what I think you're saying is that it's a receptive language problem.

T: It's hard to tell whether it's receptive or expressive because the answers I'm getting back don't match, but there's not much way for me to know if what I'm saying to Stacy makes sense. I don't get any feedback from her. It's an interesting situation because I don't know what to do with her next in comprehension.

The consultant at this point had the good sense to move into the actual reading materials that were being used, and was able eventually to formulate an intervention plan based on adequate teaching of comprehension skills.

Paraphrasing is sometimes perceived as a risky strategy for consultants who want to maintain an expert stance, since their understanding of the teacher is exposed to be less than always perfect. But the collaborative consultant is more concerned with clear communication and understanding, and paraphrases often to be certain that understanding is correct.

Perception Checking

An important aspect of maintaining a relationship is to understand not only content, as in paraphrasing, but the feelings of the communicator. We seldom know for sure what feelings lie behind another's words. Consultants may think they know what the teacher is feeling, but it is difficult to know for sure unless they check. A teacher might seem distracted in an interchange. It might be because the room is too warm, her child is at home ill, or she is feeling uncomfortable talking about this pupil. A good perception check communicates that the listener wants to understand the other person's feelings. It does not convey approval or disapproval, but merely conveys how the feelings are perceived. Inferences about other people's feelings can be, and often are, inaccurate. Perception checking therefore, not only conveys a desire to understand, but may also short-circuit a set of interactions based on misunderstanding about what the other person is feeling.

In this example, the consultant's choice of word might have been better, but the teacher's response was genuine:

> **T:** I don't get any reaction. Sometimes she says, "I'll bring that tomorrow," sometimes there is no reaction at all.
>
> **C:** It must be kind of bewildering, the fact that she is not showing any reaction to your comment.
>
> **T:** I wish you could meet her and see; you know, she looks at me, she hears it, and that's it!

Some consultants have verbalized their concern that the use of perception checking makes them uncomfortable. They are concerned about opening a Pandora's box of teacher feelings, which they believe would be inappropriate in a task-directed interview. However, the critical distinction is that it is not therapy, but clear communication that is the objective. Bersoff and Grieger (1971), in their description of the interview's place in the assessment process, emphasize that the interview is not an impersonal technique and that attitudes, emotions, and expectations are important aspects of the data gathering: ". . . At times, . . . teacher concerns about a child's behavior may be based on irrational attitudes and ideas that lead to irrational expectations, demands, and feelings, and inappropriate actions toward the child after he emits his questionable behaviors" (p. 484). Understanding the hidden agenda of feelings about the problem provides additional useful information in knowing who has the problem and what kinds of interventions can be tolerated. It can be helpful to the consultant in getting at problems of lack of self-confidence and/or lack of professional objectivity (Caplan, 1970). The sense of being understood at the emotional level also contributes to maintaining the relationship.

Active, Attentive Listening

Listening is an active, not a passive mode. In workshops, when participants are asked to practice listening skills, someone invariably comments on what hard work it is. The key to active, attentive listening is that it is a response to a message sent by a speaker to a listener. Thus, each of the techniques discussed thus far are part of an active-listening repertoire. However, in this section the focus is on the use of facial expressions, eye contact, and responses such as "yes," and "uh-huh" as part of the process.

One problem with these responses, noted in some of our more relaxed colleagues, is the potential for their overuse. In one transcript, the following pattern emerged:

C: What do you, what is he normally doing when he's at his desk and he's . . .

T: Well, he finds, there must be three million things in his desk that are interesting, from his pen to his eraser. You know, sometimes it's just nothing. He's sitting there, not motionless or "lookless," I would say; he will sit there, and he won't seem to be engaged in anything, not even in deep thought.

C: Right.

T: But I think it's gotten better, I mean, since the first of the year he was much worse, because he didn't know if I was going to be on him, if I was going to demand things.

C: Right.

T: Like "move to the front." And now it's almost every time I routinely give a direction, I look his way.

C: Ummhmm.

T: Is he doing what I want him to do, is he not. If he's not, it's a comment of, "Mr. Smith (child's name), what are we going to do over here?"

C: Right.

T: You know, either he pretends to be involved, or he actually gets to work. But, I'm worried about the friends he has in the class, because I don't think he has any, or many.

C: Ummhmm.

The interview continues to free-float. The consultant has lost control, and the focus has deteriorated. Communicating active listening is not enough by itself, although the consultant should be aware of the need to be attentive and involved at all times.

Asking Relevant Questions

Although the amount of question asking should be decreased from the usual inquisitorial mode of intake/referral interviews, it is necessary to ask focused questions about the problem. Questions should be used sparingly, however, and not used to change the direction of the interview until all the information has been extracted from the topic under consideration. Questions should be specific, and designed to elicit information related to frequency, duration, intensity of the problem, conditions under which problem behavior occurs, instructional techniques used, and desired level of performance versus current level of performance. The following transcript demonstrates how a consultant achieved a lot of information using well-focused questions directed at obtaining specific instructional information. Note also the use of paraphasing and perception checking in the process:

C: So you're saying that Larry doesn't understand the concepts of carrying and borrowing, and he doesn't possess the prerequisite skills, such as mastery of number facts.

T: Exactly. Then the book presents the examples horizontally and that is included on the tests. When Larry has to add or subtract horizontally he becomes totally confused. He doesn't know which two numbers belong in the tens column and which two numbers belong in the ones column, and he has no idea of how to carry or borrow that way.

C: Does Larry have any problem with place value or recognizing which numbers are in the ones and tens columns when he's working in a vertical format?

T: Yes, but more so horizontally. Even when I draw arrows he still gets confused and doesn't know where I'm getting the numbers and he can't figure out how to get the answer. And even if he does get the answer in the ones column, he may write it in the tens column. So he's totally confused with the whole operation and in particular what number should be subtracted from what number.

C: Well, it sounds very frustrating for both you and Larry.

T: Yes it is. But this type of example is on the test so he has to learn it, and yet he can't even perform the operations when they're presented in the regular vertical examples.

C: It sounds as if this is a curriculum problem, introducing the horizontal before the child has mastered the vertical. Is Larry the only child who is confused with this?

T: Oh, no, but Larry is experiencing more difficulty with math in general than the other children in the class.

Compare that sequence to a more typical question/answer format, again on a child referred for a learning problem:

C: From what you have told me, Susan seems to have a poor memory, is a nonreader and does not know her alphabet and its sounds.

T: That's right. Her memory is terrible. I've taught them how to write their first and last names and Susan can only write her first name. All the other children can write both of their names but not her, and keep in mind that this is the lowest first grade class. Look at this other sheet, she was told to write her name on the line at the bottom of the page. She just doesn't seem to be able to follow directions.

C: Does Susan have any visual problems?

T: No, her vision and hearing were checked and she was OK.

C: What is her attendance like?

T: Umm. She has a good attendance record and she had good attendance last year when she was in kindergarten. So far this year she's been out four days. She is never late.

C: What is her behavior like in class?

T: Susan is a nice kid. She pays attention sometimes and acts interested, but she comes to school without pencils, her notebook is sloppy, dirty, and has pages missing. She shows no pride in schoolwork and fails to do her homework on many occasions.

C: How does she get along with the other children in the class?

As is clear, in this case, the consultant is following her own line of thought, never really getting to the details that would elucidate the problems. Moreover, the pattern of dialogue does not allow the teacher to be a participant in the process. What has the consultant learned? Hard to know, since there was little paraphrasing or perception checking or clarifying. From the first responses, the teacher's etiological assumptions that the child has a poor memory and therefore can't write is left to stand.

The point here is not that questions should not be asked, but that they should be used sparingly, interspersed with other forms of interaction such as requesting clarification, paraphrasing, and perception checking. In many good interviews, clarifying requests actually predominate. Questions, when asked, should be well-focused and directed toward obtaining specific information regarding the academic problem.

Offering Information

Although the problem-identification interview is not focused on resolving the problem, there is sometimes an opportunity here to offer useful information to the teacher. The opportunity to do so can be an asset to the relationship. Parsons and Meyers (1984) present, as one of the generic costs to the consultee of engaging in the consultation process, perceiving consultation as a "cost without return—a vacuum cost" (p. 110), and suggest that consultants be constantly alert to demonstrate their value to the consultee "as a resource for need satisfaction, right from the initial interview" (p. 110). When the consultant does provide information, the consultee will apply that to the situation and determine if it is helpful. Sometimes, direct information is needed, and is one of the reasons why consultees request consultation (Caplan, 1970).

However, the consultant errs in thinking that the teacher will necessarily find the information useful. Particularly when recommendations are offered as information at this stage, they are often rejected. It is almost impossible to avoid the urge to offer advice when in the consultant role, but the problem-identification interview might not be the most appropriate time to do so. Before a clear picture of the problem emerges and a strong collaborative relationship is built, offering advice might be premature.

In the following example, the consultant offers some information to the teacher about the effects of bilingualism:

T: Although Louis speaks English well, he comes from a bilingual family in which the dominant language spoken at home is Spanish. His mother is unable to help him with his homework or studying because she doesn't speak or comprehend the English language.

C: It appears that Louis' bilingualism is making it even more difficult for him to understand math concepts. Many children who are thinking in two languages have problems because they must translate what they are learning into the dominant language. This is extremely difficult, especially for abstractions such as math.

T: Exactly. It's no wonder that he's having such a difficult time in school.

In another instance, however, the information is neither heard nor incorporated by the teacher:

T: Well, I also wanted to talk to you about her math. Her math is also very poor. There I have a fourth grade curriculum that I follow. She has problems with multiplication. She has a very difficult time remembering her facts. She has hardly passed any test this year. She failed the midterm very poorly. We are doing division now, and I don't think she understands the division concept.

C: Well, I imagine that if she did not get the multiplication in the first place, she might have a very difficult time learning the division. She needs to have mastered the multiplication in order to master the division.

T: Sometimes she might remember her facts and other times she just has a very difficult time recalling.

Here, the teacher does not grasp that moving into division was inappropriate, given the child's lack of mastery of multiplication. This piece of information goes against the curriculum-driven pressure of schools, that is, the need to get through the curriculum for the grade level, and so is not integrated into the problem definition at this point.

Examining Work Samples

An aid to communication is to examine together the child's actual work. Rather than talk about the child's work, examining the work itself together provides a useful framework for consultation interchange. In chapter 5, the use of the child's work as an assessment technique is considered. Here, the work is discussed from the point of view of aiding communication. The following dialogue, a result of a request for looking at materials, was very helpful to the consultant in understanding a number of issues:

C: It would help me understand better if you can show me some of the materials that you are using with her, both the skills series book that she is reading now and . . .

T: I am going to try to get them from the reading specialist because I don't have them myself. I got them from the reading teacher here.

(At this point, the consultant became aware of a critical issue with this case, that there were three people involved in teaching reading, and that there was little coordination occurring.)

C: And also the curriculum that you are using to teach her.

T: I don't have a written curriculum for her because she is so far behind that I don't have, say, what would be an appropriate second grade curriculum. But what I have been doing with her is getting books from the reading teacher that will help develop specific skills areas.

C: What you are saying is that you are not using the books that you use with the other children.

T: Yes, because those are not appropriate for her and I could not put her back in second grade here, I mean, that would be so obvious to the class and to her, that I think it would be very difficult for her to take in terms of her self-image.

C: Do you think that when I see the material—

T: It would be pretty obvious to see the mistakes she makes. I don't have the answer sheets because when they finish, I send them home to the parents. So I am not sure of what I have. I think that probably the best thing for you to look at is her reading book and log. And you would be able to see the kinds of mistakes she makes, words like *girl* she spells *gril*, and so forth. Her spelling is really poor and her handwriting very immature.

Several instructional issues were raised here by the interchange, including the fact that the teacher had not kept track of the child's errors on her work, sending the completed papers home with the child prior to recording them. In another example, the request to see the instructional material resulted in a valuable piece of information:

T: His handwriting is terrible. His handwriting could definitely be improved upon.

C: It sounds like you feel that improving his writing is a priority for Michael.

T: Absolutely. His physical writing skills.

C: Well, that is one problem we might want to focus on. I would like to see some samples of his work after the interview and also the materials that you use to work on writing with the children.

T: Well, I don't have a workbook. Part of his problem is my problem: I don't really teach handwriting. I should, and I don't. I have nothing to say in defense of myself. I have never found handwriting to be—I mean, I don't make a big deal about it. His happens to be abominable. But that's not his fault, it's my fault.

Too often when teachers bring instructional material to the child-study team or consultant-interview situation, it becomes used only as evidence of disability. The material is passed around, without much analysis, as documentation of the problem, rather than as information to be studied. The careful analysis of the work, and comparison of the referred child's work with that of other children, will be discussed in more detail in chapter 5.

Practicing Good Communication

Whereas most helping professionals have learned the communication skills described in this chapter, the point here was to remind the reader of them and to demonstrate how they are used in instructional consultation specifically. Bergan (1977) suggested that two types of practice are useful: recognition practice (practice in recognizing the various categories) and production practice (in which one modifies one's interviewing behaviors). Appendix A contains two exercises, one recognition- and one production-oriented, to help practitioners examine their own use of communication skills. For the reader interested in improving communication skills, they provide a place to begin. There is an interview transcript, which can be analyzed for both communication skills and content skills, as well as some exercises to provide practice in developing good communication skills. (In addition, there is a computer program to assist the user in recognizing the categories of communication responses. "Interviewing" (Rosenfield et al. 1985) is one of four components of SPIRIT I (Grimes, 1985), a computer module for continuing education of school psychologists, available through NASP.)

The Language of Interaction

Along with the communication strategies, a related aspect is that of the language used by the consultant. According to Paskewicz (1984), language structure conveys messages about the possibility of change, independent of the content of the interaction. What is said may be less important than how it is said. What is done about a school problem depends on how it is perceived. Consultation efforts to some degree are directed at changing the perspective taken by consultees stuck in their limiting world view. Certain language structures limit the possibility of change. Judgemental adjectives, abstract nouns used as explainers, and "shoulds" may structure our perspective so that change is more difficult, if not impossible.

Tombari and Bergan's (1978) work suggests how critical the influence of language can be on the teacher's role in the consultative relationship. In their research on question cuing, they have described a number of specific ways in which the questions we ask set the stage for problem analysis. For example, they have studied the effects of variations in cue type and the use of summaries on teacher verbalizations, expectancies, and problem definitions. They contrast two types of verbal cues: behavioral, such as "Tell me about _____'s behavior in your class" and "When does this behavior typically occur in your classroom"; and medical model, such as "Tell me something—anything—you would like to talk about _____" and "When does _____'s problem typically manifest itself?" (p. 214). The cues elicited responses from consultees congruent with the type of cue's respective viewpoints on human behavior. But even more striking, variations in types of cues affected the teacher's beliefs about the likelihood of solving the pupil's problem in the classroom. Teachers given behavioral cues expressed greater optimism about being able to solve problems in a classroom setting. Tombari and Bergan (1978) explained the difference in terms of the logical implications of the models:

> The medical model emphasizes remote environmental influences and internal characteristics as determinants of behavior. These variables cannot be manipulated by teachers to help children in school. The behavioral position, on the other hand, emphasizes the role of immediate environmental influences which generally can be controlled by a teacher. (p. 218)

Increasingly, we are aware that the language we use has a dramatic effect on the outcome of the consultant effort. It may not be a good strategy to allow teachers to use the initial referral interview to ventilate their frustrations and feelings about a child as an opening tack. To do so may be to allow teachers to convince themselves of the impossibility for them to cope with the child's difficulty. A variation of this problem becomes relevant again in focusing upon interventions, when the research on the effect of language on the acceptability of interventions is discussed in chapter 8.

Interview Format

Bergan (1977) developed an elaborate system for examining and coding the verbal interactions in consultation. He considered the necessity to produce different kinds of verbalizations to meet specific interviewing needs. The system developed included four categories: (1) source of the message (consultant and consultee); (2) the message content (what is being talked about); (3) the process (the kind of verbal action conveyed in a message); (4) and message control ("potential influence of a verbalization by one participant in consultation on what will be said or done by another participant," (p. 30).

Bergan (1977) describes the problem-identification interview in terms of a set of verbal behaviors in sequence:

1. The consultant "emits a series of behavior-specification elicitors to identify a behavior of concern to a consultee" (p. 58). The consultant elicits, through the nature of his or her utterances, the specific behaviors of concern to the consultee.

2. The consultant follows up with a "set of behavior-setting specification elicitors" (p. 58). The behavior-setting subcategory consists of "verbalizations referring to antecedent, consequent, and sequential conditions occurring contiguously to a client's behavior" (p. 33).

3. The consultant concludes with a summary of the behavior and behavior-setting content.

As a general framework within which the instructional consultation model progresses, Bergan's (1977) sequence has merit. However, the content aspect is modified in instructional consultation to examine academic behaviors more intensively.

To this point, the focus has been on the preparation for the interview and the communication skills needed to obtain clear communication and to maintain a collaborative relationship. The content of the interview, that is, what information is needed to complete the problem-identification stage, must also be considered.

CONTENT

Witt and Elliott (1983) delineate nine components of a problem-operational-ization interview: (1) explaining the purpose of problem definition; (2) identifying and selecting problem behaviors; (3) identifying problem frequency, duration and intensity; (4) identifying general conditions under which problem behaviors occur; (5) identifying desired performance level; (6) identifying client strengths; (7) identifying behavioral-assessment procedures; (8) identifying consultee effectiveness; and (9) summarizing the interview. A more elaborated agenda for a problem-solving interview is provided by Alessi and Kaye (1983), and by Bergan (1977) based on problem-solving models available in the literature. However, each of these valuable sources for determining the content of the referral interview is focused primarily on the child's behavior rather than on the child's academic functioning, although information about academic functioning might also be obtained. A more direct approach to academic problems is taken by other authors, however: structured interview formats focused upon academic assessment have been developed by Shapiro and Lentz (1985) and Deno and Mirkin (1977). Figure 3-4 is an elaboration of their models. Although the format described in Figure 3-4 includes information to help formulate the problem definition, that information usually will not be gathered in the order in which it appears in the format presented in Figure 3-4. Nor is it recommened that the questions be asked directly, given that the communication strategies just discussed would preclude doing that. The questions provide, however, a structure for developing a comprehensive picture of the child's academic problem. Most of the information indicated needs to be obtained before a complete picture of the problem emerges.

As the teacher and consultant strive to organize the information, the nature of the problem may become clearer. In many cases, it quickly becomes apparent that the child is being asked to work at frustration level, on objectives and in materials for which he or she is not ready. In a recent group of 26 students learning to do instructional consultation, 23 of their consultees had the referred child working in material that was at frustration level. Although knowing that the child is working at frustration level does not

When a teacher asks for consultation on a learning problem in the classroom, the following information is needed to help specify the problem. The focus is first on clarifying and describing the problem, prior to a decision about whether the child MIGHT have a handicapping condition requiring a formal evaluation.

I. Where in the scope and sequence of the classroom curriculum (reading, math, language arts, writing, etc.) does the teacher expect the learner to be in the academic area of concern at this point in the school year? This can be defined in terms of specific skills and/or placement in the basal reader or other sequenced curriculum materials used in this classroom/school.

II. What is the learner's actual current functional instructional level? (Data collected through curriculum-based assessment techniques provide this information.)

III. Is there a significant discrepancy between the learner's current level and the teacher's expected level? (Criteria need to be specified.)

IV. Is the learner currently placed, for instructional purposes, at his/her instructional level in the classroom instructional program?
   If not, what are the barriers to placing the learner at instructional level?

V. At instructional level, the following information is needed about the learner's performance:
   A. What type of error does the child make? (Error analysis techniques provide this information.)
   B. Are there prerequisite skills needed for the learner to move to the next step in the instructional sequence? What are they? (Task analysis is useful in determining these skills.)
   C. Do the curriculum materials themselves require additional prerequisite skills that the learner may not have; for example, is the learner required to know the names of the pictures on the phonics sheet? Is the learner required to write long answers beyond current writing level? (Task analysis is useful here, too.) How is this problem being handled?

VI. Concerning current instructional procedures:
   A. Describe the instructional procedures, including: instructional format, opportunities for feedback and error correction.
   B. How is skill mastery determined? Describe the evaluation procedures used.
   C. Have other teaching procedures been used? Describe, including results of mastery testing.
   D. Are there special conditions under which the learner demonstrates/can not demonstrate the skills and/or behaviors?

  E. What are the learner management techniques being used to assist the learner in maximizing on-task time?
  F. What is the current rate of progress the learner is making under current teaching/management procedures?

VII. Who else is involved in working on the learner's skills besides the classroom teacher?
  A. The above questions need to be answered by all those working with the learner on the skills in question.
  B. How do the professionals involved with the learner coordinate their work?

FIGURE 3-4.   Referral Information for Academic Problems: Specifying the referral Problems.

always solve the question of why the child is making such slow progress through the curriculum, it often provides a useful starting point for planning intervention.

The major focus of the interview, however, is the development of mutually agreed-upon referral questions which provide a basis for further assessment and/or intervention. Referral questions have several defining characteristics (Batsche, 1984):

1. Questions must be definable and measureable—observable and reportable.
2. Questions must be agreed upon by evaluation-team members and the referral agent.
3. Questions must lead to or have the potential to lead to interventions, not labels (p. 10).

The referral interview in Appendix B provides an opportunity for the reader to examine information gathered and generate referral questions that meet the criteria just listed.

The questions often generate a need for additional assessment strategies to answer them. Typically, the teacher does not have the information available that is needed to answer the questions. Indeed, one aspect of many children's lack of progress is that the teacher is not aware of the student's actual functional academic or behavior level. The consultant and teacher then must consider what questions still need to be answered and who will be responsible for doing so. The questions formulated must be answerable, that is, be definable and measureable (not historical questions, such as "Whatever did his kindergarten teacher in that other school do with him?") and must relate to developing a classroom intervention (not questions related, for example, to parent's marital status).

Whereas in most cases the teachers would be the logical ones to assess the child's academic status, often they do not have the skills and the consultant may need to do the academic assessment. (The procedures for doing so are discussed in the next chapters on observation and curriculum-based assessment.) The goal in most cases, however, is to model these procedures for teachers and to encourage them in future consultation interactions to incorporate curriculum-based assessment (CBA) and observational techniques into their own knowledge-and-practice repertoire.

The interview should not end until a plan is developed for gathering information to answer the diagnostic questions to complete the problem-identification process. Psychologists with relatively little experience in classrooms might find it useful to read the next two chapters about observation and CBA prior to conducting their first referral interview; knowing more about the kind of behaviors to be evaluated and how that evaluation is conducted is recommended.

A caution at this point: based on an examination of interview transcripts, it has become apparent that there is a flight from academic focus in these interviews. Teachers and psychologists seem to find it easier to talk about the child's behavior than about academic nitty-gritty. Often interviews end without the specific information being obtained, and consultants should not be surprised, particularly at first, to find themselves needing to go back for another interview.

SUMMARY

Problem identification should be viewed as a process. The problem identification stage begins with entry and contracting, during which teachers are introduced to consultation around academic problems in their classroom and informed of what is required of them and how the process unfolds. Consultants develop a referral process in the school to allow the teacher to request a consultation, and teachers who request consultations have a structure for arranging time to do so. The consultant enters the referral interview aware of the teacher's likely agenda, or prepared to listen for it, and to use good communication skills so that a clear picture of the problem emerges, while he or she maintains a collaborative, problem-solving orientation. Usually, the problem-identification phase is not concluded with one interview, since there is often additional information that needs to be obtained. Diagnostic questions are formulated, and methods to answer them are agreed upon, including assigning responsibility for doing so. We turn our attention now to two aspects of the process of gathering data to complete the problem-identification phase: classroom observation and curriculum-based assessment.

Chapter 4

CLASSROOM OBSERVATION

The proper unit of analysis for what people do together is what people do together.

—McDermott & Hood, 1982, p. 240

The classroom is a behavioral setting, an ecological entity with a life of its own (Sarason, 1982). The data of the classroom itself have the greatest relevance to a child's performance in the classroom. As a result, skill in systematic observation is necessary to obtain critical information for decision making about a child referred for a school learning problem. As McDermott and Hood (1982) reminded us, we need "descriptions of the intellectual task environments faced by particular children at particular times in terms of how their concerted behavior helps to organize and is organized by these tasks," descriptions of "what all parties are up to throughout a scene in which intellectual performances are at issue" (p. 244). Careful assessment of children with learning problems requires that we witness the context, with all its complexities and interactions, in which the problematic behavior occurs, as we search for "the determinants of behavior through examination of the individual's transactions with the social and physical environment" (Hartmann, 1984, p. 107).

In this chapter, much of what is known about behavioral observation is not discussed, as this information is readily available elsewhere (see, for example, Alberto & Troutman, 1982; Alessi & Kaye, 1983; Hartmann, 1982). The focus, instead, will be on two dimensions of the observation process: (1) integrating a classroom observation into the collaborative-consultation process; and (2) structuring classroom observations to answer questions about academic-referral problems.

61

IMPORTANCE OF SYSTEMATIC OBSERVATION

Observational measurement has been defined as "the process of systematic recording of behavior as it occurs, or of a setting as it exists, in ways that yield descriptions and quantitative measures of individuals, groups, or settings" (Goodwin & Driscoll, 1980, p. 110). Traditionally, classroom observation is often performed by school psychologists in a casual, haphazard, and anecdotal fashion, and is considered by many practitioners as offering "a chance to take a look at what is happening."

Although there is often some value in even a nonsystematic viewing of the setting in which the problem exists, in recent years, systematic behavioral-observation techniques have become more popular. School psychologists have received training in doing behavorial observations, using techniques such as event or frequency recording, interval recording, time sampling, and duration and latency recording. Most behavior-modification textbooks present detailed descriptions of these techniques (see, for example, Alberto & Troutman, 1982). However these systematic, behavioral observation techniques used in clinical assessment are still considered informal, that is, less-structured and less-elaborate attempts to use systematic observational procedures as opposed to the more formal observational-measurement techniques used in research (Goodwin & Driscoll, 1980; Hartmann, 1982).

Although systematic observation techniques have been associated with behavioral models, they are not limited to that orientation. As Lidz (1981) reminded us:

> An assessor can record observations in a manner directed by ethological, psychodynamic, or any other theoretical or atheoretical source of hypotheses that enables him to draw inferences from his data. . . . An assessor's theoretical orientation will determine his choice of which behaviors to record and how to interpret the data collected. (p. 76)

A major virtue of more systematic observation procedures is that they help the practitioner to minimize bias. The anecdotal observation is subject to considerable bias. It is especially difficult to observe classroom behavior because of the complexity of classroom life. No observer can monitor everything that takes place in the classroom. Therefore, what one "sees" is subject to selection bias of the observer. Certainly clinical observation does have a place. After all, one cannot avoid seeing some obvious problems in the classroom that do not need to be systematically observed, as in the case of the child described in the last chapter who was observed copying his homework from another child during an observation carefully constructed to monitor off-task behavior.

However, to provide the type of unbiased data that is required for classroom decision making, several other issues need to be clarified. First, there is an important distinction between behavior and inference. In observation, what one sees is the behavior. How one interprets that behavior requires a degree of inference. The observer does not see a poor attention span; rather, observers can gather data about well-defined off-task behavior. A child cannot be observed to be hyperactive; however, data can be gathered about out-of-seat behavior. The leap from what one sees to the evaluation of that vision is often made without recognizing that an inference has, in fact, been made.

In addition, there are considerations around reliability and validity of the classroom observation (Hartmann, 1984), if the data are to be used for instructional decision-making. Boehm and Weinberg (1977) suggested that we regularly ask the following questions: (1) "What am I trying to sample from the stream of all behavior?" (2) Why am I interested in the particular information provided by the observation procedures I choose?" and (3) "Am I reporting what I see objectively?" (p. 56)

In addition, they suggest that there are at least two conditions that must be met for valid observational measurement: (1) A representative sample of the behaviors to be measured must be observed; and (2) A complete, accurate record of the observed behavior must be made (p. 56).

In the case of instructional observation, the situation is not different. Figure 4-1, based on Boehm and Weinberg (1977, pp. 58-59), presents the validity and reliability issues salient to the classroom observer.

---

1. Is the observation system sensitive to questions you are asking about the child's problem? Is the purpose of the observation system matched to your goal?
2. Are the conditions for observer reliability met?
   a. Are behaviors defined carefully enough so that—
      they are mutually exclusive, that is, do not overlap?
      each behavior of concern can be observed?
   b. Is each category sufficiently narrow so that two or more observers would place behavior in the same category?
   c. Is inference necessary to categorize behavior?
3. Is the sampling procedure adequate to answer the questions asked?
   a. Is the procedure for sampling systematic?
   b. Is the procedure feasible, given the personnel and time constraints involved?
   c. Are the behaviors representative in terms of time, setting, and subjects?
   d. Is the coding system comfortable for the user?
4. Are the conditions for validity met?
   a. Are the behaviors observed relevant to the inferences likely to be made?
   b. Have sources of observer bias been considered and eliminated?

FIGURE 4-1. Checklist for observation systems.

Although this review of issues about observation is brief, it suggests at least that observation for instructional consultation does not differ in essentials from classroom observations for other clinical purposes. But it is helpful to keep in mind that the most critical issue is that of purpose: What referral question does this observation process help to answer?

OBSERVATION WITHIN
THE CONSULTATION PROCESS

For teachers, a classroom observation is often perceived as an aversive experience. After all, most teachers associate observation of their teaching behaviors with supervision rather than assistance. Further, if the consultation process has been working so far, the teacher has some awareness that the focus of the assessment is on the instructional match, the match between the child, the task, and his or her instruction. Therefore, attention must be paid to pre- and postobservation contacts, the interactions with the classroom teacher surrounding the observation itself.

Preparing for a Classroom Observation

During the entry-and-contracting period, in which the process of instructional consultation is discussed with the teacher, the teacher should have been informed that the consultant would likely be observing in the classroom. In the abstract, at least, the teacher should have had some warning that this is part of the consultation contract. As the situation emerges in which the consultant will actually enter the classroom, the teacher needs a fuller preparation for the event.

Most important, the teacher and consultant need to clarify what is going to be observed and how it will be observed. The more sharing about the observation process, the more the collaborative relationship will be enhanced rather than diminished by the intrusion of the consultant into the teacher's domain. It should be clear to the teacher what type of data will be gathered, and how it is related to the questions that the teacher has about the student. Using the initial interview to structure referral questions and develop assessment procedures relevant to the specific student being referred provides a logical precursor for a classroom observation.

The consultant often finds it useful to engage the teacher in discussion around the best time to observe the behavior in question and to consider together the effect of his or her presence on the classroom as a whole and on the child being observed in particular. Up front, it is necessary to discuss that one is not merely observing the child, but the child in the instructional interaction, as that is the relevant information for the process. It is not that one says, "I am observing you," but rather, "We need to know how Joe responds to your instruction and management techniques." If the critical element is the student response, we need to know clearly the stimuli that elicited the response, to evaluate the situation in terms of its actual effect upon the student.

As often as possible, it is useful to engage the teacher in collecting observational data. Moran (1978) made a strong case for teachers to use observational techniques around instructional concerns, as "the teacher's first responsibility is to be alert to response to instruction" (p. 14). However, while teachers are often keen observers of behavior, they are less often systematic in their observational style. Thus, the consultant might perceive that one aspect of the consultation process is to assist the teacher in collecting data more systematically.

However, particularly early in the consultative relationship, many teachers are reluctant to become involved in systematic observation. Whereas teachers are in the most logical position to collect reliable data over time, often they resist doing so, feeling overwhelmed by the procedures. Some degree of understanding of the pressures caused by being asked to do behaviorally oriented procedures, such as collecting observation data, is expressed by Abidin (1975). After exploring the internal events experienced by a teacher asked to be involved in a behavioral program for a child in her classrooom, Abidin used a "think out loud" technique with one teacher. He concluded that the process had some potentially negative effects on the teacher. He found, for example, alteration of perceptual experience, such as feeling tethered to the target child and a sense of having her range of movement limited; heightening of sensory awareness of sound and movement of the target child together with a reduction of awareness of the other children; body tension; and difficulty in concentrating. Using Broadbent's theoretical model, he concludes that:

> In short, whenever an individual operates in a complex stimulus input situation with an equally complex set of response requirements, the effect of intensifying stimuli emanating from a single source will be to produce a negative effect upon overall vigilance and the individual's ability to respond to other stimuli in the situation. (p. 56)

Abidin stresses that the importance of this is not in eliminating the teacher's participation in the program, but in how consultants handle the situation. He suggests that we can prepare consultees for these negative impacts, project understanding and empathy for the teacher's situation, and/or design programs that reduce the demands on the teacher. For example, suggesting simple techniques for observation is one strategy. A teacher can collect frequency data using a piece of paper strapped to the wrist, so that all the teacher has to do is make a mark with the pencil that is always in his or her hand. In many cases, though, the teacher will insist on someone else undertaking the responsibility.

Debriefing the Observation

An equally critical stage is the postobservation conference. It is important to clarify in advance that you will be discussing the observation with the teacher, and to arrange a suitable time for this discussion so that it is neither hurried nor off-the-cuff. Any anxiety that the teacher might have about her performance needs to be allayed as soon as possible. It is probably best to begin the conference by asking teachers to tell their perception of the event. Was it typical/atypical of that class and that child's behavior? Is there anything that the teacher wants to say about it?

The postobservation-feedback session should begin with the question that the observation was designed to answer. The data collected needs to be related to the problem for which the child was referred and which was agreed upon as the basis for the observation. The data themselves should be presented rather than the conclusion (inferences) drawn by the observer based on the data. It is often easy enough for teachers to reach the same conclusion that the consultant did from the data, and less resistance and/or defensiveness is generated when the conclusion is their own rather than someone else's.

In one case, a school psychologist was in a classroom to observe a child's off-task behavior. The most critical factor observed, however, was that the desk of the child had been placed out of the teacher's line of vision when he instructed the class. This fact was presented to the teacher; the consultant then asked what the implications of that arrangement might be on the teacher's concern that the child was constantly out of his seat demanding attention. It was not necessary for the psychologist to tell the teacher to move the child's desk.

OBSERVATIONAL SYSTEMS FOR CLASSROOM
INSTRUCTIONAL OBSERVATIONS

Given that direct observation is not only highly recommended in the professional literature for students referred for academic problems, but also required by law in the regulations enforcing P.L. 94-142 in many states, the concern then becomes how to collect observational data that are useful to answer questions that have arisen as a result of the referral process. Several observational systems exist that are suitable for assessment in academic referrals (Shapiro & Lentz, 1985; Ysseldyke & Christenson, 1985), and some of those will be discussed here. But it has been the author's experience that the observational process can become, in some cases, as rote a procedure as some psycho-diagnostic testing batteries, particularly when people perceive it as a required tool for placement/classification decisions under the law.

For example, at a recent child-study-team meeting attended by the author, the speech pathologist, the member of the team assigned to do the classroom observation, reported that she had "stopped in" to observe the child who was being discussed. She had indeed collected data about off-task time, which she duly reported. However, the teacher had not yet clarified the purpose of the referral with the child-study team. Moreover, the observer had been assigned by the child-study team to do the observation in this referral because she had the time. There had been no attempt to meet with the teacher first to determine what the problem was or to arrange the observation at a time during which the behavior of concern might be exhibited. In fact, in reporting the observation, neither the content of the lesson at that point nor any other factors related to the situation was presented.

With minimal training, it is not hard to select a behavior and generate a behavioral-observation system, or to develop a structured observation format that everyone in the district uses to observe a referred child. However, it is a critical first step to generate a series of questions that the observation technique will answer. First the question, then the decision about how to collect the data.

For consultants with relatively little or no classroom teaching experience (or experience at a grade level substantially different from that of the current assignment), it is useful to develop some sense of classroom life. Often, psychologists will indicate that they find observing in classrooms 'boring,' that they're not comfortable there, and/or that they are not sure exactly what is supposed to go on. Both for academic and behavioral referrals, if the focus is to be on classroom intervention, it is essential that the observer understand the culture and regularities of classroom life. Figure 4-2 suggests a procedure by which the consultant can develop some understanding of the teaching of a major source of referrals, that of reading. (See also Table 4-1 and Figures 4-3 and 4-4.)

Several formal systems of observation exist for academic problems. Three such systems are described as follows:

Student Teacher Observation Code (STOC). Shapiro and Lentz (1986) believed that certain minimal data need to be collected, including: an estimate of student "on-task" time, defined as "orientation towards task materials" (p. 40); measures of common classroom behaviors that might compete with engaged times; teacher-initiated contacts with students; teacher provision of feedback about academic performance; and compliance with teacher instructions. The Student Teacher Observation Code (Saudargas & Creed-Murrah, 1981) is a system that Shapiro and Lentz (1986) present as meeting their criteria. The STOC utilizes 30-second momentary-time samples to record behaviors having obvious durations and for which an estimate of percent of time of occurrence is desired, and frequency counts for recording discrete behaviors during the 30-second intervals between time samples. On the protocol (which is presented in Figure 4-5), space is provided for classroom rules and seating arrangements to be recorded. Table 4-2 and Figure 4-5 provide the behavior code for this system.

1. **Arrange with a teacher to do an observation in a classroom during reading and for a discussion of the lesson afterward.** It is most useful to do this in the first or second grade. Even better, arrange more than one observation across grade levels.

2. **Obtain information on the following, which should also be the focus of your observation:**

   a. *Class grouping procedures:* On what bases are the children grouped? Are there criteria for regrouping?

   b. *Specific methods used for teaching decoding and comprehension skills:* Is there a scope and sequence to the reading program? How and when are the reading skills introduced? Is a basal reading series used? What, if any, supplementary materials are used along with the basal series?

   c. *The relationship in the classroom among the various language art skills (reading, writing, listening, speaking):* Is there a specific scope and sequence for each of these areas? What do you observe about how the teacher relates these areas?

   d. *The instructional strategies that are used in the lesson itself:* Use the A.P.D.A.C. Instructional Strategy Sheet* or The Instructional Environment Scale (TIES)† to observe the teacher's use of instructional strategies. Be sure to show the teacher the list so that he or she knows what will be observed.

3. **After the observation, discuss with the teacher what problems, if any, you observed children displaying, and how the teacher thinks problems in reading should be handled.** The Teacher Interview and the Student Interviews of the TIES provide a structured format for focusing on a single child.‡

*The A.P.D.A.C. Instructional Strategy Sheet is provided here in Table 4-1.

†The Instructional Environmental Scale (TIES) (Ysseldyke & Christenson, 1985). The Teacher Interview and Student Interview sections of TIES are provided here as Figures 4-3 and 4-4, respectively.

‡See Figures 4-3 and 4-4.

FIGURE 4-2. An observational process to learn how reading is taught.

Student _____

Grade _____

TIES
The Instructional
Environment Scale

Date _____

School _____

DATA RECORD FORM

Setting _____

Teacher _____

SECTION I   TIES TEACHER INTERVIEW

---

1. To what extent was _____ 's performance on _____
   typical?   (day)

2. How does your instructional goal for _____ differ from
   his/her classmates?

3. What are your expectations for _____ ?
   (Probe for quality of work, classroom participation, task
   completion, neatness, if assistance is needed.)

4. How do you plan instruction for _____ ?
   (Probe for strengths, weaknesses, skill level, emotional needs,
   interests.)

5. How do you determine the appropriate instructional placement
   for _____ ?

6. Tell me about _____ 's independent assignments.
   (Probe for amount of practice, kind of tasks can handle
   independently, success rate.)

7. How do you evaluate _____ 's progress?
   (Probe for record keeping, decisions about what to teach next,
   mastery criteria.)

Additional copies of this form (#0649) may be ordered from PRO-ED,
5341 Industrial Oaks Blvd., Austin, Texas 78735 USA   512/892-3142

Copyright © 1987 by James E. Ysseldyke and Sandra L. Christenson

FIGURE 4-3

SECTION III TIES STUDENT INTERVIEW

1. I want you to tell me what you needed to do on these assignments.
   a. What did your teacher want you to learn?
   b. What did your teacher tell you about why these assignments are important?
   c. What did you have to do?
   d. Show me how you did the work. (Have student explain a sample item.)

2. I am going to ask you several questions. In each case, I want you to tell me your answer by using this scale, where 1 means "not very much" and 4 means "very much."
   a. Sometimes students understand their assignments. Sometimes they don't. Show me how well you understand the assignment.
   1   2   3   4
   b. How much did you believe you could do the assignment?
   1   2   3   4
   c. How interesting is this work for you?   1   2   3   4

3. Now, I have some other questions.
   a. Sometimes students cannot finish their work, and sometimes they have extra time. How much time do you usually get to finish your work: too little (1), just about right (2), or too much (3)?
   1   2   3
   b. Does your tacher call on you to answer questions in class: never (1), not much (2), a lot (3)?   1   2   3

4. What does your teacher expect you to do when he or she gives these assignments.
   a. If you are confused?
   b. If you are done with your work?

5. What does your teacher tell you about:
   a. Completing your work? (What happens if your work is not done?)
   b. Getting the answers correct? (What happens if you make mistakes?)
   c. Having neat papers? (What happens if your work is messy?)

6. Student Success Rate:
   a. Number of questions completed _____
   b. Number of correct answers _____
   c. Total number of questions assigned _____
   d. Success rate _____
   e. Kind of errors made by the student _____

FIGURE 4-4. From The Instructional Environment Scale, J. E. Ysseldyke and S. L. Christenson. Copyright © 1987 by James E. Ysseldyke and Sandra L. Christenson. Reprinted by permission.

Saudargas-Creed-Murrah   Sheet#: _____

_____ (GR: ___)   _____ M T W R F   Start: _____ End: _____ Total: _____
Student   Date   Day (circle)   Time

                                                               1. ISW: TPsnt   3. SmGp: Tled
                                                               2. ISW: TSmGp   4. LgGp: Tled
_____   _____
School   Class Activity
                                                                                      Ac. Beh
_____   _____   _____
Teacher   Observer   Referral Problem

STATES	1	2	3	4	5	6	7	8	9	10	11	12	13	14	15	16	17	18	19	20	Σ	%
SW																						
OS																						
LK																						
M																						
PLO																						
SIC																						
SIT																						
OACT																						

EVENTS	1	2	3	4	5	6	7	8	9	10	11	12	13	14	15	16	17	18	19	20	Σ	Rate
RH																						
CAL																						
OS																						
OAG																						
N																						
AC																						
OCA																						

TEACHER	1	2	3	4	5	6	7	8	9	10	11	12	13	14	15	16	17	18	19	20	Σ	Rate
TA/SW																						
TA/OTH																						
DIR-OPP																						
DIR-C+																						
APP																						
DIS																						

COMMENTS _____
_____
_____
_____

FIGURE 4-5. STOC behavioral coding sheet. From S. Shapiro and F. Lentz, "Behavioral Assessment of Academic Skills." In *Advances in School Psychology, Vol. V*, T. R. Kratochwill (Ed.), (1986), Hillsdale, NJ: Lawrence Erlbaum Associates. Reprinted by permission.

TABLE 4-1

A.P.D.A.C. INSTRUCTIONAL STRATEGY SHEET

(Copyrighted: Carol Lidz, 1977)

Child's name: _____ Date: _____

Teacher's name: _____ Subject: _____

Objectives: _____

Strategy	Does Now	Effectiveness: V=very S=somewhat NV=not very DK=don't know	A=appro. to task NA=not appro. to task	C=continue A=add

A. Setting the stage for learning: methods which introduce and present the material: methods which orient the child's attention.
1. Verbal instructions:
  a. describes task:
    (1) nature of:
    (2) terminal objectives.				

2. Begins presentation with a question which relates to the task to be described.				
3. Uses more than one modality for presentation, e.g. auditory + visual.				
4. Reduces distractions not relevant to the task.				
5. Induces motor activity of pupils as instructions are presented.				
6. Modulates tone or volume of voice to get attention.				

Item				
7. Uses physical contact with pupil.				
8. Induces recall of what is already known which relates to new material.				
9. Gestures to, points to, underlines details to be particularly noted.				
10. Calls pupil by name.				
11. Uses verbal alerting cues such as "look at this . . .", "are you ready?", "here's another . . ."				
12. Varies rate (speed) of presentation to maintain attention.				
13. Assures presence of subskills necessary to new task.				
14. Assures comprehension of each part of presentation before proceeding.				
15. If written, varies print size.				
16. Other: _____				
B. Guiding the Learning Process[*]				
1. Delays (when child begins to respond before teacher completes sentence, teacher says, "Wait a minute" and repeats sentence).				
2. Focuses for attention (asks child to repeat what was requested: "Do you remember what I asked you to do?").				
3. Repeats demand (teacher repeats what was requested or said).				
4. Synonymously rephrases (uses different word or phrase for something child did not appear to understand).				
5. Partially completes task for child (teacher begins and child completes).				

TABLE 4-1. Cont'd

Strategy	Does Now	Effectiveness: V=very S=somewhat NV=not very DK=don't know	A=appro. to task NA=not appro. to task	C=continue A=add
6. Dissects into smaller components (child completes).				
7. Relevant comparisons are offered: a. correct, along with clearly incorrect from which child is to choose, e.g., "is this number 'more than', 'less than' or 'just the same' as that?" b. introduces perceptual or verbal cue to emphasize significant aspects, e.g., teacher used fingers to show "this is five," "this is three," "which is more?"				
8. Teaches didactically: a. gives relevant facts; b. provides model demonstration.				
9. Leads child into clarification of response, e.g., "what do you mean by . . ." "tell me more about . . ." "what does it do?"				
10. Repeats demonstration (not the same stimulus value as first demonstration, as this time the child has the question to be answered in mind).				
11. Relates unknown to known (direct application of present to past, without requiring cognitive transformation).				
12. Directs pupil's action on materials in way which helps pupil recognize salient characteristics; tells child to do something so that child discovers desired response.				

13. Verbally directs child's focus on relevant features.					
14. Makes task more concrete by introducing objects or pictures.					
15. Reduces number of stimuli to which to attend or from which to choose.					
16. Changes mode of pupil response, e.g., from reproduction to matching or selecting from alternatives or imitating.					
17. Uses method of successive approximation, i.e., goes back to simpler level, and gradually builds up to more complex.					
18. Varies modality of stimulus presentation (visual, verbal, motor, imagery).					
19. Varies method of presentation as appropriate to the material, e.g., re: math, rote for computation, discovery for comprehension; wholistic vs. analytic approach.					
20. Material and presentation are rationally sequenced.					
21. Other: _____					
C. Promoting Retention and Generalization:					
1. Provides review.					
2. Allows for adequate practice (consider distributed vs. massed).					
3. Builds in "test" and review items into lesson.					
4. Promotes visual imagery.					
5. Encourages verbal elaboration and cognitive transformation.					
6. Cites a number of examples.					

TABLE 4-1. Cont'd

Strategy	Does Now	Effectiveness: V = very S = somewhat NV = not very DK = don't know	A = appro. to task NA = not appro. to task	C = continue A = add
7. Introduces "distractors" (examples of when the rule taught does not apply).				
8. Has pupils work out problems or examples not specifically included in the teaching or practice segments.				
9. Makes material meaningful in terms of everyday experiences, past learnings, or future expectations.				
10. Optimizes anxiety level (not too much, not too little).				
11. Delays information feedback.				
12. Induces encoding from one modality to another (e.g., aural-verbal to written or pictorial).				
13. Other: _____				
D. Utilization of Reinforcement:				
1. Uses intrinsic reinforcement (material which itself has value of appeal to pupil).				
2. Induces competitive responses (with self or others).				
3. Uses contingencies: a. high probability activities; b. privileges, including free time.				

4. Praises.				
5. Approves.				
6. Uses physical contact (positively or negatively?).				
7. Uses aversive reinforcement (punishing contingencies, disapproving remarks, etc.).				
8. Uses information feedback (indicates right vs. wrong, gives correct information).				
9. Uses tokens.				
10. Uses concrete reinforcers (foods, toys . . .).				
11. Gives grades.				
12. Uses contracts.				
13. Uses attention-inattention.				
14. Uses peers to reinforce.				
15. Other: _____				

*B1-13 from Blank, M. (1973)

TABLE 4-2

Behaviors Coded in the Saudargas Student/Teacher Observation Code

Student Behaviors	
Symbol	*Behavior Category Label*
SW	School work
OS	Out of seat
LK	Looking Around
M	Motor or repetitive body movements
PLO	Playing with objects
SIC	Social interaction with child
SIT	Social interaction with teacher
OACT	Other activity
RH	Raising hand
Cal	Calling out to teacher
OAG	Object aggression
N	Making noise
AC	Approach child
OCA	Other child approach

Teacher Behaviors	
Symbol	*Behavior Category Label*
TA/SW	Teacher approach to student doing school work
TA/OTH	Teacher approach to student doing other activity
Dir-Op	Teacher direction followed by student opposition
Dir-C+	Teacher direction followed by student compliance
App	Teacher approval or praise of student behavior
Dis	Teacher disapproval of student behavior

Note. From Shapiro and Lentz (1986). Reprinted with permission.

Teacher-Pupil Interaction Scale (TPIS). Another method of observation that has proved useful in instructional consultation referrals is one developed by Goodwin and Coates (1977). The Teacher-Pupil Interaction Scale (TPIS), according to the authors:

> . . . was designed to measure the sequential verbal and nonverbal interactions between pupils and teachers across the entire range of classroom activities. In contrast to instruments developed primarily for research purposes . . . , the TPIS was designed for daily use by psychologists and other consultants. The scale is easily administered and scored, thus facilitating its use by educational consultants. The information provided suggests specific ways in which teachers can modify their instruction to produce desired changes in pupil performance. (p. 51)

Four demands were considered in development of the scale. First, it was designed to collect reliable data on "a pupil's on- and off-task classroom behavior before, during, and after remedial interventions" (p. 51). A second aspect was the need to relate changes in behavior to instructional method, such that sequential patterns could be observed. Third, reliable data on interactions between other children in the class and the teacher needed to be provided. Fourth, the categories needed to be both "sufficiently discrete to pinpoint a variety of classroom interactions . . . but not so narrow that meaningful frequencies would result only from around-the-clock observations or ratings of unique classroom settings" (p. 52).

The observation system itself consists of two kinds of categories: teacher behaviors and student behaviors. There are four categories within each. The teacher behavior is rated only in terms of the teacher's interaction with the particular child being observed. The pupil behaviors are rated on a continuum from on-task to increasing degrees of off-task behaviors. Table 4-3 contains a description of the categories and their definitions.

The data for the TPIS are collected on a matrix (see Figure 4-6) of 14 blocks of 12 rows and 4 columns within each block. Space is provided for indicating the child's name, the observer's name, the specific instructional

TABLE 4-3
Categories of the Teacher-Pupil Interaction Scale (TPIS)

Teacher-Behavior Categories

1. **Instructing:**   T instructs, explains, describes, answers questions, gives directions, and provides P with information regarding his or her performance.
2. **Rewarding:**   T makes a positive verbal or nonverbal response to P's performance, appearance, or other characteristic.
3. **Nonattending or neutral:**   T attends to activities that do not include P being observed.
4. **Disapproving:**   T makes a negative verbal or nonverbal response to some aspect of P's performance, appearance, or other characteristic.

Pupil-Behavior Categories

1. **On-task behavior:**   P, during instructional periods, uses task materials, orients toward T and/or the assigned work, and, when directed, interacts with other Ps. (Activities associated with the completion of a task (e.g., sharpening pencils, submitting work, or T comment) also fall within this category.)
2. **Scanning behavior:**   P orients away from the teacher or class activity, but makes no verbal or physical contact with other Ps.
3. **Social Contact:**   P orients away from T or class activity by interacting socially or getting out of seat, but fewer than four other Ps orient towards P's activity.
4. **Disruptive behavior:**   P orients away from T and/or class activity by interacting with other Ps verbally and/or physically, and four or more Ps orient toward P's activity.

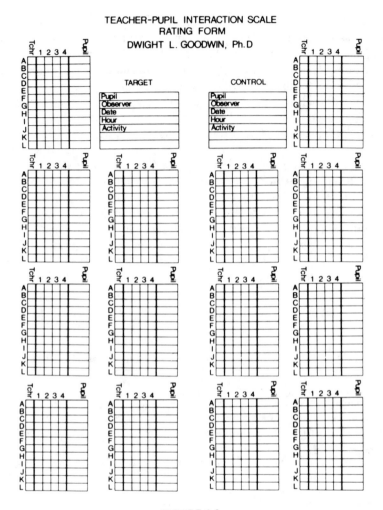

FIGURE 4-6

activity, and the day and hour. A change in activity during an observation can be noted next to the observation block in which it occurred. As a result of having the data in this sequence, changes in both the teacher and the child can be related to transitions between activities as well as to subject matter and type of instructional activity. In Figure 4-7, one of the blocks is completed. Figure 4-8 demonstrates how percentages are derived from the observational data.

At the end of each 5-second interval, the observer (O) simultaneously records both the teacher's and the child's behavior. There is no attempt to estimate behavior during the whole interval. The pupil's behavior (P) is designated by the numbers on the column, while the teacher's behavior (T) is

	1	2	3	4
A	1			
B		1		
C		1		
D		1		
E		1		
F				4
G	1			
H	1			
I			1	
J			1	
K			4	
L	1			

FIGURE 4-7

Pupil Behavior

Teacher Behavior	I	2	3	4	Σ	%
I	151	0	0	2	153	60
2	5	0	0	0	5	02
3	20	48	13	9	90	31
4	0	2	0	2	4	01
Σ	176	50	13	13	ΣΣ 252	
%	70	20	5	5		

FIGURE 4-8

described by a number (1-4) entered into the column describing the child's behavior. Each row, designated by a letter, A-L, corresponds to an interval of 5 seconds. One minute of behavior is recorded in each block. After completing a block on the referred child, O next observes a selected control child for the following minute on the space designated on the right side of the form. The authors suggest selecting control Ps by beginning with the pupil seated nearest the exit and proceeding clockwise around the room. The alternating 1-minute observations of target and control children are continued for 14 minutes, so that 7 minutes of the target pupil and 7 minutes of control children's interactions with the teacher are obtained.

Training procedures are suggested by the authors. They maintain that interobserver agreement of .80 or higher can be established with student or parent volunteers. Trainees can move from role playing an illustration of the behaviors the categories were designed to include to rating only teacher and then only pupil behaviors, to finally rating both simultaneously. Pairs of trainees can be assigned to classrooms and their rate of agreement determined. Finally, Goodwin and Coates use a criterion videotape to assure that the raters have reached mastery. Information on the validity of the TPIS for discriminating intervention effects is also provided (Goodwin & Coates, 1977).

The Teacher-Pupil Interaction Scale data are analyzed in two ways. First, matrix analysis is used to evaluate the responses of both teacher and child before, during, and after an intervention. A 4x4 matrix can be constructed for both target and control Ps, permitting comparisons both in terms of changes as a result of interventions as well as generalization of effects to peers. Summation along the rows yields frequencies of teacher behaviors, while column sums show total pupil behavior. Statistical analyses are possible, although examination of the percentage is often enough for classroom decision making. Having the data in this format also allows for subtle changes in teacher behavior to be suggested. For example, while the teacher may reward sufficiently, more selective rewarding may be needed. The matrix may help clarify which teacher behaviors produce better learning conditions for the child. Secondly, the data can be analyzed sequentially, to provide environmental assessment information, to evaluate the "precise nature of the contingencies existing between T and P" (p. 57).

Determining Performance Discrepancies in Social Behavior.   A third observational system was provided by Deno and Mirkin (1977). First, they suggest that one set of behaviors can identify the "categories of concern" (p. 101) for most teachers; these are defined in Figure 4-9.

Deno and Mirkin (1977) suggested that observers establish consistency by the use of two observers recording the same behavior at the same time at least once, and estimates of agreement be established using the formula for observer reliability:

$$\frac{\text{Smaller number of occurrences recorded by observer X}}{\text{Larger number of occurrences recorded by observer Y}} \times 100 = \%$$

If the percentage falls below 80%, the data cannot be considered reliable. Further training of the observers may be needed.

To collect the actual data, Deno and Mirkin (1977) recommended that several 10 to 30 minute periods each day for 5 to 7 days be scheduled. Although 30 consecutive minutes for 5 days is preferable, they indicate that a minimum of 10 to 20 minutes per day for 7 days is also acceptable. A protocol for their system is found in Figure 4-10, and they note that any form used should record the incidence of the target behaviors per minute for both referred child and peers, as well as marking the starting and ending times for the observation.

A number of random-sampling methods to select the peers to be used as control subjects against which to measure the target child are suggested. The observer may go up and down rows, move from one table to another clockwise, or alternate from left to right. They warn against choosing children who sit near the target child and to switching during the observation to a child exhibiting a behavior of interest.

To record, 0 enters a tally in the appropriate box for each occurrence during the timed minute. If the behavior continues for the whole minute, only one mark is entered; if the behavior does not occur, a zero is entered. Observations are alternated between the referred child and the control children, focusing on a different alternate each time: during minute one, the target child is observed; during minute two, peer no. 1 is observed; during minute three, the target child is observed; during minute four, peer no. 2 is observed, etc.

The data are analyzed in terms of rate/minute for the target pupil compared to the average per minute rate of peers. At the end of all the observation periods, the median per minute rates for each behavior for each

---

1. **Noise:** Any sounds created by the child which distract either another student or the teacher from the business at hand. The noise may be generated vocally (including talking out or unintelligible sounds) or nonvocally (tapping a pencil or snapping fingers).

2. **Out-of-place:** Any movement beyond the either explicitly or implicitly defined boundaries in which the child is allowed movement. If the child is seated at a desk, then movement of any sort out of the seat is out-of-place.

3. **Physical contact or destruction:** Any contact with another person or another person's property that is unacceptable to that person. Kicking, hitting, pushing, tearing, breaking, taking, are categorized as physical contact or destruction.

4. **Off-task:** Any movement away from a prescribed activity which does not fall into one of the three previously defined categories. Looking around, staring into space, doodling, or any observable movement not related to the task at hand is included.

5. **Other:** Although the above-mentioned behaviors serve as a reasonable basis for most observations, individual cases may arise in which other behaviors should be recorded. Children may be identified who do not communicate or who do not interact. In such instances, either self-initiated utterances or self-initiated contacts may be added, defined, and recorded. Generally, however, the first four categories will encompass many of the discrete categories that might be considered, and the "other" category should be used only if absolutely necessary to clarify the problem identified by the teacher.

FIGURE 4-9. Definition of categories for data-based program modification system. Adapted from *Data-Based Program Modification: A Manual* (p. 103) by Stanley Deno and Phyllis Mirkin. Published by the Leadership Training Institute/Special Education, University of Minnesota.

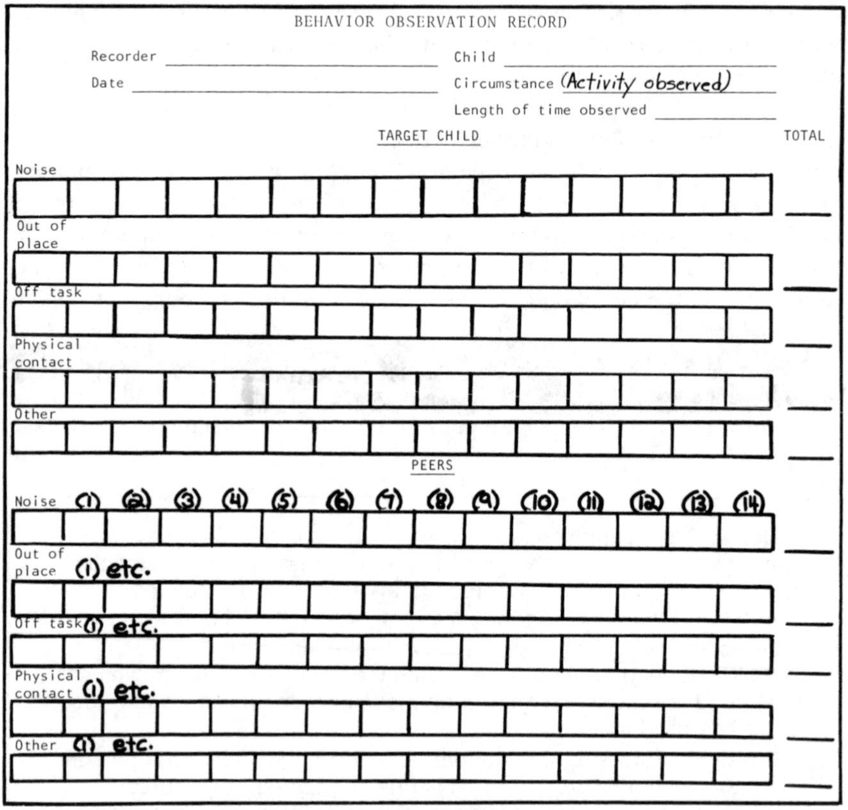

BEHAVIOR OBSERVATION RECORD

Recorder ______ Child ______

Date ______ Circumstance (Activity observed)

Length of time observed ______

TARGET CHILD — TOTAL

Noise

Out of place

Off task

Physical contact

Other

PEERS

Noise (1) (2) (3) (4) (5) (6) (7) (8) (9) (10) (11) (12) (13) (14)

Out of place (1) etc.

Off task (1) etc.

Physical contact (1) etc.

Other (1) etc.

FIGURE 4-10

day of observation are determined for both the target child and peers (all the peer data are aggregated, as though it were emitted by one person). The data are then graphed. Examples of how this method is used can be found in Deno and Mirkin (1977, pp. 101-108).

Use of an Observational System. While many other formal systems exist, these three (STOC, TPIS, and the DBPM) provide the consultant with some structured formats with which to organize an observation. It is possible to make useful modifications in any of these three systems (or to use them as they are) provided the consultant understands the concerns noted earlier in this chapter regarding collecting reliable and valid observation data. Two examples (Observation Cases 1 and 2) of how instructional consultants conducted observations are provided in the appendix to chapter 4.

OBSERVING THE ACADEMIC PROBLEM

It is a rare case in which direct observation is not useful for gathering data on a child with an academic problem. Ethnographers in education have convincing evidence that instruction is an interactional activity, that the patterns in the ways teachers and children interact with each other enable us to identify factors that support and/or constrain participation and learning:

> . . . the academic task is defined through the social, interpersonal context. . . . the academic task (e.g., silent reading, vocabulary development, story discussion) is produced during interactions among teacher, students, and texts; academic tasks are not the preset or explicitly stated tasks provided in curriculum guides, teacher guides, or lesson plans. . . . What actually constitutes the academic task depends on how it is delivered during the social and communicative interactions of teachers and students. . . . That is, the ways in which the task is delivered (e.g., what is done, to whom, for what purpose, in what ways) defines what is actually required of students. For example, recent work has shown that two teachers may have the same materials, similar groups of students, similar training, and the same stated task (reading and discussing a story) and not produce the same academic task. Differences in delivered task result from the ways in which the teacher distributes turns, the types of questions asked, the point at which questions are asked, the types of information to be discussed, the ways in which students respond, and so forth. (Bloome & Green, 1985, p. 168.)

The observation systems of the types presented thus far in this chapter are useful for obtaining measures of the behavioral corrrelates that often accompany learning problems. But they do not usually provide information on the academic performance in its context. At the most basic level, too often children placed at frustration level in the scope and sequence of the curriculum are observed on classroom behaviors, such as off-task behavior. How long would most college students spend on-task in a Greek 3 class if they never had the earlier, prerequisite courses? They would drop the course. Elementary school children rarely have that option! Instead they drop out of the activity (translated as "off-task" behavior). Many children are asked to function in a set of activities for which they do not have the prerequisite skills. To then measure their on-task behavior is mindless. Thus, a critical question prior to the observation of off-task behavior must be whether the work itself is at the child's instructional level. The next chapter will cover in detail the techniques of curriculum-based assessment, which are used to answer the question of task suitability for the child.

The following case example describes the interaction between curriculum match and off-task behavior:

*Case Demonstrating Instructional Mismatch
and Its Relationship to Off-Task Behavior*

The following observation was conducted in a fourth grade class in an urban parochial school, as a result of a referral. Tammy was referred mainly for math problems, in particular problems with division and multiplication. The teacher and consultant agreed that it would be beneficial for the consultant to observe the class during math period. We agreed to focus on Tammy's on- and off-task behaviors. We wanted to know why she was having such great difficulties in math. I would look at the teacher's strategy for teaching Tammy and her interaction with her.

The observation occurred on a Thursday afternoon between 1 and 2 PM. The students had just returned from lunch and were settling down to the afternoon math class. The class was going to review division because the children were having a test the next day. This was also the last day the teacher was teaching division to the class because she had to move on in the curriculum to teach measurement the following week.

We had also decided that I was going to be a nonparticipant observer and that I would sit close to Tammy. The methods for collecting data were the following: (1) narrative; (2) record sheet for collecting on- and off-task behaviors, and (3) the A.P.D.A.C. Instructional Strategy Sheet.

Following is the sequence of events as they occurred that Thursday afternoon. In the first place, the teacher appeared to be in control of the class. The students were grouped in approximately four tables around the classroom. Both Tammy and another child (known as very disruptive and as being far behind in academics) were seated next to the teacher's desk. The class in general ran very smoothly. The transition from one exercise to the next was done easily. For instance, at one point when the teacher grouped the children for peer tutoring, this was done in a matter of minutes.

Analysis of the Instructional Design:

Setting the stage: the teacher used 6 out of the 15 strategies in this category. She introduced to the class the agenda for the day, used both auditory and visual modalities to explain material, and reminded the students of what had been already taught related to division, such as subtraction and multiplication.

Guiding the learning process: the teacher asked children to repeat what was requested, rephrased it, provided model demonstrations, and led children into clarification of her explanations. She made tasks more concrete by introducing object to the explanation of tasks, and used a method of successive approximation.

Reinforcement: the teacher's use of reinforcers was limited to a few phrases or nonverbal signs of praise and approval upon students' responses. She also employed peer tutoring to reinforce other students. No other kind of reinforcers were observed.

Interval recording procedure: I devised a record sheet for collecting data on Tammy's on- and off-task behaviors, by comparing her to a control pupil in the classroom and recording on- and off-task behavior in 5-minute blocks of 10 seconds each for a 40-minute period. On-task behavior was defined by the following activities: looking at the teacher if she was talking, looking at the book when class was doing some exercises, following directions given by the teacher, looking at the blackboard if the teacher was doing some exercises, sitting in her seat in the classroom, and any other activity that had to do with the task at hand, such as sharpening the pencil to write up exercises in the notebook. Results indicated that Tammy was on-task only 25% of the time, contrary to the control child, who was 100% on-task. Here is a description of some of her behaviors: Tammy spent a considerable amount of time talking to the child next to her or calling for his attention. For the first 20 minutes or so of the class Tammy was making calendars in her workbook and playing with her pencil and a ruler. When the teacher specifically asked for the class's attention to explain an exercise in the blackboard or demanded the class's attention, Tammy never paid any attention. On the contrary, Tammy was always looking for something (off-task) to do. Tammy daydreamed at times, too (crossing her legs, looking to the opposite side of the room, whispering words). When the students were assigned for peer tutoring, Tammy was matched with another girl. While the other child was doing all the work, Tammy was not doing anything, or would just do the easy work such as separating the counters by color. When Tammy was asked by the other child to do one exercise, Tammy stood up to look at another child's response and wrote it in her workbook.

Feedback to teacher: The first thing I did when I reported the observation data to the teacher was to ask her if the lesson I observed was a typical lesson. She said that on the average it was. So, I started by giving her positive feedback with respect to the instructional strategy. The school social worker, Eileen, who was also at the conference, contributed a great deal in giving the teacher positive feedback. When I presented the data on Tammy's behavior, the teacher reacted as very surprised. She had not noticed that Tammy was off-task with such frequency. We discussed that because Tammy is off-task in such a quiet way. Tammy never drew her attention by being loud or out-of-seat. When we talked about the peer tutoring, the teacher asked for my opinion about it. I told her that, indeed, the peer tutoring was a very positive thing to do, but that it would be better carried out if the children knew the purpose of it. In Tammy's case the girl who was supposed to help Tammy just sat there and did all the exercises by herself without getting Tammy much involved in the process. We discussed that one hypothesis for Tammy's off-task behavior was the level of difficulty of the material presented to her in class. Since Tammy does not know what goes on in class most of the time, she looks for things to do in the meantime. When I asked if she had noticed that Tammy and the child next to her were disruptive to each other, it did not come as a surprise to her. She added that it was probably for the same reason as Tammy, because the other child was very far behind academically, too. She reacted very positively to the observations and said she was going to do something about it.

In view of this observation and a task analysis of Tammy's problems in math, it can be concluded that Tammy's on- and off-task behaviors during math class are due to an instructional mismatch between Tammy's skill level and the tasks demanded by the curriculum.

Sometimes it is useful to demonstrate to teachers the difference in a child's on-task time when the material is at the child's instructional level compared to when it is at frustration level. Many teachers seem to view off-task time as a personality trait (distractibility, impulsivity, etc.) rather than as a possible reaction to material that is too difficult. Demonstrating the child's differential performance is often helpful to counter this perception and stifle the referral to the neurologist for a suggested ADD (Attention Deficit Disorder). However, it is also true that many children who have been off-task for long periods in their learning history as a result of inappropriately difficult work do have trouble settling down even when their curriculum is adjusted to their instructional level. Observation of on- and off-task time at that point becomes a baseline for intervention.

But direct observation procedures can also be developed to answer particular questions related to the instructional context. For example, we have used observation to help clarify at what point in the instructional sequence a child goes off-task. In many cases teachers are aware that the child is not completing seat work. Is the child off-task during the time the directions are presented? Does a change in the procedure for starting seat work (such as providing one direction at a time, helping the child with the first example, etc.) make a difference in either latency for beginning the task or total on-task time? Does the child begin the work and then stop after one problem? How many problems can the child complete before going off-task? Does the child stop working or appear interrupted by another child or another classroom distraction? Sometimes teachers are unable to concentrate on the target child because of their need to attend to the multiple other classroom interactions, and answers to these focused questions can be obtained best by another observer. However, it should be clear that ability to generate an observational focus necessitates the consultant knowing the variables in instruction that make a difference: "The issues involved in simultaneously capturing the academic and social interpersonal dimensions of . . . instruction derive, in part, from knowledge about the nature of . . . instruction" (Bloome & Green, 1985, p. 169).

Yesseldyke and Christenson (1985) have recently developed an extensive observation system designed to assess systematically the instructional environment in which the student is functioning. The Instructional Environment Scale (TIES) has two major purposes:

1. To systematically *diagnose* the extent to which students' academic or behavior problems are a function of factors in the instructional environment, and

2. To identify starting points in *designing appropriate instructional interventions* for individual students (p. 5).

They also suggest some secondary purposes for the TIES, including use in consultation, Individual Educational Plan (IEP), development, teacher training, process monitoring, and research.

TIES is viewed as a clinical instrument enabling users to make qualitative judgments about the instructional environment. The user gathers three kinds of data to make a qualitative rating: (1) classroom observation of the student; (2) an interview with the teacher; and (3) an interview with the student. TIES is designed to assess 12 domains of effective instruction, each of which is defined with specific descriptors: instructional presentation, classroom environment, teacher expectations, cognitive emphasis, motivational strategies, relevant practice, academic engaged time, informed feedback, adaptive instruction, progress evaluation, instructional planning, and student understanding. A target student is the focus of the observation, and the rating describes what occurs for the individual student. Equally important is that the descriptors specify the components of good instruction, and thus can be used to lead directly to intervention strategies when they are found to be lacking. The descriptors provide a short course in the effective-teaching literature.

Other observational techniques are used to obtain a more direct assessment of academic performance itself. These involve watching the child perform during the academic subject in which the child is having difficulty. Error-analysis and think-out-loud techniques that enable the teacher to understand the thinking of the child in the learning process are also discussed in depth in the next chapter. However, on occasion it may be decided by the teacher and consultant that the latter should observe the child in the instructional setting and provide feedback to the teacher about the child-teacher instructional interaction and the child's performance. Since Bennett et al. (1984) indicate how hard it is for many teachers to engage in useful error analysis, the consultant could be helpful to the teacher by observing the instructional interaction and engaging in a dialogue about the child's performance.

Another method, often discussed under observational techniques in the behavioral literature, is that of direct measurement of permanent product (e.g., Alberto & Troutman, 1982). Sometimes called "outcome recording", this method of data collection begins after the behavior itself has occurred through analysis of the product. Additional discussion of permanent product recording will also be found in the next chapter.

SUMMARY

Direct observation in the setting in which the academic performance is (or is not) exhibited can provide useful information for the problem-identification and intervention-planning stages of instructional consultation. However, for the information to be helpful, the criteria of reliability, validity, and efficiency must be met. The observational procedures must be systematic, so that observer bias is minimized. In general, observation to collect data for instructional consultation does not differ from the rules of good observational methodology.

However, the observer must also consider carefully the pre- and post-observation contacts with the teacher so that the collaborative consultation relationship is maintained or even enhanced, rather than damaged by the observation procedures. Moreover, it must be understood that the observational systems usually recommended in the literature are measures of behavioral correlates of learning, and should not be used to focus on the child's behavior when the learning task itself is inappropriate for the child. Finally, the creation of observational procedures to measure specific academic interactions related to the child's particular difficulty is suggested.

In planning the observational phase of the assessment, the consultant must consider the child in interaction with the task and instruction. Without an understanding of the task as it is delivered in the classroom, the consultant will lose important information. It is further essential to view the child in comparison to other children in the classroom, rather than against an arbitrary criterion that may not reflect the reality of the referring teacher's classroom. To truly see the child in the classroom is to see the child in the social, interpersonal context that defines the academic task (Bloome & Green, 1985).

APPENDIX
CLASSROOM OBSERVATIONS

Observation Case Example: Case 1
Classroom Observation of Teacher-Child Dyad: Mike, Grade 3

Structuring the Observation

In initial and subsequent interviews, the teacher and I "clarified" that the social/behavioral problems she had perceived at the time of referral to be the result of attitudinal problems/"deficits" in Mike might more realistically and productively be viewed in terms interactive with setting and skills. For example, we discussed specificlly whether or not the frequency and duration of his out-of-seat behavior are perhaps related in some way to the level of difficulty of assigned academic work and/or whether his "unwillingness" to work independently in actuality reflects his inability to do so because of inadequate entry skills and/or lack of "understanding" (for whatever reasons) of the instructions. Therefore, we agreed that during my classroom visits, I would observe Mike's behavior during instructional periods as well as independent work periods.

Sarah, Mike's teacher, was definite in her feeling that out-of-seat behavior was the behavior to be targeted since it "bugged her" the most and was a disruptive factor in the classroom with which she wanted help. She further indicated that this behavior was most troublesome to her during instructional periods such as 9:30-10:15 AM. It was agreed that I would do a number of observations to observe teacher-student/class interactions, antecedents/correspondents of out-of-seat behavior (circumstances involving classroom routine, setting and/or peers), behavior of a comparison child, and strategies (and their effectiveness) currently being used to address Mike's out-of-seat behavior. Baseline data for out-of-seat behavior would be collected and recorded through one-minute interval recording in 15-minute blocks. The Teacher-Pupil Interaction Scale (TPIS) (Goodwin and Coates, 1977) and Goodwin's ABC analysis-intervention materials (Gutkin and Curtis, 1982) would also be used.

Data and Feedback

Teacher event-recording data (3/12/85; 3/13/85; 3/14/85) indicating that in each of six 15-minute segments of time Mike was out of his seat three or four times verified Sarah's concerns. During my initial classroom visit (3/19/85: 9:30-10:00 AM), however, Mike remained in his seat until the last two minutes, a period following the instruction to begin working on seat work which had been described. When the independent work "signal" was given, Mike left his seat immediately as if "on cue." In addition, I noted that during the instructional period observed Mike was frequently off-task—eating, turning sideways, apparently watching other students, playing in his desk, etc.

Subsequently he was unable to begin independent work without one-to-one teacher assistance. When Sarah and I discussed this initial observation, she indicated she would observe antecedents of out-of-seat behavior and we agreed that, in subsequent observations, I would collect baseline data on off-task as well as out-of-seat behavior.

One-minute interval recording data collected on 3/19/85 (three 15-minute segments) indicated 0% to 20% of intervals in which out-of-seat behavior occurred during class instructional periods and 60% out-of-seat behavior during seat work. Once again the instruction to begin working independently seemed to initiate immediate out-of-seat behavior marked by running in the room, talking to peers, playing with and trading pencils, etc.

However, during these same periods, percentages of one-minute intervals off-task were 60%, 74%, and 87%. Once again Mike needed one-to-one teacher assistance with each seat-work task assigned. TPIS data indicated off-task behavior in Mike in 67% of five-second intervals as compared to 15% for the comparison student, Jerry. TPIS teacher behavior was high in instructing and class-positive verbal reinforcement. Mike's frequent off-task behavior was marked by talking to peers, playing with shoes, wiggling in seat and looking out of the window. Sarah's effort, "Mike, are you listening?" at one point had seemingly little to no effect in changing his off-task behavior.

In our feedback conference, Sarah reported high correspondence in her observations between the initiation of independent work periods and out-of-seat behavior. She had not previously realized either how much of Mike's time during instructional periods was off-task. In addition, it has become apparent that Mike frequently requires one-to-one assistance with tasks for which his entry skills are adequate. Out-of-seat behavior frequently appears to follow off-task behavior, which has apparently led to uncertainty regarding instructions for independent work.

As a result of this observation-feedback process, we have now agreed that the behavioral intervention should attempt, initially at least, to increase on-task behavior during instructional periods (so that Mike will be clear about instruction for independent work) and that doing so may result in significant decrease in out-of-seat behavior as well as increase in both quality and quantity of academic work completed.

Observation Case Examples: Case 2

Previous to class observation, Observer and Teacher had met and agree on which behaviors were going to be observed. The behaviors to be observed consisted of:

- On-task behavior
- Class participation (volunteer)

Teacher pointed out to Observer a child who has average on-task behavior and participation, to be used as a comparison child.

The purpose of this observation was to confirm Teacher's report on our initial interview regarding Tom's limited class participation and his "day-dreaming" or limited on-task behavior during whole-class and small-group instruction. The following symbols were used to facilitate recording of these observations:

T = Teacher
O = Observer
C = dyad child (Tom)
X = comparison child.

Tom was observed for two periods of 50 minutes each on two consecutive days.

On Day 1, observation was conducted while the teacher instructed the whole class.

On Day 2, observation was conducted during Tom's small-reading-group instruction.

Day 1

Behavior to Be Observed: On-task behavior:
1. Tom will use task materials
2. Tom will orient toward Teacher.
3. Tom will orient toward the assigned work.

Observation: The teacher instructed whole class to look for their sight-word vocabulary cards. Tom was the last student who got ready to begin the drill.

Observations were recorded every two minutes for Tom and X (see Table C-1). X was sitting at Tom's left, because it was easier for the examiner to record their behavior together.

TABLE 4-4

Student	Number of on-task behaviors (Total number: 25)	%
C	17	68%
X	20	80%

Results: Tom's on-task behavior was recorded 17 times out of possible 25, indicating a 68% on-task behavior. However, it was noted that Tom looked at the cards and spelled the words looking at the back side of the cards, therefore looking at the letters backwards.

The results for comparison child X were 20 out of possible 25, indicating an 80% on-task behavior.

Day 2

Behavior to Be Observed: Participation in class activities.
Tom will raise his hand to volunteer answers from reading selection.

Observation: The teacher guided reading of the selection in a group of eight students. Tom read his assigned page with some hesitation. He made two word substitutions which the teacher corrected.

The teacher asked a total of 20 questions which included questions before and after each page was read.

Observations were recorded after each question that the teacher had asked the group. A comparison child, X, sitting at Tom's left was used for this observation. (See Table C-2.)

TABLE 4-5

Total number of questions asked	Number of times hand was raised	%
C	5	25%
X	12	60%

Results: Tom raised his hand 5 times out of possible 20 times; resulting in 25% class participation to volunteer answers.

The results of X, consisted of 12 times out of possible 20 times; therefore child X showed a 60% participation to volunteer answers.

Discussion: Results from these two observations concurred with referral. As these results indicate, Tom showed limited participation to volunteer answers when the teacher asked general questions and, also, his on-task behavior needs to be improved.

Observer shared her findings with the teacher. She was made aware of what Tom did during instruction time. The teacher offered to help Tom to keep on task more often by calling his attention to look at the cards the correct way.

In order to increase Tom's participation during reading lesson, the teacher will go around table asking each child a question instead of asking a general question and waiting for Tom's participation.

We will meet again to discuss if there have been some changes in Tom's observed behaviors within two weeks.

Chapter 5

ASSESSMENT
OF ACADEMIC LEARNING

> *At present, tests . . . typically are not designed to guide the specifics of instruction. . . . They serve as an index to the standards of schools but they are not designed to effectively shape progress towards these standards—and can do so only indirectly, if at all. In the twenty-first century, tests and other forms of assessment will be valued for their ability to facilitate constructive adaptations of educational programs.*
> —Glaser, 1985, p. 1

In this chapter, assessment is considered as it relates to guiding the decisions teachers make about instruction in the classroom. Gickling and Havertape (1982) indicate the four stages of the assessment cycle as screening, identification, instruction, and measurement of progress. Typically, psycho-educational assessment has been focused on the stages of screening (early recognition of problems) and identification (discriminating, based on a normative framework, whether a student requires some kind of special service). Those two types of assessment, which have formed the bulk of the assessment literature in school psychology, do not, however, readily translate in a functional way to teachers who are responsible for a child's instruction (Gickling & Havertape, 1982). We need, therefore, to turn our attention to assessment, that is related to instructional decision making, that is, assessment for instruction and measurement of progress.

Curriculum-based assessment (CBA) (Tucker, 1985), also called direct assessment of academic skills (Shapiro & Lentz, 1985), is a set of procedures "for determining the instructional needs of a student based upon the student's on-going performance within existing course content" (Gickling & Havertape, 1982, p. 17). It "properly includes ANY procedure that directly assesses student performance within the course content for the purpose of determining that student's instructional needs" (Tucker, 1985, p. 200). The underlying assumption of CBA is that "the essential measure of success in education is the student's progress in the curriculum of the local school"(Tucker, 1985, p. 199). CBA is a process of data collection, interpretation, and application that provides information to guide instructional decisions. Three central questions are answered: (1) Is the student placed in curriculum materials where he or she has the prerequisite skills to master the material? (2) What is the nature of the discrepancy between the student's functional level and the one at which he or she is expected to perform, within the classroom curriculum itself? (Shapiro & Lentz, 1985); and (3) What is the nature of the error(s) made by the child?

School psychologists in the past have not been trained to use CBA procedures. In fact, many child-study-team members, including school psychologists, assume either that CBA is regularly conducted by the classroom teacher (since it can actually be considered a "teaching practice that is as old as education itself"; Tucker, 1985, p. 199) and/or that it has only a limited place in the assessment process. The latter is especially true if team members are not clear on the distinctions among the different reasons for assessing children in the school setting; for example, the distinction between assessment for classification and for other types of purposes, or if they believe that the cause for the learning problem is basically internal to the child. However, if the goal is to assist the teacher in the classroom to provide a more productive learning environment for the child, CBA provides the most important type of assessment data. Further, in our experience as instructional consultants, these data are rarely available when a referral is made by a teacher and their absence makes it difficult to assist the teacher in modifying the instructional environment.

This chapter begins with discussion of what a curriculum task is and what it encompasses. Then, different methods for doing curriculum based assessment, that of Gickling and Havertape (1982) and of Deno and Mirkin (1977), are described. Next, an in-depth exploration of error analysis is presented. Finally, the use of the computer to do CBA is examined. When the reader has concluded this chapter, he or she should be able to conduct a precise assessment of a student's learning performance.

The results of the academic assessment will enable the instructional consultant to help the teacher place the referred child in the task at which instruction needs to begin in the academic area in question. Assessment will have made it possible not only for the intervention plan to begin at the child's instructional level, the "window of learning" between frustration and boredom that exists for every child (Tucker, 1985, p. 201), but also to be prescriptive for the type of error or error pattern of the child. Moreover, the nature of the discrepancy between the child's current functioning level and the expected level will have been clarified.

ASSUMPTIONS UNDERLYING
ACADEMIC ASSESSMENT

Several assumptions underlie this type of assessment. First, it is assumed that the evaluator has a working understanding of the scope and sequence of the various academic curricula in which the child is placed (Gickling & Havertape, 1982). That often means examining the instructional materials that are used for teaching the skills. As has been consistently documented in the literature (e.g., Anderson et al. 1985), the choice of a basal reading series or math program is usually what decides the scope and sequence of a school subject in a given school. Further, as Woodward (1986) lamented:

> Many of the teachers I observed (both experienced and less experienced) followed their textbooks almost word for word. . . . In the basal reading programs, there appeared to be a rigid adherence to a highly managed series of teaching and learning activities presented in the teacher's guides. It seemed as if the textbook program contained everything that could possibly be needed, and it was rare indeed for spontaneous activities or activities that departed from the teacher's guide outline to occur. (p. 26)

Teachers have been led to believe that if they follow the lesson plans, skill strands, and testing systems of the series their students will succeed, and they are fearful of departing from the series sequence and format because their administrators expected them to fully implement each step and stage (Woodward, p. 28). (The interested reader should obtain Woodward's, 1986, article, for a historical perspective on the teacher's role with regard to published teaching materials.)

However we have also discovered, in some cases, when there is no adopted textbook series, that the teacher *had no scope and sequence* in a particular curriulum area in which a child was experiencing difficulty. The lack of an organized progression of skills in itself is alarming. When the teacher is concerned about a child's progress in a particular area and still has no scope and sequence, that is, an orderly and sequenced series of skills to be learned, the child is indeed in trouble. In chapter 3, an example of this was provided in the case of the teacher who had no writing curriculum for a child who was experiencing difficulty in handwriting. In fact, when there is no text or workbook series, as is often true in handwriting, spelling, and other language arts, there is often no clear scope and sequence to the instructional program.

Moreover, it is apparent to this author after years of contact with teachers that many do not regularly assess children's progress in the curriculum in the classroom, but make instructional decisions without information about the child's mastery of prerequisite skills. For some teachers, this is because the emphasis is on getting the curriculum-driven express moving, that is, exposing children to the entire curriculum assigned to a given grade level, rather than assuring that they have mastered the skills presented. For others, it is because the teachers do not have the skills to assess children's mastery of content. In a recent workshop with reading teachers in a school district, it was clear that they were aware that while the basal series had both placement tests and criterion-referenced mastery tests, neither were being used appropriately by most classroom teachers. The criterion-referenced tests, for example, were given by the teachers, scored, and carefully entered into the child's folder. But instruction was not planned based on the results!

Special-service providers are sometimes disbelieving of this lack of skill and focus by classroom teachers. In a CBA workshop for school psychologists, they were assigned to read the Gickling and Havertape (1982) self-study guide. They returned to the next session with the point of view that CBA was not their responsibility, that it was the role of the classroom teacher. One of the school psychologists, however, who had believed also that it was the teachers' role, had independently talked to the teachers in her school and was shocked to discover that they did not regularly assess the children's mastery of content or make instructional decisions on the basis of what children know and do not know. Her input made it clear to the other workshop participants that information about instructional level and match was not widely utilized in their school system. Both of these examples confirm the research literature that suggests that teachers are not regularly using assessment of learning data for instructional decision-making.

A second major assumption of Gickling and Havertape (1982) with regard to CBA is that the curriculum material is not neutral, that the curriculum material can, in fact, help or hinder the learning of the child. Thus, it is important to know how to modify and manipulate the material to make it work for the child (topics which are considered in chapter 7). Simply switching to another series will not usually break the pattern of failure for the child. Knowing the child's ability to perform within the classroom curriculum is crucial information for classroom decision making.

A MODEL OF THE ACADEMIC TASK

Elkind (1976), noting the embarrassing glibness with which most psychologists talk about curriculum, attempted to clarify this concept more fully. He described three types of curricula: (1) The developmental curriculum, which is composed of "the complex of abilities and knowledge that children acquire more or less on their own in order to adapt to their world" (p. 54); including such concepts as conservation and causality that Piagetian techniques, for example, have provided some additional ways to assess; (2) the personal curriculum, which consists of "the child's own hierarchy of needs, interests, values, and attitudes that determine his willingness to participate in the activities of the school" (p. 54), oftentimes necessitating motivational strategies by teachers when this curriculum does not include school subjects; and (3) the school curriculum itself, "the body of information accumulated and recorded by mankind over the centuries and which it is the prime function of the schools to transmit"(p. 54). He concluded that the school curriculum is at the heart of the educational enterprise, and the other two types of curricula, often the focus of psychologists, cannot be substituted as priorities. The goal of psychologists in the school must be, at least in part, to help teachers with their real task, that of coordinating all three curricula.

Curriculum Scope and Sequence

Effective academic assessment is based on the assumption that evaluators understand both the scope and sequence of the academic subject and how it relates to the child's individual needs (Gickling & Havertape, 1982). According to Gickling and Havertape, an evaluator must consider: "what skills or sets of skills are being taught, the order in which they are presented, and the types of adaptations which are feasible within the child's classroom" (p. 34). While educators may not be in total agreement about the scope and sequence for any given subject, the concept itself implies that skills are presented and developed in a logical order, or if not a hierarchy, at least, that there is a list of skills that need development. Speaking specifically of the reading scope and sequence, Glicking and Havertape concluded:

> An evaluator must be aware that an exact scope and sequence is contingent on various factors, the first being the structure and type of reading program, and curriculum used within the particular classroom. The skills and their sequence of development will be different depending upon whether a phonics, linguistic, or content approach is being taught. There will also be variations in scope and sequence in different publishers' versions of these three general approaches to reading. (p. 36)

But over and above the structure of the curriculum, there are individual differences among teachers in the ways they present materials (e.g., Anderson et al. 1985; Gickling & Havertape, 1982; Steely & Englemann, 1979). One teacher may choose to follow the teacher's guide of the basal reading series on a daily basis, activity by activity, rarely straying from the manual. Other teachers may espouse a free classroom, and find it against their educational philosophy to provide highly structured programs for their classes. These choices represent the teacher's personal value systems and professional philosophies, and should be respected as such—unless the result is a classroom full of curriculum casualties, that is, children unable to benefit from the teacher's methods.

The Instructional Task

However, whereas the concept of scope and sequence has been described in the literature, less attention has been paid to the concept of the instructional task. The scope and sequence as presented on a day-by-day basis is a series of instructional tasks, and yet, according to Bennett et al. (1984), "Models of task processes are rare" (p. 9). Although some attention has been paid to instructional objectives (e.g., Alberto & Troutman, 1982; Mager, 1962; Moyer & Dardig, 1978), a more useful analytic model is provided by Bennett et al. (1984). They suggest that for each assigned task (and Gickling and Havertape (1982) suggest that there may be over 750 of them in a year for an elementary school child), it is essential to know:

1. The teacher's intention in assigning the task.
2. How that intention was manifested in the particular task set.
3. The teacher's task instructions, that is, how it was presented and specified.
4. The pupil's perceptions of 3.
5. The materials available for the task.
6. The pupil's task performance, including interactions with the teacher or other pupils.
7. An assessment of short-term learning outcomes, that is, immediately following the task.
8. An assessment of longer-term learning outcomes, for instance, at the end of each term, in order to evaluate development and retention of learning over series of curriculum tasks (pp. 10-11).

Thus, once the child is placed in the scope and sequence, the assessment process still must include a more fine-grained analysis of the task itself and the instruction, as well as the child's unique response to it.

ASSESSMENT PROCEDURES

The complexity of the classroom learning task requires assessment methods that examine those features Bennett et al. (1984) delineate, as well as those related to the scope and sequence of the subject content. The point of direct assessment of school subject areas is to "provide a structure for controlling the differences between what the teacher is trying to teach and what the student is able to learn" (Gickling & Havertape, 1982, p. 21). The process begins with an evaluation of the pupil's placement level in the scope and sequence of skills, followed by analysis of the student's error patterns. Too often error analysis is conducted at the student's frustration level, that is, at a level too far removed from the student's window of learning. Examining reversals or off-task behavior before knowing the child's instructional level can lead to misdiagnosis of the child's difficulty. For example, it makes little sense to examine specific comprehension difficulties in material the child can not decode. Once the instructional level is known, the child's errors and cognitive approach to the material need to be examined in some detail in order to know how to intervene most effectively.

Finding Instructional Level

Conceptually, instructional level is the critical point at which the child has the prerequisite skills to enter the scope and sequence of the classroom curriculum and can maximally benefit from instruction. To establish this point, data are collected on both the progress and performance of the child within the curriculum materials used by the child's teacher. In addition, to determine if there is a discrepancy between this child's instructional level and the norm of the rest of the class, a standard for progress and performance is established, largely based on the functioning level of average children in that classroom or school. The essential question asked is whether there is a discrepancy between desired and actual performance, using as the reference point the performance of other students in the curriculum materials.

Deno and Mirkin (1977) introduced Data-Based Program Modification, a process in which two types of data need to be collected on students. First, progress or mastery data are collected to record the time the student is taking to master the instructional objectives in the curriculum. The second type of data collected is performance data, which provide information on how the child's academic performance changes on a single task over time. Graphs are used to demonstrate the discrepancy between the progress and performance of a referred pupil and that of average students in the classroom. In Appendix A (at the end of the book), Deno and Mirkin's (1977) method for obtaining these two types of data is presented in detail as a guideline for use.

In many school systems, reading and math specialists are expert in doing informal inventories and can often be involved in the process of constructing and administering them. However, it is even more useful to obtain the cooperation of the teachers in learning how to administer and construct informal inventories in school subjects. Teachers who become accustomed to making instructional placement decisions based on data obtained from these techniques have a higher probability of meeting children's instructional needs. One experienced special-education teacher of emotionally disturbed children at the middle-school level, when introduced to the method of using informal inventories, expressed her gratitude for finally knowing how to place a child in a reader. In fact, teachers using this type of assessment model have been reported to find them more meaningful and jargon-free than psycho-educational assessment techniques, relevant to their classroom instruction, motivational to both themselves and their students because of awareness of progress, and helpful in terms of knowing when to change current instructional interventions (Tindal, Wesson, Deno, Germann, & Mirkin, 1985). But it cannot be taken for granted that teachers have skills in this area and the consultant may need to help teachers learn to construct and use informal inventories effectively.

Reliability and validity issues related to these procedures have been addressed. Studies have been conducted to develop curriculum-based assessment methods that meet criteria of reliability and validity (Deno, 1985; Germann & Tindal, 1985; Marston & Magnusson, 1985; Tindal, et al., 1985). Deno and Mirkin and their associates have provided evidence for a system based on the following, (as reported by Tindal et al., 1985):

> READING—One-minute reading aloud from randomly selected passages from the basal curriculum and/or one-minute reading aloud from a list of vocabulary words selected at random from the basal curriculum: Number of words read correct and incorrect (Deno, Mirkin, & Chiang, 1982).
>
> SPELLING—Two-minute spelling samples using dictation of a random selection of words from the basal spelling curriculum: Number of words or letter sequences spelled correct and incorrect (Deno, Mirkin, Lowry & Knehnle, 1980).
>
> WRITTEN EXPRESSION—Three-minute writing sample in response to story starters or topic sentences: Number of words or letters written or the number of words spelled correct (Deno, Martson, & Mirkin, 1982).
>
> MATH—Two-minute samples of computation problems appearing in the basal text, one for each function (addition, subtraction, multiplication, division, fractions, and decimals): Number of digits computed correct and incorrect (Tindal et al., 1985, p. 228).

Based on this research, there is now a methodology that can provide reliable and criterion-related data for instructional decision making in the classroom. School psychologists, with their substantial training in assessment and measurement, can provide an additional resource to help each school/school system to develop local norms based on its curriculum and student population. An example of the procedure for doing so was described by Shinn (1985).

The data-collection system just described could be introduced on a schoolwide basis. However, for individual consultants and teachers to move toward this model may be perceived as unrealistic or too time-consuming. An intermediate step is suggested by Gickling and Havertape (1982) and Moran (1978), who also present models of direct assessment of academic performance. Their approaches might be considered less comprehensive but more accessible as a transition to a schoolwide or systems model of CBA. Moran's model of informal inventories provides an especially useful resource for school psychologists to aid teachers in developing and interpreting informal classroom inventories in reading, mathematics, language, handwriting, and spelling.

Glicking and Havertape (1982) present CBA procedures for reading and math as well. In assessing reading, they suggest that there are only two types of reading tasks: reading tasks that involve "rapid and sequential sight-word recognition with accompanying comprehension" (p. 22) and drill activities, defined as essentially everything else related to reading. Given these two types of tasks, there are three categories of performance for children on each task item: know items, hesitant items, and unknown items. How well students function on the task and task items determines level of performance. Performance can be at one of three levels, instructional, independent, or frustration. The model is pictured in Figure 5-1.

The process of conducting an informal-reading inventory can be found in most remedial reading texts or in Moran (1978). Generally three passages are selected from each level of the reading series used in the school. The length of the passage selected is, typically: 50 words from the Preprimer and Primer; 100 words from Grades 1-4; 150-200 words from Grades 4-6; and 250 words from junior high school text books. Comprehension questions are created for each passage, usually a minimum of four per passage. The types of questions

INSTRUCTIONAL DELIVERY MODEL

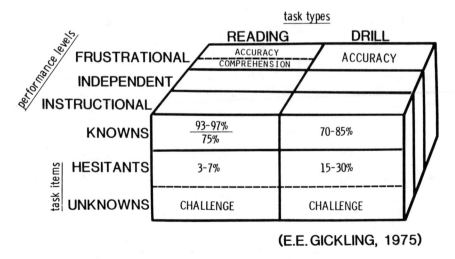

FIGURE 5-1. Instructional Delivery Model.

most often include: definition, immediate recall, main idea or conclusion, and inference; other types include sequencing and outcome-predication questions. However, the most useful criterion for selecting type of comprehension question is that of using skills that the student is expected to demonstrate at each level of the curriculum.

A word list for each reader is also helpful. At the upper levels, 20% of the words from the reader can be used for the word list, selecting every Xth word (depending on how many are needed to make a list of 20% of the words). Each reader usually has a complete list of words at the back of the book. Two word lists can be developed; one is used to examine the child's decoding skills, whereas the other is used to determine the student's automatic recognition (flash recognition at 1/2 sec. exposure). Word recognition errors from the first list can be analyzed for type of error.

A copy of each passage for recording purposes should be prepared; the comprehension questions can be placed on the same page. A notation system to indicate the types of errors made by the reader is often helpful (e.g., omissions, substitutions, insertions, repetitions, need for assistance). Comprehension responses should be recorded verbatim.

To begin the inventory, the teacher can often help in estimating the child's reading level. The passage reading should be timed, using a stopwatch (Table 5-1 provides some normative data for time to read by grade level). The reading of passages should be continued until the highest level is reached at

TABLE 5-1
Normative Data for CBA in Reading by Grade Level

Medians: Grades 1-3		
Frustration Level	Instructional Level	Mastery Level
29 words/min. or fewer	30-49 words/min.	50 words/min.
and/or	and	and
less than 80% comprehension	80% comprehension	80% comprehension
and/or	and/or	and
8 or more errors/min.	3-7 errors/min.	2 or fewer errors/min.
Medians: Grades 4 and Above		
Frustration Level	Instructional Level	Mastery Level
49 words/min. or fewer	50-99 words/min.	100 words/min. or better
and/or	and/or	and
less than 80% comprehension	80% comprehension	80% comprehension
and/or	and/or	and
8 or more errors/min.	3-7 errors/min.	2 or fewer errors/min.

Note. From Deno and Mirkin (1977) pp. 84-85.

which the student reads with 93-97% word accuracy and 75%-80% comprehension. That is considered the student's instructional level. At the instructional level and at the point just above that, the word list can be read to evaluate the child's errors diagnostically.

The informal inventory is used to find the level at which the child should be placed for instructional purposes. Once the appropriate placement in the scope and sequence is established, an in-depth analysis of the task and the child's approach to the task can be undertaken.

However, another approach to placement, one which uses standardized tests, is the Degrees of Reading Power (DRP) Program (College Board, 1986). It consists of tests designed to measure students' ability to comprehend English prose and a mechanism to translate the test results for instructional purposes, through readability analyses of instructional materials. The DRP tests measure how well students, in grades 3-12+, understand the meaning of passages, using a cloze procedure. Scores, based on a latent-trait model, are reported in terms of DRP units. Along with the manual comes the Readability Report (College Board, 1985), which lists the difficulty level of over 3,000 published texts in reading and content areas, with readability given in DRP units, that is to say, in the same metric that the test results provide. Thus, for instructional purposes, teachers can match DRP test scores to test difficulty level and select materials at the student's instructional level. For materials not listed in the Readability Report, there is a software program for microcomputers—Mic=RA→DRP—to enable the school to assess the readability level in DRP units of materials not found in the Readability Report.

Once the concept of curriculum-based assessment is understood, it becomes apparent that there is a need to be able to determine entry level in each curriculum area. Assessment tools are easily devised for finding the child's entry level in particular skills. Appendix C, Part II includes numerous assessment formats for finding the child's entry level in particular curriculum-skill areas, including reading, handwriting, math, and language arts. In many cases, the formats provide a data-collection method for recording the student's progress past the baseline point of entry at instructional level to mastery.

Task Analysis

Once the student is placed in the scope and sequence, it is possible to examine the next objective to be learned. Task analysis is the "detailed assessment of the specific skills a learner must acquire to reach a specific goal" (Sloane, Buckholtd, Jensen, & Crandell, 1979, p. 149). The process begins with the identification of the behavioral or target objective, and then consists of analyzing that objective in two ways:

1. Entry-level analysis, in which the skills or behaviors assumed to have been acquired by the student before instruction on this objective can begin are defined; and
2. Subskill analysis, in which there is a sequential definition of the skills that the learner acquires in moving from current level of functioning (entry level) to mastering the behavioral objective.

Instruction begins with a description of what the outcome of effective instruction will be. The critical question is not what the student will be studying but what students will be able to do after they have mastered the objective (Gagné & Briggs, 1979). Precision in defining objectives is required for two reasons. First, there is a need for clear communication among teachers, students, and parents about the purposes of instruction. Second, objectives facilitate the evaluation of instruction. Gagné and Briggs were convincing in their argument that clear objectives insure "that what is evaluated and what is communicated as an intended learning outcome have a common meaning" (p. 118).

Often teachers tend to conceptualize the goals of learning in terms of the number of pages of curriculum materials completed. In order to be more effective in providing instruction, it is necessary to consider whether the curriculum materials provide coverage of the objectives that the teacher is concerned about, or whether the teacher needs to modify or supplement the content of the curriculum, text, or program to ensure mastery of the objectives that need to be covered. For example, according to the research of Steely and Englemann (1979), basal readers in fourth through sixth grades need additional examples in order to develop the comprehension skills that most teachers would like to see their students attain.

The skill of constructing behavioral objectives has been described extensively and ranges from complex models (e.g., Gagné & Briggs, 1979) to simpler descriptions (e.g., Alberto & Troutman, 1982; Mager, 1962; Sloane et al., 1979). At their most straightforward, behavioral objectives consist of three components:

1. A statement of the performance of the learner, that is, the behavior the learner will do, stated in terms that are directly observable and measurable.
2. A statement of the situation in which the behavior or performance will occur, or the conditions. This might include the type of prompts, aids, or cues that, in part, define the situation in which the behavior will be expected to occur, or the evaluation format that the teacher will use ("Given 20 words presented orally . . .").
3. A statement of the criteria for mastery, or acceptable performance, of the objective, the standard for evaluation of minimally acceptable perfor-

mance. The statement may be in terms of frequency of response, accuracy of response, percentage of accurate response, or performance within an error limitation.

There are several problems to be aware of in developing behavioral objectives, each of which has been widely described in the literature. First, in describing the behavior component of the objective, it is important to avoid the use of vague but commonly used terms in education, such as "to know" or "to understand." What does a teacher mean when she indicates that she wants a child "to know his vowels"? However, that is not so much a problem with the concept of behavioral objectives as a function of knowing how to write them appropriately, using precise descriptions of behavior. Unless teachers understand that knowing subtraction has to be stated as a specific perform- ance, such as "John will be able to subtract one-digit numbers from two-digit numbers with borrowing, given a group of 10 written problems, with 90% accuracy in 5 minutes," knowledge of the child's mastery of subtraction skills remains fuzzy.

A second problem with behavioral objectives is the possibility of trivializ- ing them. This is often the case when the objectives focus on completion of a particular task as opposed to demonstrating a skill. Objectives that focus on completing a certain number of pages in a text, for example, rather than on mastery of the skills involved, are considered more useful in contingency contracts than as behavioral objectives for setting instructional goals (Sloane, et al., 1979).

Classification of objectives has received considerable attention, and a number of taxonomies of educational objectives have been developed (e.g., Bloom, Englehart, Furst, Hill, & Krathwohl, 1956; Krathwohl, Bloom, & Masia, 1964). Objectives are most commonly divided into the cognitive, affective, and psychomotor domains. Sloane et al., (1979) suggest that teachers might find a more practical breakdown, one that groups behaviors into academic (e.g., learning certain phonics skills), social-emotional (e.g., learning to cooperate with others), and work skills (e.g., on-task behavior).

After the goals and objectives for instruction have been set, by developing behavioral objectives, task analysis moves into the next step of ascertaining whether the learner has the entry-level behaviors, or prerequisite skills, required to begin learning the objective. While the analysis of entry-level behaviors could go on endlessly, it is usually most efficient to test down from the desired (or current placement) level of functioning for a particular student until instructional level is obtained, using the techniques suggested earlier in this chapter. Once the instructional level is ascertained, reasonable objectives for the child within the curriculum area can be set. Then the focus can shift to conducting a subskill analysis using the methods of task analysis.

Conducting a subskill analysis includes four steps (Sloane et al., 1979):

1. Specify subskills: Specify all the behaviors needed to perform the behavioral objective.
2. Determine the interdependencies among the subskills; which are prerequisite to others and which depend on prior skills.
3. Place the skills in the order for instruction, based on the analysis of interdependencies.
4. Develop a monitoring system to determine when the child has mastered each subskill and can be moved to the next step.

While all tasks can be broken down into units of performance, there is, unfortunately, no simple rule to assist in selecting the appropriate method to conduct the subskill analysis. Moyer and Dardig (1978) suggested that extensive practice in task analysis is necessary to become skilled, and that at the beginning the process may be time consuming. However, they suggest six different types of task-analysis methods to select among, depending upon the particular task at hand:

1. The "Watch a Master perform" method: Given a psychomotor task, the analyst can watch the performance of an expert in the task, and write down all the steps in correct temporal order as accurately and concisely as possible. Examples of situations in which this might be useful are making a phone call or setting a table.

2. Perform the task yourself: The analyst gathers the required props and verbalizes each step while performing the behavior (a tape recorder can be used to avoid having to write the steps down as the analysis is going on). Then the task is performed a second time, following the steps outlined, adding or eliminating steps in the process. Examples of when this might be useful are tying a shoe or multiplying by two-digit numbers.

3. Work backwards from the terminal objective, constructing a pyramid of tasks leading to completion of the goal: The analysis starts with the objective; the behaviors that are at the preceding level of difficulty are logged. Each of these behaviors, in turn, is treated as the goal. When the entry level of the learner is reached, the analysis is discontinued. An example of where this might be useful is in objectives involving word problems in mathematics.

4. Brainstorming: This is a less-systematic method, but may be used for the analysis of complex tasks that are not strictly sequential. All the subtasks are written down, without regard to order. A logical order is then developed from the list.

5. Sequentially consider how to modify or simplify the condition's component of the objective to make it easier for the pupil to perform: A series of increasingly difficult conditions are generated as approximations to the final objective itself. Some of the changes that could be made are changing the

number or amount of stimuli (e.g., asking the student to copy one word, then five words, then the whole message for the day) or providing additional prompts or cues (in essence, the sequence is a fading process). Of course, the systematic approximations must be eliminated so that the learner masters the behavioral objective under the set of conditions stated in the terminal objective.

6. Identify the specific behaviors that signal goal attainment: This method is most useful for objectives in the affective domain. Mager (1962) suggested the following process for complex affective goals:

   a. List the goal.

   b. List the observable behaviors that would need to be exhibited for the learner to show that the goal has been attained.

   c. Discard from the list behaviors that can be excluded and identify those in need of further clarification.

   d. Determine how often or how well the behaviors must be performed.

   e. Determine whether behaviors on the list represent comprehensive goal attainment.

Good work habits or leadership behaviors are examples of the kinds of complex affective behaviors that this model of task analysis would be helpful in analyzing.

A checklist (Figure 5-2) has been developed by Moyer and Dardig (1978) to help review the quality of the task analysis. But the ultimate test is the feedback on how well the learner makes progress in the program designed on the basis of the task analysis. The analyst must be prepared to add, correct, or delete steps in the process. Once the steps have been indentified and sequenced, the student is ready for instructional intervention. Brief probes must be designed, so that the student can be monitored regularly (daily, if possible) to measure progression through the subskills. That way, there is minimal risk of placing the learner in instructional materials and lessons that are inappropriate and a waste of instructional time. Sometimes also the subskill analysis allows progress to be made in a different order. If it is determined that all the skills are not prerequisite to one another, frustration in one skill can be briefly set aside, as the child makes progress in an alternative skill that is parallel but not dependent on the problematic skill in the sequence.

In recent years, research to confirm the learning-hierarchy model and compare it to other models has been conducted by Bergan and associates (Bergan, 1980; Bergan, Stone, & Feld, 1984; Bergan, Towstopiat, Cancelli, & Karp, 1982; Cancelli, Bergan, & Jones, 1982). Bergan (1980) presented some theoretical limitations to the learning-hierarchy concept, and presented some alternative ways of conceptualizing learning other than through the type of hierarchy assumed to underlie the task analysis model of prerequisite skills.

1. Are all of the subtasks stated in observable, measurable terms? Would all persons looking at the subtasks interpret them the same way?
2. Are any critical steps omitted? Could a learner perform the major task after mastering only the subtasks?
3. Are all the subtasks relevant to the major task? Are unnecessary subtasks included?
4. Are any of the subtasks so minute as to be unnecessary? Could any be combined without losing information?
5. Are the subtasks arranged in logical order?

FIGURE 5-2. Checking a task analysis. From "Practical Task Analysis for Special Educators" by J. R. Moyer and J. C. Dardig, 1978, *Teaching Exceptional Children, 11,* p. 18.

For example, Cancelli et al. (1982) studied acquisition of mathematic's rules related to fractions, and found that "hierarchical ordering may be based on qualitative changes in children's thinking patterns" (p. 49) through rule replacement, a premise fundamentally different from a simple building of skills. Much as in cognitive development theories, the suggestion here is that qualitative changes occur in the course of learning complex skills. Bergan (1980) made explicit the underlying assumption made by learning hierarchies, that "there ought to be some relationship between the patterning of skills in a hierarchy and the order in which skills should be taught" (p. 643), and suggested a need for further research to document this. The questions raised in the work of Bergan and others make clear the need for ongoing assessment of a student's learning progress, and the need for continuing research into the most efficient and effective ways to sequence instructional objectives.

In sum, the diagnostic value of task analysis is to set clear goals for the instructional process, to place the child in the appropriate subskill in the scope and sequence, and to then teach one by one the necessary subskills that the child needs to master the skills. The child avoids frustration by ensuring that entry-level skills are in place before moving on to the next instructional objective. The components of each objective are assessed, so that the child's progress is sequential. Mastery is evaluated regularly, and evaluation is used as a source of information for instructional decisions.

Process Analysis

Our understanding of a learner's approach to academic content would not be complete without an analysis of the way the student approaches the task. This assessment strategy is based on a fundamental assumption:

> Here it seems that the child's own READING of the situation is what we must look to. . . . Underlying this suggestion there is a whole set of very fundamental notions about the ways in which we relate to the world. Of these, the most important is the idea that this relation is *Active* on our part from the beginning. We do not just sit and wait for the world to impinge on us. We try actively to interpret it, to make sense of it. We grapple with it, we construe it intellectually, *we represent it to ourselves.* (Donaldson, 1978, p. 67)

According to Donaldson, it is important never to underestimate the child's tendency to engage in active invention.

In fact, there is research to support the importance of the student's internal thinking relating to academic achievement. Peterson, Swing, Stark, and Waas (1984) found that: "Students' reports of their understanding of the lesson and their cognitive processes during classroom instruction may be more reliable and more valid indicators of students' classroom learning than observers' judgments of student attention" (p. 512). The critical factor is to gain access to the child's thinking process.

Thus, an assessment includes a diagnostic evaluation of the child's error pattern and thinking process. In fact, there is considerable evidence that teacher analysis of children's daily performance, with instructional decisions based on error and correct-response patterns, will result in substantial increases in student performance (Haring & Gentry, 1976; Kerr & Strain, 1978).

According to Gickling and Havertape (1982), there are several techniques for evaluation of error patterns. An error analysis of the actual answer (or product) as well as how the child produced the answer can be conducted in several different ways. First, the child's product can be evaluated. Second, the child can be observed working on the task. Third, students can describe their thinking processes as they perform the assignment. Finally, the amount of time it takes for the pupil to complete the assignment can be measured.

Error Analysis.   Grimes (1981) identifies three major types of errors that children make in their academic subjects. Through the use of probes, that is, samples of student performance on standard curriculum tasks under standard conditions (Grimes, 1981), teachers can examine errors further:

1. *Random errors.* These are also called "won't do errors," or careless errors. The child can make the correct response, but does not produce it consistently because the effort is perceived to be too great for the reinforcement offered. If this type of error is involved, an analysis of consequences is needed. Kratochwill and Severson (1977) suggested a posssible aptitude-treatment interaction of reinforcement on children's learning performance, and it may be necessary to conduct trial teaching lessons that vary the types and amounts of reinforcement prior to recommending a particular method of reinforcement for a particular child.

2. *Errors in concept formation.* In this case of "can't do" error, the child has misunderstood the concept, picked up an incorrect idea and/or developed an inaccurate rule. Glaser (1985b) also suggested that the diagnostic task goes deeper than identifying incorrect or correct answers. Rather, the diagnostic task is to:

> synthesize from a student's performance an accurate picture of misconceptions that lead to error. . . . It attempts to identify the nature of the concept or the rule that the student is employing in some systematic way. The assumption is that in most cases the student's behavior is not random or careless, but is driven by some underlying misconception or by incomplete knowledge. (p. 4)

Children's math-operation errors are sometimes in this category. The correction process here is to help the child develop *more accurate* discriminations about the rules and characteristics of the concept.

3. *Errors in unlearned concepts.* The third category, also a type of "can't do" error, occurs when the child lacks information for correct performance. The role of the instructor here is to help the pupil define the new concept by means of discrimination and rule learning.

Diagnostic Interviewing. Several approaches to structuring a setting for diagnostic interviewing or probing error patterns have been developed. Bennett et al. (1984) attempted to train teachers to use a diagnostic process in three phases:

1. The child is observed performing the task at issue.
2. Based on the child's performance, provisional hypotheses (or hunches) are formed about what the pupil's difficulty (if any) might be.
3. The hunch is then evaluated by presenting the child with a problem related to the task performance. Additional questions may be asked, and new hypotheses formed and evaluated as they occur.

Bennett et al. (1984) found this process extremely difficult for teachers to do in the classroom setting for several reasons, even though the teachers in their program had volunteered to learn the process and considered the skill worthwhile. First, the teachers often found it difficult to manage the rest of their class while they conducted the diagnostic interview with the child. The need for excellent classroom management techniques was apparent. Second, teachers had difficulty in adopting the concept of entertaining an hypothesis. Problems were seen as self-evident, and the teachers rushed to intervention and prescription prior to a clear understanding of the issue for the child. They asked few questions. According to Bennett et al., "the teachers did not interview; they taught. They did not diagnose, conjure alternatives, or check possibilities" (p. 200). Here again, the assessment and hypothesis-generating skills of school psychologists can provide a substantial contribution to the process, in modeling and teaching these diagnostic interviewing procedures over time. At first, however, it may be necessary for the consultant to conduct the diagnostic interviews, rather than assume that teachers have the skills to assume this responsibility.

One technique to use during the diagnostic interview was suggested by Meyers (1985), who provided a rationale and procedure for the use of the "think-out-loud" method to assess the process of learning as the student interacts with an instructional task. This approach, based on meta-cognitive and information-processing theory, allows the evaluator to examine the pupil's strategies for problem solving. Meyers applied the think-out-loud procedure to evaluation of reading comprehension. Rather than determine how much the reader understands, a product approach, the think-out-loud technique determines how the reader goes about trying to understand the reading material. This leads to a more direct link to instructional intervention.

The method for think-out-loud begins with asking the student to read a passage of about 15 to 20 sentences one by one. Each sentence has been typed on a separate line, and the evaluator or pupil uncovers the story one sentence at a time. Students are instructed to verbalize all of their thoughts after reading each sentence:

'. . . tell me what you are doing and thinking about as you try to understand the sentence. This is just like talking to yourself or thinking out loud.' Then, various metaphors are used to help the child understand the task even better, for example, 'It is just like a News Broadcast in which you are the reporter, and you report each of your thoughts as they occur.' Finally, we stress the importance of verbalizing thoughts when the passage is difficult to understand. (Meyers, 1985, p. 18)

He introduces as a scoring system the code developed by Lytle (1982; cited in Meyers, 1985), which includes moves, strategies and styles. "Moves," according to Lytle's system, are discrete responses reflecting the reader's activities to understand the material. The six major categories of moves that Lytle scores are:

1. Signaling understanding: responses which indicate the reader understands the text, such as, a paraphrase of a sentence's meaning.
2. Monitoring of doubts: statements or questions indicating reader recognition of some lack of understanding of the material, such as stating the need to re-read a passage to figure it out.
3. Analyzing text features: comments by the reader on the author's style (rarely found in elementary school student protocols).

4. Elaborating on the text: responses that add to or expand the text, such as stating that the reader imagined scenes to help clarify the text.
5. Judging the text: evaluation by the reader of the quality of the text according to a specified criterion.
6. Reasoning: responses by the reader that indicate the use of problem-solving approaches to resolve doubt and interpret the text.

Meyers describes the application of the approach to a particular child and suggests the implications for instructional interventions using the process approach. He also cautions that there is a need for additional research using this model of assessment.

Peterson et al.'s (1984) research study used a different approach, which has practical implications for understanding the thinking processess of the student. Students were videotaped during their lesson. Following the lesson, the videotaped students were then interviewed, using a stimulated-recall technique. They first viewed tape, and then were individually interviewed about their thinking processes during the teaching of the concept and/or the seat-work segment of the class. Questions about seat-work were designed to elicit their cognitive processes while doing the problems as well as their understanding of the problems. A blank copy of seat-work problems was given to the students to facilitate their recall. Modifications of this approach might be developed for assessment of student processing.

Error analysis.   An example of the kind of error analysis procedures that might be useful has been presented by Gickling and Havertape (1982). They identified five common sources of error that children make in mathematics. They suggested that children's work samples in mathematics should be examined for the following:

1. Teacher's assumptions about the student's knowledge of facts and concepts. Whereas a child might get the right answer, the process might involve an error. This type of error can be evaluated during a diagnostic interview of the type described above. Having the child talk through the process will reveal the problem. Children sometimes use their fingers for counting, arriving at the correct answer but using an inappropriate or inefficient strategy. Or, they sometimes copy their work (as exemplified in the case excerpt presented in chapter 4, misleading the teacher into thinking that they have mastered the material because they get the right answers. Teachers often describe children as inconsistent or as having known the answer yesterday but not today. A more careful analysis of these errors, rather than attributing them to faculty memory processes, is advised. The next four types of problems can be determined often through evaluation of the child's products as well as in a diagnostic interview.

2. Incorrect use of place value. The child may not correctly be using the ones, tens, and hundreds columns, or understand their meaning. As regrouping becomes necessary, this source of error becomes more apparent.

3. Use of faulty algorithms. Algorithms are the basic rules used to solve problems. The four operations of arithmetic (addition, subtraction, multiplication, and division) each have a unique set of algorithms which must be performed in the correct sequence. Sometimes children create their own sets of procedures. It is suggested that the evaluator look for patterns rather than isolated events. Finding the creative solutions children sometimes develop is an analytic activity all its own.

4. Insufficient mastery of facts and accompanying random responses. When children are lacking the correct facts, they tend to emit more random responses. In fact, Russell and Ginsburg (1984) provide evidence that children with math difficulties had considerable difficulty in rote mastery of math facts, and this aspect of functioning should be evaluated carefully. A differentiation between "can't do" and "won't do" types of errors in this area is particularly important in generating the correct instructional intervention.

5. Errors in choice of operations. Sometimes children choose the wrong operation because of insufficient attention to the sign.

Each type of error requires a different type of instructional intervention. It is a useful exercise (as well as a challenge) to attempt to diagnose the errors in the exercise in Figure 5-3, using Gickling and Havertape's categories.

Word problems in math require additional types of error analysis than the ones described by Gickling and Havertape (1982). For example, reading problems may interfere with the child's ability to decode the problem itself. If the child can complete the problem when it is presented orally, does well on computation, and is known to have a reading problem, the diagnosis is not difficult to make.

Problems in language or in understanding the conceptual level of the problem can also be explored diagnostically. These issues go beyond mathematics. One source of diagnostic information in this area is the Boehm Test of Basic Concepts—Revised (Boehm, 1986), which has been designed "to assess children's mastery of the basic concepts that are both fundamental to understanding verbal instruction and essential for early school achievement" (p. 1). The test, appropriate for children in kindergarten, Grade 1, and Grade 2, includes relationship concepts that are essential in order for children to:

• understand and describe relationships between and among objects; the locations and characteristics of persons, places and things; and the order of events;
• follow teacher directions;

Locate the source of error in each set of math problems. First categorize the error as either a PLACE VALUE error, an error in ALGORITHMS, a RANDOM RESPONSE error, or an error in OPERATIONS. Then explain the nature of the error. Finally, comment on where you think instruction for remediation should begin.

(a)
14	26	41	31
x3	x2	x5	x6
12	24	20	18

Source of error: _____

Explanation: _____

_____

_____

_____

Recommended instructions: _____

_____

_____

_____

(b)
316	126	279	756
+47	+75	+84	+78
353	191	253	724

Source of error: _____

Explanation: _____

_____

_____

_____

Recommended instructions: _____

_____

_____

_____

(c)
	12	24	18	13
	x4	x5	x6	x3
	16	29	24	16

Source of error: _____

Explanation: _____

_____

_____

_____

Recommended instructions: _____

_____

_____

_____

(d)
	29	16	75	54
	–6	+4	–4	+8
	35	20	79	62

Source of error: _____

Explanation: _____

_____

_____

_____

Recommended instructions: _____

_____

_____

_____

(e)
	51	46	72	33
	x4	x8	x3	x6
	204	222	256	216

Source of error: _____

Explanation: _____

_____   _____

_____

_____

Recommended instructions: _____

_____

_____

_____

(f)　　12　　38　　75　　41
　　　+25　　+46　　+16　　+59
　　　　37　　714　　811　　910

Source of error: _____

Explanation: _____

_____

_____

_____

Recommended instructions: _____

_____

_____

_____

(g)　　24　　18　　51　　16
　　　 +6　　 +9　　 +8　　 +2
　　　　12　　18　　14　　 9

Source of error: _____

Explanation: _____

_____

_____

_____

Recommended instructions: _____

_____

(h)
12	53	83	19
+13	+64	+22	+42
25	77	65	53

Source of error: _____

Explanation: _____

_____

_____

_____

Recommended instructions: _____

_____

_____

_____

FIGURE 5-3. Analyzing children's math errors. Developed by Carol Righi and Florence Rubinson to accompany the Self-Study Gickling and Havertape module, 1982.

- comply with the demands of instruction in the areas of language arts, mathematics, and science;
- comply with the procedural aspects of teacher-made and standardized tests; and
- engage in problem-solving activities that involve classifying, sequencing, comparing, and identifying multiple attributes (Boehm, p. 2).

Along with the 50 concepts tested individually, there is an applications booklet to evaluate the child's ability to use the same concepts:

- in combination;
- to make intermediate position comparisons, such as identifying a tree taller than one, but not the tallest;
- to place objects and events in order; and
- to follow multiple-step directions (p. 26).

The test results provide norms by socioeconomic level and grade, by item, and for the total score. Equally, if not more important, is the interpretation section of the manual, in which suggestions are made for classroom instruction based on the results. An error-analysis procedure is described, so that the teacher may be clear about how to assess the difficulty for the child before planning the instruction.

COMPUTERIZED CBA

While the rationale for direct assessment of the learner's academic level and skills has been presented here, many educators feel that the procedures described are labor intensive, that is to say, too time consuming and tedious to be conducted on a regular basis. Others are concerned about the effort needed to train classroom teachers to conduct learning assessments. Although none of these reasons should be an excuse for not discovering ways to incorporate the essential features of CBA into the repertoire of teacher behaviors, one alternative for facilitating the process involves the use of microcomputer technology in the assessment.

Much software development and literature currently have focused on noninteractive uses for the microcomputer, that is, its use in scoring, analyzing, and writing reports on some of the more widely used, norm-referenced tests. Time is saved basically in terms of clerical tasks. Certainly the results generated by the measures of direct assessment recommended by Deno and Mirkin (1977) could be fed into a computer program to complete the essentially clerical tasks associated with this method.

However, there is a second type of computer use, involving interaction of the child with the computer actually to conduct the assessment. Interactive assessment tools have been developed to facilitate this process (e.g., Hasselbring, 1983; Hasselbring & Kinzer, 1984).

This interactive computerized-assessment process has potential application for both norm-referenced testing and curriculum-based assessment methods. For example, Hasselbring (1983) computerized the Test of Reading Comprehension (Brown, Hammill, & Wiederholt, 1978). However, Hasselbring and Kinzer (1984) also developed a computerized version of the cloze procedure as an informal testing device. Text samples of curriculum materials are entered using word-processing capability. Their Computerized Cloze Program (CCP) then converts the text into cloze passages. The student types in the missing words, after which the CCP scores the responses.

Similarly, Hasselbring's (1983) Computerized Test of Spelling Errors (CTSE) administers, scores, analyzes, and summarizes a child's spelling performance. A computer-controlled, cassette-recorder tape pronounces the target word, followed by its use in a sentence, and then the word in isolation again. The student types in the spelling, after which the next word is presented, a method in which the pace is entirely controlled by the child. The scoring includes an error analysis, as each spelling response is checked against 13 error types. The error analysis allows the teacher to identify areas of strength and weakness for instruction in spelling. Research on the program has indicated that the computer-generated data are as valid and reliable as those obtained using paper-and-pencil formats, with less time required of the teacher.

Hasselbring (1984) suggested that computerized academic assessment is still in its infancy. "Expert systems" programs, evolving from the field of artificial intelligence, will eventually be useful in determining how the learner goes about the problem-solving process and will be used to coach the learner to a more effective performance. One current example of an expert system for direct assessment of an academic area is DEBUGGY (Burton, 1982). This program diagnoses student "bugs" (errors) in simple mathematical operations. A set of math problems and the child's answers are entered, and the program compares the responses to a model of possible bugs, attempting to diagnose the learner's procedural errors. An interactive version, IDEBUGGY, actually presents the students with problems, and then generates a possible diagnosis based on the answers. As each response is assessed, the program determines whether to give an additional problem or whether enough information has been generated to make and report a diagnosis. It is these more powerful expert systems that may eventually enable the state-of-the-art in direct assessment of academics to be applied to a wider population of children.

Hasselbring (1984) optimistically concluded:

> The diagnostic and assessment programs currently available are only precursors to the more elaborate and powerful expert systems currently under development. It is conceivable that, in the next five to ten years, expert systems will be developed which contain much of the knowledge and skill of the country's best educational diagnosticians. These systems will be able to guide an assessor through the necessary steps for the assessment of any special-needs student, test the student directly where appropriate, analyze the assessment data, and prescribe appropriate instructional strategies for remediating the student's problems. (p. 18)

Although it is not likely that computers will eliminate all of the need for direct assessment of learning by consultants and teachers, it should be possible to enhance the assessment process in this domain.

SUMMARY

In this chapter, several stages are presented for direct assessment in the academic skills area. The process begins with placing a child in the scope and sequence of curriculum skills for that classroom and/or school, and analyzing the discrepancy between a referred child's performance and that of the average functioning child in that setting. Procedures for an analysis of the task designated for that child's instruction and error analysis are specified, so that prior to the instructional intervention, the teacher is clear about the task the child should be learning and the type and pattern of error and/or steps in skill development around which planning is necessary.

Probes for constant monitoring of progress are part of an ongoing assessment, much as data collection functions in behavioral approaches. The teacher has a clear idea of baseline academic skills, and the progress resulting from different interventions. Without this fine-grained analysis of the learning area, it is difficult to know where to begin instruction and how effective the instructional intervention has been. This information provides the starting point for the next stage, instructional planning. Developing and conducting an instructional intervention, therefore, are the topics of Section III.

Section III

INSTRUCTIONAL INTERVENTION— PLANNING AND IMPLEMENTATION

For while teaching will forever be in part an art, its foundations can and should rest on the sciences of human behavior.
—Gordon, DeStefano, & Shipman, 1985, p. 63

Thus far the focus has been on problem identification and analysis. The purpose of the assessment process is to gather data to construct an instructional intervention with the child in the least restrictive environment. For most children the classroom is the setting for the instructional intervention, and the teacher is responsible for planning, if not carrying out, the intervention. In this section, a framework for planning and implementing a classroom-based intervention is constructed.

In chapters 6 and 7, the format for planning and conducting interventions is described. Chapter 6 introduces the intervention model and describes techniques for managing the learner. Chapter 7 focuses on instructional management. Although some of the problems encountered in this stage are discussed in chapters 6 and 7, chapter 8 focuses on the barriers to implementation in the school setting, and the consultation issues involved.

Chapter 6

PLANNING AND CONDUCTING AN INSTRUCTIONAL INTERVENTION
Management of the Learner

Those who can, do. Those who understand, teach.

—L. Shulman, 1986

If the problem-identification stage has been completed effectively, there is now substantial and useful information available from which to formulate an instructional intervention. However, the intervention has to be one that is perceived as both acceptable and "do-able" to the teacher. There are, in other words, two aspects to classroom-based treatment: (1) what will enable the child to make progress; and (2) what those professionals (usually the teacher) responsible for mediating that program will accept. Thus, both the consultation process and the knowledge of instructional alternatives become intertwined in this stage. In this chapter, a process for developing a plan, and one aspect of the knowledge base, techniques for the management of the learner, are the center of attention.

DEVELOPING DIAGNOSTIC HYPOTHESES

Diagnostic Decisions

The first step in the planning process is to integrate the information that has been obtained in the previous stage, that is problem identification and analysis, in terms of a series of decisions. It also becomes apparent as the decision-making process unfolds whether the questions that have been raised are answered or whether other information is required before a plan can be

125

formulated. At all times, however, the consultant avoids confronting the teacher with what the teacher *should* do, but focuses on what the child needs for instructional progress to be made. As the diagnostic questions are addressed, the consulting team has the basis for planning the intervention.

1. Is There a Discrepancy that Needs to Be Addressed?   The team must first decide whether or not there is a discrepancy that requires a special plan. While in most cases, the assessment process helps to define the discrepancy in more detail, occasionally it provides information that suggests that current interventions are working effectively. For example, in one case, a child-study team (CST) received a referral regarding a first grade youngster who was making slow progress in learning to read. The teacher had, however, begun an intervention that seemed to be effective, and the child was beginning to make progress. The decision of the team was not to modify the intervention until further data had been gathered on the success of the plan currently in place. In this case, the important recommendation of the CST, which had not occurred to the teacher to do, was to encourage her to maintain data on the child so that progress under the current plan could be followed. Deno and Mirkin (1977) provided a formula (as described in Part I of Appendix C) for calculating a discrepancy ratio should one be needed for placement/classification decisions. Moreover, it is possible for the school staff to determine how much of a discrepancy would require an instructional intervention, using the Deno and Mirkin's formula or one developed within the school by the staff. If a significant (as determined by the school staff) discrepancy is uncovered by the team, they would proceed to the next decision.

2. Is the Child Placed at Instructional Level or Expected to Work at Frustration Level Skills?   This is a critical question in instructional planning. There is little point in developing an instructional plan to assist the child if the child is not placed in materials at instructional level on a daily basis. Few children will maintain high on-task times in material that is not possible for them to complete successfully. To intervene to maintain high on-task times in such situations is to encourage a "be still, be quiet" philosophy (Winett & Winkler, 1972). Whereas such a program may have value for the mental health of the teacher or eventually be necessary for the child when he or she is placed at the correct level in the material, it is not enough by itself for academic progress. Many irrelevant errors, such as reversals, appear when children are at frustration level. These errors often disappear when children are placed at the appropriate level in the scope and sequence of objectives and receive adequate instruction. Using curriculum-based assessment data, the team may both determine if the child is at instructional level and if not, where instructional level actually is in the academic domain of concern. If the child is at instructional level and not making progress, they should proceed to the next decision regarding instructional design.

However, if the child is not at instructional level, the child should be placed in the scope and sequence at the point where he or she has the entry-level skills to make progress. This is often a more complex decision than it appears. Teachers may be resistant to moving children back in the curriculum for a number of reasons, all of them legitimate if we examine it from their point of view. Some of the major reasons include: (1) the child has already gone through that material, so what good will it do to go back and do it again? (2) The teacher does not have the time/energy to have a separate reading group for this child; (3) the child will feel badly about going through the material again; and (4) the teacher's supervisor insists that the teacher cover the entire scope and sequence (usually defined in terms of curriculum materials—e.g., completing the reading series for grade 3 during the school year). To deny the validity of any of these reasons is to court an ineffective consultation outcome.

In each case, the consultant avoids debating with the teacher about what the teacher should do, and focuses on what the child needs:

- "The child has already gone through the material, so what good will it do to repeat it?" That may be correct, and an instructional plan needs to be formulated to ensure that the child *masters* the materials this time around.

- It is impossible to set up a separate reading group for this child." The focus then is shifted by the consultant to how the resources for additional help can be obtained, without blaming the teacher for feeling overwhelmed by her current load of responsibilities.

- "The child will feel badly about returning to material already failed." A discussion with the teacher on how to approach this issue with the child is often helpful, as is considering the possibility of packaging the material for the child in a somewhat different format. To change reading series, however, presents a whole new set of problems, and often succeeds in making the task more complex for the child (e.g., a different set of sight words, a different sequence of instructional objectives), and should be avoided.

- "The supervisor (principal, etc.) has required the teacher to go through the entire curriculum for each child in the grade." The consultant may need to run interference with the supervisor for the teacher. Occasionally the principal will not bend on this requirement, but more often, if there is a plan with an evaluation component to monitor the child's progress, the principal may allow an "exception." Success in this process then encourages the principal or supervisor to allow further exceptions in the future. However, often the consultant takes on the role of advocate in this situation, both for the teacher's freedom to make an appropriate instructional decision and for the child's chances to make progress.

3. How Effective Is the Current Instructional Program?   If demonstrated to be ineffective, what changes need to be made in the instructional design? If the problem is a "won't do" one, what changes in management of the learner need to be made? If the problem is a "can't do" type, what changes in the management of learning need to be considered?

When the decision is made to modify the instructional program of the child, a number of specific factors need to be considered. There are, essentially, four components to the program that can be manipulated: the child's work setting; the curricular materials; the instructional procedure; and the arrangement of consequences based on the learner's performance (Haring & Gentry, 1976). After examining in detail the current status of these four components and the type of problem of the child ("can't do" versus "won't do"), the program modification can be planned.

It is critical at this juncture to understand that each modification is in itself a hypothesis, a hunch, based on knowledge of instruction, about what this child needs in order to progress most effectively and efficiently. To reverse Berliner's (1985) comment, clinical work is always idiographic, but nomothetic generalizations become the basis for idiographic hypotheses. Doyle (1985) suggested how sparse our knowledge base is about "the dynamic orchestration of student characteristics and instructional variables . . . there are few specific guidelines for designing instructional treatments to fit specific learning characteristics or dimensions of students" (p. 93). He concluded that it is more important for teachers to have a "broad understanding of how students learn, [to] continuously monitor students' progress, and adjust in a myriad of ways to evolving circumstances in the classroom" (p. 93), while admitting that the empirical basis for these adjustments is not very precise. Thus, a trial teaching paradigm provides a more realistic basis for the intervention. It implies that ongoing evaluation of the effectiveness of the program must be part of the plan. It also makes it even clearer why a collaborative rather than an expert consultation relationship is valuable, as two professionals together attempt to resolve the learning problem of the student at hand. This is not to say that the intervention plan is based on trial and error, but that there is a realistic possibility that the plan may need to be modified and/or adapted to meet the specific nature of the problem and the complexity of the classroom setting.

The remainder of this chapter includes a discussion of selected aspects of the knowledge base for planning instructional alternatives, based on the two modifiable categories identified by Haring and Gentry (1976) related to management of the learner: the work setting and the arrangement of consequences based on the learner's performance. Chapter 7 covers the management of learning, that is, curriculum materials and instructional procedures.

STRATEGIES FOR MANAGING THE LEARNER:
MODIFICATIONS IN THE WORK SETTING

Often recommendations are made to change the child's work setting in an administrative sense; for example, move the child to a smaller class, a remedial class, a resource room, or a transition class. Alternatively, teachers are told to provide the child more individual attention. Rather than these broad and indirect measures to increase the instruction and time provided for a child (in fact, we have found many times that the size of the reading group in the remedial reading class is larger than the group in the child's regular classroom), a set of specific teacher behaviors involving improved classroom management techniques is presented for two purposes: to increase the amount of time that a child will actually spend on-task in a productive way and to enable teachers to have a sense of control that will free them to attend more to the instructional program itself. If a classroom is poorly managed, teachers spend considerable energy and time on issues that do not result in productive encounters with instructional tasks.

The teachers we have encountered rarely have had a course in classroom management (in fact, few teacher training programs require them to do so). At best, they may have had a course in behavior modification, which tends to focus more on the consequences following student behavior than the antecedent events, "factors existing in the environment prior to a behavior that make that behavior more or less likely to occur"(Paine et al., 1983, p. 12). Kounin's (1977) research makes it clear that early intervention, before problems have a chance to develop, is the most effective management.

In working with teachers, we have found it useful to recommend a basic management text when teachers request help on classroom management techniques to improve their general classroom control (for example, Paine, et al., 1983, *Structuring Your Classroom for Academic Success;* Emmer, Evertson, Sanford, Clements, & Worsham, 1984, *Classroom Management for Secondary Teachers;* Evertson, Emmer, Clements, Sanford, Worsham, 1984, *Classroom Management for Elementary Teachers*. The latter two books cover the same material, but for different grade ranges.). Whereas the books are written for teachers and are fairly straightforward (Paine et al. even include specific scripts for the teacher to use in developing new classroom behaviors), they are also useful for in-service work. However, teachers often have questions about actually implementing the techniques, and the consultant needs to be available to provide feedback for the teacher. Figure 6-1, "Guidelines for Classroom Observation" taken from Paine et al. (1983) provides a structured set of guidelines for teachers or observers to use to evaluate the basic classroom management skills of the teacher.

Guidelines for Classroom Observation

Name _____

Affiliation _____ Date _____

Welcome to our classroom. Some of the activities you observe here may be different from those in other classrooms you have visited. This is a classroom *structured for success*, that is, a preventive, whole-class approach to classroom management. It is designed to prevent many of the problem behaviors that might otherwise occur in the classroom and uses a variety of procedures and positive consequences. While this approach involves the whole class rather than focusing on individual students, it does not mean that individual differences and needs are overlooked. There remains considerable room to accommodate various student learning rates and preferences. However, the procedures focus on structuring success for all class members and for all class components that make up a routine day.

Please use this guide as you observe student and teacher behaviors in this classroom. The guide will help you focus on the key preventive management procedures used, and your comments will provide me with valuable feedback. Before you leave the classroom, please return this form to me or leave it in the designated spot. Thank you for any input or feedback you can provide.

I will be happy to talk with you outside of class to answer any questions you may have. Please feel free to call me at _____ . The best times to reach me are _____ . Thank you for your interest. We hope you will visit us again.

	Yes	No	Did Not Observe
A. The use of *praise* is a positive way to manage classroom behavior.			
1. Teacher states student's name and behavior being praised.	_____	_____	_____
2. Teacher praises academic behavior.	_____	_____	_____
3. Teacher praises on-task behavior.	_____	_____	_____
4. Teacher praises socially approved behavior (being nice to others).	_____	_____	_____
5. Teacher praises often.	_____	_____	_____
6. Teacher praises other students while working with individuals.	_____	_____	_____
B. Cards are used to *request assistance*; students can continue to work while they wait, which maximizes students' time on-task.			
1. Teacher acknowledges cards: "I see your card."	_____	_____	_____

2. Students continue to work while they wait. _____ _____ _____
3. Teacher assists students as quickly as possible. _____ _____ _____

C. *Transition time* is the time it takes to change what you are doing. Students are taught how to change what they are doing quickly and quietly to maximize time spent on academics.
1. Students move quietly. _____ _____ _____
2. Students put books away and get ready for next activity. _____ _____ _____
3. Students move chairs quietly. _____ _____ _____
4. Students keep their hands and feet to themselves. _____ _____ _____
5. Teacher praises students for correctly following rules. _____ _____ _____

D. Suggestive praise combined with a mild consequence is used to *deal with misbehavior*.
1. Teacher first praises other students who are exhibiting correct behavior. _____ _____ _____
2. Teacher clearly states, "This is a warning." _____ _____ _____
3. If misbehavior continues, teacher puts name and point on board. _____ _____ _____
4. For every point on board, student loses a privilege (e.g., access to academic game, reading time in library, chance to be line monitor). _____ _____ _____

E. Research has shown that *point systems* can positively manage student behavior.
1. Teacher marks points immediately after transition time. _____ _____ _____
2. At end of period teacher marks points for receiving no more than one warning. _____ _____ _____
3. Teacher directs student attention to point chart when posting points. _____ _____ _____
4. Students need 90% of total points for day to participate in activity at end of day (e.g., academic game, "free" reading time, peer, or cross-age tutoring). _____ _____ _____

F. Students *correct some of their own work* to receive immediate feedback and focus on their errors
   1. Students leave pencils at their desks. _____ _____ _____
   2. Students are quiet at correcting station. _____ _____ _____
   3. Students come back to seats to correct errors. _____ _____ _____
   4. Students work while they wait if correcting station is full. _____ _____ _____
   5. Students file completed papers in box or basket at station. _____ _____ _____
   6. Students go on to next assigned activity. _____ _____ _____
G. Rules are posted to inform teachers, students, aides, volunteers, and others of important classroom contingencies so that rules may be applied and followed consistently.
   1. Rules are posted so that they are clearly visible. _____ _____ _____
   2. Rules are stated positively (e.g., "Stay in your seat" instead of "Do not leave your seat"). _____ _____ _____
   3. Students follow rules. _____ _____ _____
   4. Teacher applies rules consistently for all students. _____ _____ _____
H. Desks that are arranged in straight, evenly spaced rows minimize unnecessary student interaction.
   1. Desks are arranged with adequate spacing to allow teacher to circulate around room and to monitor student progress. _____ _____ _____
   2. Desks are arranged so teacher can see all students. _____ _____ _____
   3. Desks are arranged so students can see teacher and chalkboard. _____ _____ _____

I. Certain time-related criteria are essential for student learning: sufficient time must be allotted for academic instruction and practice, and the schedule of allotted time must be followed. Public posting of a time-efficient schedule helps the teacher and students adhere to the schedule.
   1. Schedule is posted where teacher and others can see it easily. _____ _____ _____
   2. Teacher adheres to schedule. _____ _____ _____
   3. If teacher does not follow schedule, more time is spent on academic activities than on nonacademic activities. _____ _____ _____

Comments on the structure or procedures used in this class

_____

_____

_____

_____

_____

_____

_____

_____

_____

_____

_____

_____

_____

FIGURE 6-1. From *Structuring Your Classroom for Academic Success* (pp. 161-165) by S. C. Paine et al., 1983, Champaigne, IL: Research Press Company. Copyright 1983 by Research Press Company. Reprinted by permission of the publisher.

There is considerable evidence that time needed for learning is an important variable to consider (see Gettinger, 1984, for a review of this topic). Further, it appears that managing allocated time well serves both a preventive function and a remedial one. Many children seem to need more on-task time to learn without falling behind; when children do not progress at the same pace as their more average peers, they need the time even more to catch up and to maintain progress. The question then becomes how to assist teachers in managing the work setting most effectively when a discrepancy is found between a child's current level of functioning and the desired level. Managing the work setting is rarely a solution in and of itself, but effective management can increase the time available to tackle the task, and thus assist the child in moving most efficiently to the desired level of functioning. The answer is not simply to move the child into another room with a different child/teacher ratio for a small proportion of the school week. In fact, our observations have shown us that smaller classes do not necessarily have higher levels of allocated and actual time, unless the teachers have mastered and use the management strategies described below.

The following topics are especially critical in this area: the physical arrangements in the classroom, the management of time, and the management of classroom "assistants." A fourth topic, that of cooperative learning techniques, is also described in this section.

Physical Arrangements in the Classroom

The most basic question to ask is whether the classroom is arranged so that noise and disruption are minimized. According to Paine et al. (1983), students seated at separate desks are less likely to talk, and more likely to work and pay attention. The seating arrangements are also related to the level and quality of student interactions (although some other important issues need to be considered in this regard). In many classrooms, we have observed children visiting and copying when seated at groups of desks or at tables. If the teacher is expecting constructive peer interaction, that needs to be monitored and planned for by the teacher, rather than expected or determined by seating arrangements alone (see the section later in this chapter on "cooperative learning techniques").

Important questions to ask, then, are: How does the seating arrangement affect the target student? Is the student next to other disruptive students? Can the teacher directly observe the student during direct instruction periods? If the student has a visual or hearing problem, is the physical arrangement planned with that in mind?

The last has been, in our experience, a surprisingly overlooked factor. It tends to be most serious in cases in which pupils have glasses or hearing aids that are broken, lost, or not worn for whatever reason. Teachers will be upset about the lost or broken glasses, but not move students to a place where they can see properly *without* the glasses. Also, children with chronic *otis media*, often generating unpredictable hearing losses, depending upon the current status of the condition, need to receive consideration. Because their hearing problems are sporadic, teachers are often unaware of their need.

Managing Time

If time spent on-task is a critically important factor, how is time managed in the classroom? Teachers need to make the best possible use of every minute they have available for all students. For children who need more time to learn, the need to use time well is even more compelling. The teacher is, as manager of the classroom, the person responsible for managing instructional time. However, if the teacher does this job well, all the others (aides, parents, and students) are involved cooperatively in the process.

What is the concept of time in the classroom and how do we protect instructional time? It begins with encouraging high attendance rates, and decreasing lateness and absences. Many children who have academic problems have spotty attendance records. Knowing that children need time on-task to learn can add incentive to the teacher and parents in setting up management strategies for attendance and on-time behaviors.

A corollary is to anticipate for many learners decreases in their academic progress if instructional time is decreased through excessive absences. Rather than send a chronically absent child for a learning evaluation, a more parsimonious strategy might be to increase instructional time. This problem seems to be a serious one with some immigrant children, especially those who did not attend school regularly. The students are sometimes labeled learning disabled, rather than seen as casualties of instructional time. A special project (Martorell, personal communication, October, 1986) in the New York City schools has been designed to provide services to high-school-age immigrant children who had experienced infrequent school attendance in their native homes, without labeling them handicapped—the previous approach for providing them with services.

In addition, it is necessary to minimize interruptions and time spent in transitions. In one classroom of special children, a low enrollment class of boys demonstrating difficulty in meeting school behavioral and academic demands, the principal had been in the habit of "visiting" every day. Once the teacher began to understand the importance of her instructional program to the progress of the children, she requested that he not interrupt the class during instructional time (Ford & Rosenfield, 1980).

Paine et al. (1983) suggested specific procedures for analyzing the current schedule: (1) computing actual number of minutes in the school week; (2) determining the number of minutes per activity; (3) subtracting the number of minutes for lunch, recess, and organizational activities, resulting in an amount of time for instructional activities; (4) determining the percent of time for each instructional activity; and (5) ranking each activity area based on the time priority given to each of them. After constructing this analysis of the

	Monday	
9:00- 9:40		
9:40-10:00		
10:00-10:45		
10:45-11:15	Reading—Mrs. Parker	
11:30-12:00	Lunch	
12:00-12:25	Recess	
12:35- 1:10	Music	
1:10- 1:40	Remedial reading	
1:40- 2:00		
2:15- 3:00	Chorus	

	Tuesday	Wednesday
9:00- 9:40	Remedial reading	Remedial reading
9:40-10:00		
10:00-10:45		
10:45-11:15	Reading—Mrs. Parker	Reading—Mrs. Parker
11:30-12:00	Lunch	Lunch
12:00-12:25	Recess	Recess
12:35- 1:10		Art
1:10- 1:40	Gym	
1:40- 2:00	Trumpet	
2:15- 3:00	Band	Band

	Thursday	Friday
9:00- 9:40		Computer
9:40-10:00		Computer
10:00-10:45		
10:45-11:15	Reading—Mrs. Parker	Reading—Mrs. Parker
11:30-12:00	Lunch	Lunch
12:00-12:25	Recess	Recess
12:35- 1:00		Gym
1:00- 1:30	Library	
1:30- 2:00		
2:20- 3:00	Remedial reading	Remedial reading

FIGURE 6-2. TJ's daily schedule showing how much time he is actually available for instruction in the classroom.

schedule, the teacher can determine whether the current schedule minimizes organizational time for the children in the areas where he or she perceives the most need for instruction. Strategies for managing transition time, the time it takes to change from one activity to another, are also included in the Paine et al. book, and can be utilized by the teacher who sees that too much instructional time is being lost in moving from one activity to another.

The strategies presented here are applicable to the entire class. Teachers who feel in control of their classroom during transitions and who know classroom time is being well used are often more willing to develop a plan for use of time for a particular child.

In one case a highly competent teacher referred a child to the school's *Child Study Team* because she was concerned about his academic progress. As the referral interview progressed, the teacher began to express her underlying concern that she had TJ so rarely in class that her instructional time was limited with him. TJ, a fourth grader, was attending remedial reading five times per week. Further, the fourth grade moved across teachers for their developmental reading program (the regular teaching of reading), and he had a teacher other than his homeroom teacher for reading. It was suggested that she construct a calendar of his schedule. The data are presented in Figure 6-2. Between the remedial reading, developmental reading, and the specials, the amount of instructional time she had with him in class was indeed limited, and became the focus of the intervention. Actually, she was greatly relieved to see the reality base for her feelings of frustration about time.

A particular issue with regard to transition time, however, is related to the student in a pull-out program, whether it be the resource room or a chapter program (or even a gifted program). Transitions between classrooms and teachers need careful management, and Evertson et al. (1984) provide a series of valuable suggestions for teachers whose children are involved:

Managing Transition Time for Pull-Out Program Students

1. Coordinate time so that it maximizes appropriate instructional time for the students. If the child is pulled out for reading instruction, it should be during classroom reading time. While this is not always easy to do in practice, remember that the child's use of instructional time is critical. If a child is struggling with reading in the regular classroom and is pulled out during social studies class, he then risks being disadvantaged in an additional subject as well.

2. Stay on the prearranged schedule as much as possible, especially if the times have been carefully arranged. If the classroom teacher tends to forget, be sure someone else in the class (perhaps even a student) has the responsibility to remind the teacher. A schedule of children's out-of-class times is necessary. As a last resort, set a timer!

3. Have activities for the student to do while waiting for instruction, both on arrival in the special class and upon return to the classroom. It is not always possible for the lesson to end just on schedule, and as little time should be lost in the transition as possible. A clear transition structure for the student to follow should be taught and enforced.

4. Assist students in remembering what they should take between classes. Either remind students or help them develop a self-reminding format. Often students are reprimanded for forgetting instructional materials, rather than a plan put into effect to help them remember. If the child has to trek continually back and forth between classes to retrieve missing items, instructional time is lost.

Another important way to maximize student engaged time is to make provision for students when they are stuck and still expected to continue working independently. During seat-work time, for example, classrooms often become more noisy and disruptive when teachers are constantly interrupted to answer students' requests for help. Those who have to wait for assistance are usually not doing any constructive activity when they get stuck, and may, in fact, be distracting to others. Paine et al. (1983) described several techniques to ensure that this disruption does not occur; for example: "Each student is given a three-sided card and a folder. The card is taped to the student's desk, and the student uses it during seat-work time to signal the teacher for help needed. . . . The folder contains work that the student can turn to for practice while waiting for the teacher's help" (p. 110).

The teacher follows good procedures of acknowledging and reinforcing students who use the procedure correctly and ignoring those who do not. The result is that students can make a "continuous request for assistance without disrupting their work time, constantly interrupting the teacher, or bothering other students" (p. 110).

Managing "Assistants"

Teachers often respond to the request to do something different in the classroom with the legitimate complaint that they do not have the time to do anything else. We have heard this complaint from teachers with 35 children, those with 25 and even those with 15 children (although it should be acknowledged that they usually only have 15 if the children are considered difficult in some way). This perception of being overwhelmed by responsibilities is not to be denied, nor is it to be given the status of an excuse. Rather, the issue should be stated differently: How can time and resources be managed so that the work setting provides the amount of supervision that the learner needs? We will consider at a later point how to build the student's capacity to work alone, without supervision. But using others to assist the teacher in the classroom may make it possible for the child at risk to receive extra personal attention.

According to Paine et al. (1983), assistants, including aides, paraprofessionals, parents, community volunteers, peers, or cross-age peers, can engage in such activities as: listening to students read, drilling them on basic math facts or sight words, correcting papers or helping students self-correct them, directing small group activities, or developing and supervising enrichment activities such as in art, music, cooking, etc. In some cases, the assistants can free the teacher from other tasks to work more productively with children who need additional intensive instructional support. Paine et al. (1983) also remind us that principals, janitors, cooks, bus drivers, and secretaries have potential value, too, and can engage in activities such as making phone calls to parents, listening to children read, praising students for on-task behaviors, and allowing the students to be assigned to them as helpers in return for completed work. Teachers should be encouraged to seek community volunteers: "good help is worth a thorough search" (Paine et al., 1983, p. 31).

A school psychologist in a school district developing a prereferral-intervention model undertook to develop a cadre of volunteers for the pilot school. She contacted numerous community groups, ranging from senior citizens to parent groups. Her efforts provided a group of people able to free teachers from having to do everything. With adequate training and supervision, volunteers can enable teachers to use their time more effectively.

However, teachers never abrogate their responsibility as instructional managers. At the beginning and throughout the work in which assistants are involved, the teacher (and consultant, if one is engaged at this point with the teacher), need to clarify what the assistant's role is to be and to supervise the process. Orientation time needs to be set aside, without the children underfoot, to be specific about such items as: where materials are found, where they will work with the child, what the classroom rules are, what the instruction should look like, including how long and how to present the tasks, and how to deal with possible problems. We have observed aides supervising reading groups, using management and instructional strategies that are counterproductive, based on their lack of knowledge of teaching.

Similarly, peer tutoring is not effective unless it is carefully planned. A detailed list of steps for a peer-tutoring program is presented in Figure 6-3.

Sometimes the "assistant" is the consultant, who may take on a variety of classroom roles to help the teacher. Sometimes the consultant may model for the teacher the kind of instructional intervention that needs to be provided. At other times the consultant takes over the class for the teacher, so that the teacher can find the time and energy to conduct the intervention. In one case, a consultant who was attempting to develop a better process for mainstreaming children in her school, took over a teacher's class so that the receiving classroom teacher, who was reluctant to accept the child, could meet with the sending special education teacher to talk about the student's instructional needs and to be reassured about the child's readiness to return to the mainstream setting. Or, the consultant may train the other "assistants" for the teacher. Particularly with teachers new to the process of consultation, providing the additional help, and allowing the program to demonstrate its effectiveness, are important factors.

Cooperative Learning Techniques

Related to the use of others, including peers, is the possibility of incorporating cooperative learning methods (Slavin, Sharan, Kagan, Hertz-Lazarowitz, Webb, & Schmuck, 1985) into the classroom management strategies of the

Peer-Tutoring Program Checklist

_____ 1. Specify goals
      _____ for learners
      _____ for peers
_____ 2. Specify reasons for implementing program
_____ 3. Specify peer role
_____ 4. Specify practical constraints
      _____ learner
      _____ peer
      _____ procedural
      _____ setting
      _____ target skill
_____ 5. Develop monitoring system
      _____ who will monitor
      _____ procedure
      _____ schedule
      _____ materials needed
_____ 6. Develop management system
      _____ peer behavior
            _____ type of reinforcer
            _____ schedule
            _____ who delivers
            _____ type of response cost
            _____ schedule
            _____ who delivers
      _____ learner behavior
            _____ type of reinforcer
            _____ schedule
            _____ who delivers
            _____ type of response cost
            _____ schedule
            _____ who delivers
_____ 7. Develop and organize materials
_____ 8. Determine schedule and setting for tutoring
      _____ where interaction will occur
      _____ during what time of day interaction will occur
      _____ how long each interaction will last
_____ 9. Recruit volunteers
_____ 10. Select peer managers
      _____ develop job sample tasks
      _____ develop rating criteria
      _____ observe performance on job sample
_____ 11. Match peers with learners
_____ 12. Train peers
      _____ specify peer tasks
      _____ develop performance criteria statements
      _____ develop training tasks
_____ 13. Manage the peer-learner interaction
      _____ monitor
      _____ apply contingencies
_____ 14. Revise as indicated by the data

FIGURE 6-3. From *Structuring Your Classroom for Academic Success* (p. 37) by S. C. Paine et al., 1983, Champaigne, IL: Research Press Company. Copyright 1983 by Research Press Company. Reprinted by permission of the publisher.

teacher. Theory and research on cooperative-learning techniques have convinced many teachers that these methods not only have a positive affective value, but also "enhance the learning of the traditional academic curriculum" (Schmuck, 1985, p. 1). Cooperative learning methods are defined by Slavin (1985) as:

> structured, systematic instructional strategies capable of being used at any grade level and in most school subjects. All of the methods involve having the teacher assign the students to four- to six-member learning groups. . . . Each group is a microcosm of the class in academic achievement level, sex, and ethnicity.
>
> All cooperative learning methods are based on social psychological research and theory. . . . However, they have been adapted to one degree or another to meet the practical requirements of classrooms and to solve problems introduced by the use of cooperation itself (such as maintaining individual accountability as well as group responsibility). The engine that runs cooperative learning is always the same: heterogeneous groups working toward a common goal. (pp. 6-7)

Slavin (1985) based on his review of the effects of cooperative learning on student achievement, concludes that the method is effective in improving achievement when the learning of every group member is critical to group success and group success is rewarded. The studies indicate that low achievers gain at least equally from the cooperative experience as their better-achieving peers.

Several methods that use cooperative learning are described by Slavin (1985). These include:

1. Student Team Learning (Slavin, 1980). This set of methods includes STAD (Student Teams Achievement Division), TGT (Teams-Games-Tournament), and Jigsaw II. Scores of each student contribute to his or her team's total, but the outcome is based on an individual's improvement over his or her past performance. The team with the highest score is then recognized/rewarded in some way.

2. Jigsaw (Aronson, 1978). In this technique, each student is provided unique information on a topic being studied by the whole group. Students become expert in their area and provide input to the work group. Students teach their teammates, and a quiz is used to determine both individual and team scores.

3. Learning Together (Johnson & Johnson, 1975). Here student work groups complete a single task, for which praise and recognition are given to the group. The emphasis is on training the participants as good group members and ongoing evaluation of the group's functioning by its members.

4. Group Investigation method (Sharan & Sharan, 1976). In this method, the students select what they will learn, how they will organize themselves for that purpose, and how they will communicate to the larger group what they have learned. Group members allocate tasks among the members.

Slavin considered how the different methods avoid the danger of low-achieving students having little to contribute and being resented or belittled by higher achieving students. In some methods, each student contributes to the total team score to the degree that his or her previous quiz score is exceeded. In others, the teacher makes sure that each student has something of value to contribute through providing the student an area in which to become knowledgeable.

It takes time and training for teachers to become expert in the use of cooperative learning techniques. However, the instructional consultant can facilitate this process by becoming aware of the techniques, mastering them, and then being a resource in cases where they are appropriate (see Bohlmoyer & Burke, 1987, for a guide to the different techniques). Given the double effect on achievement and affect, these techniques are worth developing.

ARRANGEMENT OF CONSEQUENCES

The concept of arranging consequences based on the learner's performance is an aspect of instruction that is not news to anyone who has ever taught or been involved in traditional school settings. The use of grades, commendations, and the whole assortment of reinforcement and punishment techniques found in the schools, over and above the internal motivation to learn, is obvious to the most casual observer. The behavior-modification literature has only provided a more systematic approach to the process, and made explicit some rules for using consequences most effectively.

There are a few basic principles involved in arranging consequences: attending to the positive; ignoring the behavior you do not want to encourage, while you are also attending to positive behavior; and rewarding approximations to the desired behavior. However, in working with teachers of children experiencing academic difficulties, one sees these few basic principles consistently violated. Children's successes are often ignored because they are still so discrepant from the teacher's expectations and much attention is focused on their deficiencies rather than on catching them engaged in desired behaviors.

There is considerable research and practice on the effects of arranging consequences, using behavior modification techniques, that indicates their effectiveness. There is also some concern about teachers' unwillingness to engage in systematic use of these techniques for children who might need them (Rosenfield, 1985). Chapter 8 focuses on some of these issues of teacher acceptance of interventions.

In addition, there is a growing research base on the effect of certain forms of positive consequences on children's intrinsic motivation to engage in academic activities (for a review, see Brilliant, 1986), which suggests that caution must be exercised in the use of some of the techniques with children who have intrinsic motivation. According to the McCloyd (1979) study, high value rewards may motivate children to engage in interesting activities, but when a child is interested in the activity, reward may diminish subsequent interest. Moreover, if the child feels he or she can do well, rewards should be related to the competence demonstrated, whereas if the child is unable to do well, it may be more effective to target rewards at first to task-related factors (Karniol & Ross, 1977). Thus, the effective use of rewards requires the instructional consultant to have a substantial knowledge of reinforcement effectiveness.

In applying behavioral interventions to children systematically, most programs sequence the following steps:

1. Decide on the behavior to be modified.
2. Determine a procedure to measure the baseline of the behavior as well as the effect of the intervention.
3. Develop an intervention plan, with different techniques depending upon whether the goal is to increase, decrease, or teach a new behavior, and upon other factors including the particular setting in which the change is to occur.
4. Evaluate the effect of the intervention by continuing to record the target behavior.
5. Modify the intervention, depending upon its measured effectiveness.
6. Plan for maintenance of the behavior (after removal of the intervention program) and generalization to other settings, times, or behaviors, if that is needed.

While use of good behavioral principles will assist teachers in increasing engaged time, four specific techniques will be discussed here that are particularly powerful. These are the use of: (1) positive attention; (2) good-behavior charts; (3) contracts, and (4) self-control techniques.

Teacher Attention and Praise

Teacher attention is a powerful tool when used appropriately. Most children, particularly at the lower elementary school grades, value teacher attention and regard. Classroom attention techniques are useful both for total classroom management effectiveness and for focusing on particular children who might need help in developing more appropriate classroom behaviors. Paine et al. (1983) suggest four components to the use of effective attention in the classroom, which incorporate not only behavioral principles, but also aspects of Kounin's (1970) classroom management research.

The first two components are "moving" and "scanning." Moving involves the teachers' moving around the classroom while students do independent activities; the teachers do so in an unpredictable pattern, so that students are encouraged to work more steadily. When teachers pause to work with a student individually, they should glance up at least every 15 to 20 or 30 seconds. Scanning is the procedure whereby teachers look around the room at various students, sweeping the entire room or repeating various segments. Given that many students may be expert at fooling the teacher, appearing to look busy while being off-task, it is necessary to look often and to look long enough at certain students to be sure they are actually on-task. Both moving and scanning enable the teacher to be withit (Kounin's term), to be aware, and to be perceived by the students as being aware, of what is occurring in the classroom. The goal is to facilitate engaged time, by catching small problems before they become big ones and catching students being good so that reinforcement can be delivered.

Praising skillfully is itself a process that many teachers need to learn. It involves noticing "when students are doing well; calling out their names publicly or speaking to them privately (whichever is most appropriate to their age and ability level); and describing clearly, but briefly, the behavior you want to encourage" (Paine, et al., 1983, p. 46). Effective praise relies on good timing, so that the praise is contingent, that is to say, students are actually doing what you are ready to praise them for, and the praise is immediate; that it is descriptive ("Good for you, Howard! You really got those arithmetic problems solved well and quickly!"), and uses the student's name; and that it is convincing, varied, and nondisruptive.

Convincing praise is not always easy for a teacher to deliver, because it relies on the teacher really meaning what is said. Often teachers are angry and disappointed in a particular student, and catching them being good at first can make a teacher almost choke on the praise. In Caplan's (1970) terms, the teacher may have a problem with objectivity with a given child, and convincing praise is not easy to produce. Consultants can facilitate this process by rewarding and supporting the teacher for using praise with a student the teacher finds particularly difficult.

Varying praise can also be a problem for some teachers. Their repertoire of statements may be limited. Brainstorming together different ways to provide praise has been found helpful to some teachers. Lists of praise statements abound in behavioral texts, but assisting teachers in rehearsing their own versions can produce a more varied and useful list for the individual teacher.

The possibility of a disruptive effect in using praise is an issue for some teachers who introduce praise in somewhat awkward ways. They may be too loud, a bit artificial, or visibly strained. Older children may notice and react to this more strongly. However, we have seen children relish what appeared to us the most artificial praise from their teacher, and begin to reward the teacher for using praise by more appropriate behavior. In most cases, feedback to the teacher on praising technique is helpful.

A fourth aspect of praising raised by Paine et al. (1983) is termed "following up" (p. 46), in which the teacher communicates indirectly to an off-task student by praising one or two others who are engaged in appropriate behavior. While the first step is to ignore the inappropriate behavior and praise nearby students who are engaged in desired behaviors, the critical factor is in following up: the teacher determines if the target student is engaging in the desired behavior after the others have been praised and then praises the target student for the appropriate behavior.

In many classrooms and for individual children, where off-task behavior is entrenched, stronger interventions than the positive use of attention may be needed. Techniques such as the use of tangible rewards, token economy systems, and time-out from positive reinforcement procedures may be employed. These techniques are described in detail in most textbooks on behavior modification.

One comment on time-out procedures needs to be made here, though. Any technique that removes the child from work time must be used carefully, and provisions made to make up the work time lost. Short time-out periods are desirable for many reasons, not the least of which is that the child should be removed from work for as short a period as possible. Punitive techniques that have students sitting idly in principals' offices or in hallways are a waste of time that could be spent engaged in learning, as well as being often a reinforcing means to escape from an aversive situation, the classroom.

Charting

Another technique recommended by Paine et al. (1983) is the use of a feedback chart. This intervention is based on the performance feedback system of Van Houten (1979, 1980), which makes use of "instructions, feedback, public posting of student performance, and praise to motivate students to do their best in school" (Paine et al., 1983, p. 148). A chart is constructed to display the student's name, the different subjects, and sections to record behavior with respect to transition time, accuracy level or following directions, completion or working during the whole period, and no more than one warning for misbehavior. At the end of each activity the student is given a plus or minus for each section. The pluses translate into special activities at the end of the day. The chart is publicly posted; it thus provides a visual display of progress, can be used for praise by the teacher, (and there is research to indicate that "public posting of students' performance increases work completion and accuracy" p. 141). It can be laminated for repeated use.

Additional interest can be incorporated by use of the Good Behavior Game, in which students are divided into teams. Student teams do not necessarily have to compete against each other. They can compete to top their own personal-best scores or try for perfect scores several days in a row. The technique can be incorporated to encourage interest in the feedback chart. Both techniques can be faded when the behaviors are well established.

Contracting

A third technique, one which has the added advantage of providing a transition to self-control of behavior, is the use of contracts. Contracts provide clear information about what the child is supposed to do and set up a statement of the consequences for accomplishing the goal. A good contract incorporates the following into the written agreement: (1) it says what must be done and what you get for doing it (i.e., specifies the target behavior and reward); (2) it says who gives the reward; (3) it is written, and includes the signatures of the involved parties; (4) it is agreed upon by both parties (seriously so; sometimes teachers and psychologists give only lip-service to this criterion); and (5) it is fair and perceived as fair by all parties involved.

If the contract does not work, it may have loopholes or errors, and the contract should be fixed. Often a failed contract is perceived as another stone in the building of a case for special education for a child ("Look, even contracting doesn't work!"), rather than examined for flaws in the contracting process itself. Figures 6-4 and 6-5 are examples of contracts that have been used by teachers. Pictorial contracts can be used with younger children (see Dardig & Heward, 1984, for the use of contracts with younger children), while older children may be more responsive to verbal formats. Each of the contract formats could be used for either academic or behavioral targets. Dunn and Dunn (1972) provided suggestions for using contracting for academic instruction, and Figure 6-6 demonstrates a model contract for specifically academic behaviors.

Homme (1970) described how contracts can differ with respect to teacher-child input. Teachers can control both the target behaviors and rewards with the child's consent, the teacher and child could jointly have input, the child could present either the target behavior or the reward, or the child could present both with the teacher's consent. The transition to student-controlled contracts allows the student increasingly to take over control of academic performance.

While the concept of "contracting" has found its way into the vocabulary of school personnel, often the contracts built are little more than monitoring systems used coercively with students. Consultants with behavioral expertise

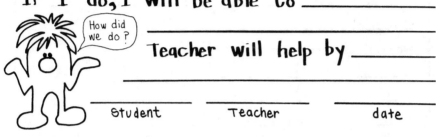

_____'s
Good Citizen Contract

I think I can _____

_____ by _____

If I do, I will be able to _____

_____

How did we do?

Teacher will help by _____

_____

_____   _____   _____
Student   Teacher   date

FIGURE 6-4. Sample contract 1. From *It's Positively Fun: Techniques for Managing Learning Environments* by R. Kaplan, J. Kohfeldt, and K. Sturia (Denver: Love Publishing, 1974). Copyright 1974 by Love Publishing. Reprinted by permission.

I've Got An Offer You Can't Refuse

If _____

_____

_____ by _____

Then _____

_____

_____

_____   _____   _____   _____
date   Student   witness   Teacher

FIGURE 6-5. Sample contract 1. From *It's Positively Fun: Techniques for Managing Learning Environments* by R. Kaplan, J. Kohfeldt, and K. Sturia (Denver: Love Publishing, 1974). Copyright 1974 by Love Publishing. Reprinted by permission.

Contract for _____ Date _____

Today I will do these tasks: Done

1. Reading _____ _____

2. Math _____ _____

3. _____ _____

4. _____ _____

5. _____ _____

When I finish my work, my choices to do are:

1. _____

2. _____

3. _____

I enjoyed _____ Because _____

_____

_____

I need help with _____

_____

_____

Signed: _____

FIGURE 6-6. Sample learning contract.

have a serious role to play in assisting classroom teachers and child-study-team personnel in creating negotiated contracts in which students are actively involved. Contracts may also provide an introduction to self-control, the ultimate goal of the educative process.

Self-Control Techniques

In self-control procedures, the child "becomes the primary agent in directing and controlling his or her behavior in order to lead to preplanned and specific behavior changes and/or consequences" (Morris, 1985 p. 92). According to Morris, the essence of the approach involves a training sequence incorporating the following steps:

1. The trainer performs the task while asking questions aloud about the task, giving self-guiding instruction, and making self-evaluations of performance.
2. The child imitates the trainer's overt self-instruction while doing the task.
3. The trainer performs the task while modeling self-instruction in a whisper.
4. The child imitates the trainer's performance with whispered self-instruction.
5. The trainer models covert self-instruction while performing the task.
6. The child imitates the trainer's performance and covert self-instruction (pp. 92-93).

Kendall, Padawer, Zupan, and Braswell (1985) provide a detailed manual for a 12-session self-control program with a research base. In each session the therapist teaches the child to use self-instructional procedures via modeling on a variety of impersonal and interpersonal problem-solving tasks, beginning with psycho-educational tasks similar to those required in the classroom. Then the process shifts to specific behavior problems exhibited by the child and the role playing of problematic situations. Essentially, the child is taught to understand the use of self-instructions before applying them in emotionally arousing situations. Both response-cost contingencies for violations of treatment session rules and social reinforcement and self-reward for successful and appropriate behavior are encouraged. Helping the learner to manage him/herself is an important goal for many students who exhibit learning problems, and a direct approach to this area is a valuable adjunct to the consultant's and teacher's set of strategies.

SUMMARY

This chapter has considered ways to modify the work setting for the learner as well as ways to assist the teacher in arranging effective consequences. Modifying the work setting was related to three areas, described in the following questions: Is the physical setting arranged to minimize distraction and maximize attention? Is time being managed efficiently and effectively, so that little allocated time is wasted on transitions and enough time is allocated to high-priority tasks? Are people resources being used effectively, so that the teacher can maximize instructional interactions?

Several guidelines and alternative intervention techniques are presented here to assist the teacher in arranging consequences for both on-task behavior and successful completion and correctness of the content of academic work. They clearly, however, do not cover the wide range of interventions to be found in the literature on classroom management and behavior modification. Valentine and Hubbell (in press), for example, provided a useful procedure for dealing with difficult discipline problems in the school based on clear and consistent communication that the child is expected to engage in appropriate behavior and the use of parent support in demanding appropriate behavior from the child in the school setting.

But the procedures described above do provide a foundation for assisting teachers in providing appropriate consequences to children for certain behaviors. Although they may be most effective for "won't do" problems, the frustration of many children in approaching academic tasks after years of failure make them equally useful for many children who have had "can't do" problems. While the work may have been modified to be at the learner's current instructional level, the student may not have yet developed adequate classroom behaviors. However, it is not necessary, and may be counterproductive, to introduce elaborate reinforcement procedures to children with intrinsic motivation in academic areas (Brilliant, 1986). An understanding of the literature on reinforcement, as well as some of the resistance of teachers to providing more structured and systematic consequences for desired behavior (see chapter 8) needs to be incorporated into the working knowledge of the instructional consultant.

Chapter 7

PLANNING AND CONDUCTING AN INSTRUCTIONAL INTERVENTION
Management of Learning

> *The best teacher will be he who has at his tongue's end all the explanation of what it is that is bothering the pupil. These explanations give the teacher the knowledge of the greatest possible number of methods, the ability of inventing new methods and, above all, not a blind adherence to one method but the conviction that all methods are one-sided, and that the best method would be the one which would answer best to all the possible difficulties incurred by a pupil. . . .*
>
> *Every teacher must . . . by regarding every imperfection in the pupil's comprehension, not as a defect of the pupil, but as a defect of his own instruction, endeavor to develop in himself the ability of discovering new methods. . . .*
>
> —Leo Tolstoy, "On Teaching the Rudiments"

In the school-psychology literature, much more has been written about the topic of the previous chapter, the management of the learner, than on the management of learning. Recent advances in instructional psychology (Gagné & Briggs, 1979; Resnick, 1981; Rosenfield, 1985a) have provided a significant literature, both theoretical and empirical, about instruction. However, application of the research findings by teachers to their classroom decision making is not yet widespread (Anderson et al., 1985; Berliner, 1985). In this chapter, some parameters of quality instruction and their application to students experiencing learning problems are described.

THE MANAGEMENT OF LEARNING

Modifications in Curriculum Materials

An argument could be made that curriculum materials are in and of themselves neutral, and that it is the use of materials by teachers that is the critical factor. Gickling and Havertape (1982), however, stress the point that curriculum materials are not neutral. They view curriculum materials as "normative in as much as they demand the same amount of performance from each student regardless of ability" (p. 38). From that perspective, it is important for teachers to learn how to modify and manipulate materials if they are going to make them work for the student. The availability of a variety of materials to use in teaching can be an asset only if there is a conscious and continuous decision process through which the material is matched to the learner's instructional level.

Teachers have three options with regard to materials; they can adopt a set of commercial materials, adapt the materials, or create teacher-made materials. If they choose one of the latter two options, there are two parameters to vary; one can vary either the content or the format in which the content is presented. In modifying materials, Gickling and Havertape (1982) make an additional point; they suggest that teachers should worry less about interest level than about difficulty level for the beginning or disabled student. Interest is, according to them, "soon smothered as the child discovers it is too hard to read" (p. 39).

It is also useful to keep in mind that the process of matching is ongoing, that there is a need for continuous assessment beyond the point at which one first establishes entry level. For example, even within one reader, the difficulty level between stories can vary such that "within the primary grades . . . the reading difficulty of basal readers will vary six months to two years, and within the intermediate grades, one year to four years" (Gickling & Havertape, 1982, p. 39). Assessment must be built into the classroom process on a continuous basis to ensure that children are kept at instructional level, rather than allowed to slip into frustration level.

Teachers often underestimate the effect of poorly written texts on students' progress. Readability measures rarely capture the difficulty level of most texts in the content areas (Anderson & Armbruster, 1986). In addition, Anderson and Armbruster found texts filled with writing problems that make them difficult to comprehend, including "poorly structured discourse; choice of either too-technical or too-general words; abrupt changes in idea flow without signaling the reader; misleading titles and headings; causal sequences that have no effects; and pronouns with unclear referents" (p. 154). The result is that "children read many pages of poorly written text" (p. 162). They stress the importance of "textual coherence," including global coherence—"text characteristics that facilitate the integration of high-level, important ideas across the entire discourse" and local coherence—"simple links that connect ideas together within and between sentences" (p. 154).

Text linguistics, a new field that is providing analytic techniques beyond the simple readability formulas of the past, should increasingly help authors to design materials "at relatively specific levels of comprehensibility and provide a basis for determining what makes a text easy or difficult (Farr, Carey, & Tone, 1986, p. 142). For example, Langer (1983) has identified four major characteristics of texts that in part determine their difficulty level:

1. Extreme density of ideas, especially if listlike or lacking explicit connectives.
2. Overreliance on the reader's background knowledge to make sense of a passage, yielding implicit rather than explicit text.
3. "Imitation genre" in which a genre is implied (e.g., joke, riddle, or exposition) but where the test question may not be appropriate to the genre.
4. Deceptive simplicity, in which a passage appears simple (based on a readability formula), but the concepts are in fact difficult or unknown to the reader (Farr, Carey, & Tone, 1986, p. 143).

As Gickling and Havertape (1982) note, curriculum materials are not neutral.

Modification in the Content of Curriculum Materials

Certainly there is a presumption that the teacher has expertise in the content of the subject matter being taught, although there is some evidence that this may not always be an accurate assumption (Shulman, 1986b). Research is currently being directed at developing a coherent framework for the "domains and categories of content knowledge in the minds of teachers" (Shulman, 1986b, p. 9). Shulman distinguished among three categories of content knowledge: subject matter content knowledge, pedagogical content knowledge, and curricular knowledge. Subject matter content knowledge refers to "the amount and organization of knowledge per se in the mind of the teacher" (p. 9), including an understanding of the structures of the subject matter (e.g., how the biology teacher decides to organize the discipline of biology). Pedagogical content knowledge goes beyond the subject matter itself to knowledge of how to teach a particular content area, including:

> the most useful forms of representation of . . . ideas, the most powerful analogies, illustrations, examples, explanations, and demonstrations . . . , the ways of representing and formulating the subject that make it comprehensible to others.

> . . . an understanding of what makes the learning of specific topics easy or difficult; the conceptions and preconceptions that students of different ages and backgrounds bring with them to the learning of those most frequently taught topics and lessons. If those preconceptions are misconceptions, which they so often are, teachers need knowledge of the strategies most likely to be fruitful in reorganizing the understanding of learners, because those learners are unlikely to appear before them as blank slates. (Shulman, 1986b, pp. 13-14)

For example, Hiebert and Wearne (1985) described a model of how students construct and execute decimal-computation procedures. The model then predicts the relative difficulty students will have in computing decimal items and the specific errors that are most likely to occur on each type of problem. Similarly, Russell and Ginsburg (1984) compared the formal and informal mathematical knowledge base of children with low mathematics achievement with their achieving peers, and suggest where the most common problems will occur for children with math difficulties. They found, for example, that their third and fourth graders displayed consistent types of problems, whether they were low functioning in math or not, but that low math achievers had a significant deficit in the area of knowing number facts (later in this chapter, a discussion of how to teach math facts to automaticity is presented).

A third area of content knowledge is that of curricular knowledge, the variety of curricular alternatives for instruction in the various subject matter areas: the alternative texts, software programs, visual materials, films, and lab exercises. An impressive demonstration of this type of expertise was observed by the author in a school for the physically handicapped, where the teachers demonstrated maximum knowledge and use of alternative learning strategies and curriculum materials. In many schools, there is not an extensive array of alternative materials, and the consultant not well-versed in this area might consider developing a relationship with local curriculum experts in the content areas either in the district, at local universities, or at instructional materials centers.

The categories of knowledge just described provide a framework for understanding content modification. However, on a more concrete level, there are some specific modifications that can be utilized in working with students experiencing difficulty with materials. For example, Gickling and Havertape (1982) present six basic rules for preparing curriculum material for children. The first rule is: Keep the percentage of knowns high. To do this, they recommend use of the "sandwich technique," by which unknown items are sandwiched in between known ones. The child is never confronted only with unknown material, even in drill. This process keeps the motivation of the child high, as there are always known items in the curriculum material. Actually, this technique provides for the low-achieving child the same learning environment that exists for the higher-achieving children, who usually have already mastered much of the material that they are asked to work on during the school day.

The second rule, related to the first, is: Confine new material to the child's margins of challenge. In reading, the range of known material should be 93-97% in content reading and 70-85% known material in drill. That leaves relatively little room for new material. The margin of challenge is carefully controlled.

Teachers often gasp when these figures are presented to them, and become concerned that they will not make fast progress at that rate in spite of the fact that they may not have been making any progress at all by introducing too much new material. With many vulnerable children, these ratios provide a genuine basis for learning progress, and the consultant needs to hold fast to the principle and help the teacher to experiment with implementing the concept. The goal is to keep the material within the comfort level of the child because there is clear evidence that doing so leads both to better achievement and classroom behavior (Harris, 1979). This is often a case in which trial lessons, sometimes conducted by the consultant, can demonstrate to the teacher the child's ability to learn under appropriate conditions. Teachers often comment, upon having this program implemented with a slow-learning child, how unbelievable it is to them to see how much the child could learn.

The third rule is a corollary to the second: Items of undetermined status are treated as unknown. If the teacher does not know whether a word is known or unknown to the child, it should be treated as unknown. If the child is hesitant about an item, it is treated as falling within the margin of challenge. Again, the caution is to err on the side of making sure that the child is not asked to function at frustration level.

The fourth and fifth rules involve preparation and presentation of drill and reading; Prepare the content before the drill; and although you prepare content before drill, you always reverse that order when assigning work to the child. In reading, for example, the drill emphasizes and complements what the student is going to be reading, and is preparation for the culminating activity, whereas much workbook drill is not connected, in terms of content, to the reader. The student needs to have practice with the material, so that when the reading passage is the task at hand, the child can concentrate on meaning in connected discourse.

Finally, the sixth rule is: All tasks must be carried to their logical conclusion. The task needs to make sense to the child, to be explained in terms of the content to be learned. Sometimes phonics tasks are presented to children in ways that give the children no sense of why they are engaged in the activity, such as cutting out letters from magazines.

The Gickling and Havertape (1982) model is essentially a ratio system in which there is a careful balancing of knowns and unknowns in the development of materials. Prepared materials are usually adequate for well-functioning students, in that the steps in the materials are within the child's capacity to acquire new skills. But for children who are experiencing difficulty, or for at-risk children, teacher-prepared materials are often needed to shape the new skills.

Creating teacher-made material in reading includes the option of developing transition stories. If the child has been placed for instruction at the correct point in the basal reading series and the amount of new material to be mastered between stories in the basal reader is still beyond the child's rate of acquisition, the use of teacher-made stories is a possible curriculum-material modification. In this process, the curriculum material is the basis of the teacher-made story, so that the goal of keeping the child in the regular curriculum as much as possible is achieved.

Using the Gickling and Havertape (1982) method, it is possible to create transition stories either to augment a basal-reading series as a preventive, developmental measure for children (Leventhal & McCarron, 1985) or to provide individualized assistance to a child already experiencing difficulty. Procedures for the creation of transitional stories include:

1. The number of transitional stories needed to interject between each basal reading story may vary, depending upon the number of knowns and unknowns and the difficulty of the words for the children. This would be equally true in creating an individualized, transitional story intervention for children experiencing difficulty and for a group of children for whom this approach is deemed useful in a preventative sense. Depending upon the number of unknown to known words, the number of transitional stories needed would vary.

2. The number of new (unknown) words introduced in the stories is based on the ratio principle and upon the expected difficulty level of the words. On average, for beginning levels, only two or three new words are used per story; fewer if the child has a very limited range. Leventhal and McCarron suggest that if a word is likely to be known from another subject, it may be included as an additional new word. For example, a word such as cat that is used in phonics may be introduced as an added new word. This is an additional advantage of using complementing materials in the different language arts subjects.

3. It is recommended that stories contain a number of words from basal stories recently read to continue to reinforce the new words. As Leventhal and McCarron comment, many times new words in a basal reader do not reappear for several additional stories, and the children need reinforcement of these words between stories so that they have the opportunity to practice and learn them.

4. Comprehension skills should be included as part of the lesson in the use of transition stories. But recall that comprehension is content, too. The

questions need to be presented to the child in a format that the child can handle. Leventhal and McCarron suggest presenting the stories in small booklets and allowing the children to draw a cover for the story as a check on their comprehension of the theme of the story. The children have to decide what the story is about (the main idea of the story) in order to decide on the drawing content.

5. In preparing transition stories, punctuation and sentence structure should be considered, to give the child reinforcement in these areas as well.

6. Once the story is created, drill activities need to be developed in which the unknowns are sandwiched in with knowns, so that the child experiences success and will continue to be attentive to the task. Games that involve the words should be developed. Most teachers know (and most remedial-reading books suggest) a variety of word games for this purpose (an example here of how curricular knowledge, Shulman, 1986, can be helpful). If the small-word-book format of Leventhal and McCarron is used, the children are encouraged to take the books home to read to their parents for reinforcement of both the words and the feeling of competence in reading.

Figure 7-1 contains two of the transition stories developed by Leventhal and McCarron, based on the Holt Basal Reading Series.

The transition-story process for children experiencing difficulty needs to be monitored carefully. It is not always easy to predict in advance how many new words can be introduced to a particular child even within the margin of challenge. Since we want to move the child along as efficiently as possible, we should determine the limits, always remaining within the ratio of 70-85% known in drill and 93-97% known in the story itself. The rate of acquisition within the margin-of-challenge ratio needs to be tested with the particular child. If the child begins making more errors in the reading itself, falling below the instructional level, we are moving too quickly.

In math, as in reading, it may be necessary for the teacher to provide tailor-made instructional material, in which item selection is based on what the child needs to learn and an instructional ratio of 70-85% knowns to a margin of challenge of 15-30% unknowns or hesitants. Some teachers may prefer to modify existing work sheets rather than construct new ones from scratch. The former strategy is less time-consuming, but has the drawback of not necessarily including all the particular child's needed material on one page. As in reading, unknowns should be sandwiched among known material when teaching facts. Short, timed drill material in the teaching of facts, to raise the level to automaticity, needs to be incorporated as part of the curriculum material, as it is not enough to have the child merely complete a series of work sheets. The last step here too, is to provide a concluding task, in which the student uses the new information.

Clarita is *grumpiest* in the morning. Teddy is the grumpiest at night. Tim is grumpiest when I make *noise*. Teddy liked the noise. Clarita *liked* the noise at night. She didn't like the noise in the morning. Clarita likes to sleep in the morning. Tim didn't like the noise in the morning or at night.

1. _____ is _____ in the morning.

2. _____ liked the noise.

3. _____ didn't like the noise.

4. Clarita likes to _____ in the morning.

Someone

Was Jim in the water? Was Gus in the water? Was the cow in the water? *Someone* was in the water. Someone likes to play in the water. Was *it* Jim? Was it Gus? Was it the cow?

1. _____ Jim in the water.

2. Was the _____ in the water?

3. _____ likes to play in the water.

4. Was _____ Jim?

FIGURE 7-1. Sample transition stories.

For teaching number facts, creating small cards on which the number facts are written is often extremely helpful to individualize materials for the child. The set of cards can be organized and reorganized to suit the need, with known facts stored for review. Children can create, with supervision, their own materials (set of number-fact cards), and the teacher then is responsible for managing their use. In one such case, the child's grandmother was able to provide the guided-practice sessions at home, under the direction of the consultant. However, some children do not respond to these drill-card materials, and alternative procedures need to be available (Schmidt, 1985).

One additional point should be made in the area of content modification regarding materials. Gickling and Havertape (1982) suggest strongly that the concept of complementing tasks be considered in the development of curriculum materials. They advise that we not ask children with learning problems to handle more than one set of new tasks at a time, and that whenever possible we build a variety of curriculum materials and tasks around similar concepts. More is not better, in teaching content, so that children who are taught reading or math by more than one teacher should not be using different types of skills or content built into the materials. In language arts, whenever possible, reading, spelling, and writing should be integrated, using the same sets of words. Words with which the child is having difficulty in the reading area can also be used in writing and spelling assignments. Relating assignments provides increased practice and a sense of familiarity and competence for the child.

Modifications in Format

Curriculum materials not only have content, the material to be learned, but are also presented in a particular format. For each piece of curriculum material, task analysis can help the teacher and consultant determine how modification of the material itself can be helpful to the child. The structure of the learning material can be modified through various prompts and cues, or through changes in complexity of the material.

The behavioral literature contains many examples of the uses of fading and prompts to teach academic skills. The effectiveness of colors and various pictorial or verbal prompts has been documented, although it has been suggested that there is some need for matching the particular type of cue used with the child's learning style (Schmidt, 1985). Schmidt found some children more responsive to fading and some to flash-card presentation in learning number facts. In fading, a supporting stimulus is gradually eliminated until the child is able to produce the required response without help. Such techniques have been used in reading, arithmetic, and handwriting (e.g., Haupt, Van Kirk, & Terraciano, 1975; Schmidt, 1985). Examples of some cues and prompts are provided in Figure 7-2, 7-3, and 7-4. The cues and prompts should be directed, as closely as possible, however, to the specific type of problem that the child is experiencing. Merely constructing materials with cues, without consideration of the nature of the error pattern of the child, is not often helpful. For example, watching a child do a writing assignment might suggest to the teacher that the child needs a cue about where to begin making his or her letters.

The difficulty or complexity level of a set of materials can also be modified. A task can be presented in ways that make it more or less difficult. For example, fewer items per page or fewer distractors in multiple-choice formats are changes that can be implemented in materials. Instructions and response modes can be changed. Students are often confused more by the instructions to a task than by the task itself. Instructions that are too difficult for the child to read can be read to the child, or some directions may need to be rephrased if they contain vocabulary or content beyond the entry level of the learner; the teacher can work through some problems with the child until the instructions are clear. Bilingual children are often unable to complete phonics work sheets that present pictures of items with which they are unfamiliar. The Boehm Test of Basic Concepts-Revised (1986) can provide useful information here regarding the instructional vocabulary, and is available in English and Spanish versions.

The response mode is often a source of difficulty. Giving children the opportunity to say the answers rather than writing out extensive responses can make the material less difficult for the child. An oral test as opposed to a written one can make a big difference. Sometimes children's conceptual level surpasses their writing skill and/or motor coordination level, but teachers are unaware of the child's potential in the task at hand because the answer is

---

Verbal prompts used in the instruction of addition with regrouping
Problem type:

| 36 | "Work from the right to the left." |
| +25 | "Be sure to regroup when needed." |

Verbal prompts used in the instruction subtraction with regrouping
Problem type:

38 306	"Work from the right to the left."
-19 -29	"Be sure to regroup when needed."
	"Always subtract the bottom number from the top number."
	"Watch for zeros when you regroup."

Verbal prompts used in the instruction of multiplication
Problem type:

38	"Multiply by the one's column first."
x27	"Remember to line up the numbers carefully."
	"Remember to cross multiply."

FIGURE 7-2.   Use of verbal prompts in the teaching of math operation. Source: From A. Archer and E. Edgar, "Teaching Academic Skills to Mildly Handicapped Children." In *Teaching Mildly Handicapped Children in Regular Classes* (p. 57), S. Lowenbraun and J. Q. Affect (Eds.), (1976). Reprinted by permission of the Charles Merrill Publishing Company.

Faded visual prompts in the instruction of one-digit-plus-two-digit addition with carrying

$$
\begin{array}{r}
\textcircled{0} \\
3\,|\,4 \\
+\ \ |\,8 \\
\hline
-\,|\,-
\end{array}
\qquad
\begin{array}{r}
0 \\
3\,|\,4 \\
+\ \ |\,8 \\
\hline
-\,|\,-
\end{array}
\qquad
\begin{array}{r}
0 \\
34 \\
+\ 8 \\
\hline
-\ -
\end{array}
\qquad
\begin{array}{r}
0 \\
34 \\
+\ 8 \\
\hline
\end{array}
\qquad
\begin{array}{r}
34 \\
+\ 8 \\
\hline
\end{array}
$$

Faded visual prompts used in the instruction of one-digit into two-digit division

$$
4\overline{)52}
\qquad
4\overline{)52}
\qquad
4\overline{)52}
\qquad
4\overline{)52}
\qquad
4\overline{)52}
$$

Faded visual prompts used in the instruction of one-digit-times-two-digit multiplication

$$
\begin{array}{r}
0 \\
4\,|\,2 \\
\times\ \ |\,7 \\
\hline
-\,-\,|\,-
\end{array}
\qquad
\begin{array}{r}
4\,|\,2 \\
\times\ \ |\,7 \\
\hline
-\,-\,|\,-
\end{array}
\qquad
\begin{array}{r}
42 \\
\times\ 7 \\
\hline
-\,-\,-
\end{array}
\qquad
\begin{array}{r}
42 \\
\times\ 7 \\
\hline
\end{array}
\qquad
\begin{array}{r}
42 \\
\times\ 7 \\
\hline
\end{array}
$$

Faded visual prompts used in the instruction of two-digit multiplication

$$
\begin{array}{r}
32 \\
\times\ 24 \\
\hline
+\ \ \\
-\ -\ \times
\end{array}
\qquad
\begin{array}{r}
32 \\
\times\ 24 \\
\hline
-\ -\ - \\
-\ -\ \times
\end{array}
\qquad
\begin{array}{r}
32 \\
\times\ 24 \\
\hline
-\ -\ - \\
\times
\end{array}
\qquad
\begin{array}{r}
32 \\
\times\ 24 \\
\hline
\end{array}
$$

FIGURE 7-3. Use of visual prompts in teaching math operations. Source: From A. Archer and E. Edgar, "Teaching Academic Skills to Mildly Handicapped Children." In *Teaching Mildly Handicapped Children in Regular Classes* (p. 54), S. Lowenbraun and J. Q. Afflect (Eds.), (1976). Reprinted by permission of the Charles Merrill Publishing Company.

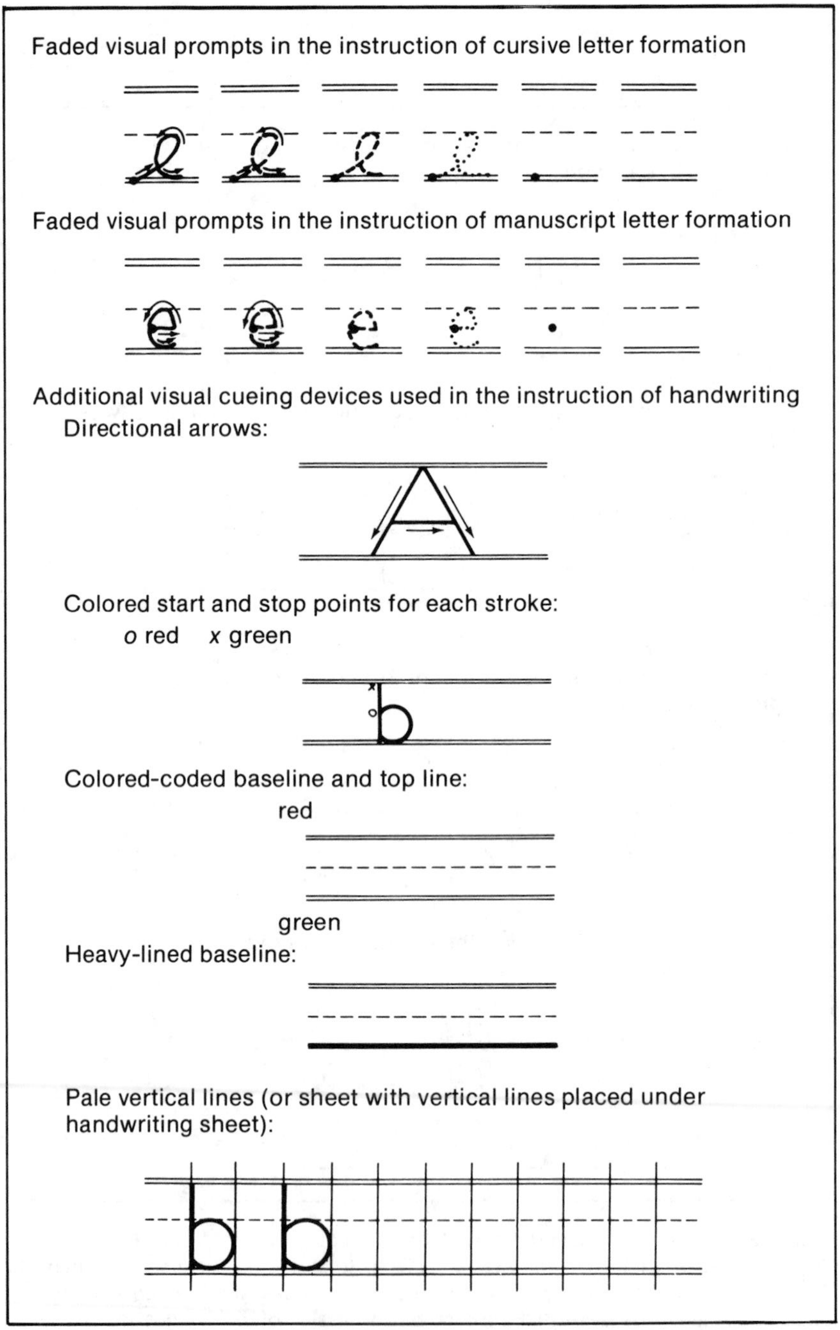

FIGURE 7-4. Use of visual prompts in teaching handwriting. Source: From A. Archer and E. Edgar, "Teaching Academic Skills to Mildly Handicapped Children." In *Teaching Mildly Handicapped Children in Regular Classes* (p. 55), S. Lowenbraun and J. Q. Afflect (Eds.), (1976). Reprinted by permission of the Charles Merrill Publishing Company.

required in written form. However, reassuring the teacher that it is appropriate (and not unfair) to vary the response mode is often a necessary step for the consultant.

Similarly, children with reading problems are often unable to read their assignments in other subjects. There is a need to provide the task content in a different form. The child who cannot read the social studies or science text or the written arithmetic problem is penalized by the nature of the material itself in completing a task that may well be within the child's competence level otherwise. Having a tape recording of the text available (which can be done by volunteers or peers who need reading practice), or simply pairing up students so that one reads to the other, or having parents read the text to the student— creative use of such techniques often require far less teacher time than anticipated by teachers. In these cases, the teachers are often only responsible for planning rather than carrying out the intervention strategy.

The discussion above about the nature of poorly written texts is also relevant here. Texts that are not well written make the task more difficult than learning the concepts would be if they were well presented. Examining the texts and developing strategies to explain the concepts more clearly or building in entry-level skills to understand the text are useful ways to modify the format. Needless to say, acquiring better written texts is a long-term strategy.

Summing Up

A task analysis of the demands created by the material can enable the format to be modified. Sometimes the modification takes the form of shaping, as when prompts and cues are utilized; these must, of course, eventually be faded. Other times, however, the format of the material is truly irrelevant to the concept to be learned. So long as the learner is unable to handle the material in its current format, the modification should be continued, as in the case of the child with a reading problem having the social studies text read aloud.

PROVIDING QUALITY INSTRUCTION

Theoretical Models

Because there is a literature that indicates that instruction is often inadequate (Rosenfield, 1985c), it is important to begin with a description of what kind of instruction is needed for students who might be at risk. As a result of a substantial body of research, it has been demonstrated that the teaching practices called "direct instruction" (Rosenshine, 1976, 1980) lead to improved student outcomes in reading and math (Becker, 1986). Becker, in his review of the extensive literature, notes that gains were found for both elementary and secondary students when the following pattern of teaching behavior exists:

> The teacher is an active planner and leader of instructional activities . . . , paces instruction rapidly, requires frequent student responding, provides feedback and corrections, and uses teacher-directed rather than individual or self-directed activities. These findings are interpreted as procedures that foster more academic engaged time and mastery learning. Rosenshine also calls this basic model a demonstration-practice-feedback approach. (p. 155)

According to Rosenshine and Stevens (1986), research now indicates that effective teachers teaching well-structured subjects:

- Begin a lesson with a short review of previous, prerequisite learning.
- Begin a lesson with a short statement of goals.
- Present new material in small steps, with student practice after each step.
- Give clear and detailed instructions and explanations.
- Provide a high level of active practice for all students.
- Ask a large number of questions, check for student understanding, and obtain responses from all students.
- Guide students during initial practice.
- Provide systematic feedback and corrections.
- Provide explicit instruction and practice for seatwork exercises, and where necessary, monitor students during seat work (p. 377).

Rosenshine and Stevens (1986) concluded that there is a limited number of teaching functions that are part of the systematic teaching strategy just described: "Review of previous learning; demonstration of new materials; guided practice and checking for understanding; feedback and corrections; independent practice; and periodic review" (p. 389). However, there are a variety of ways that each can be fulfilled. They suggest the possibility that each function can be met in three ways: "By the teacher, by a student working with other students, and by a student working alone—using written materials or a computer" (p. 389).

Becker (1986) connected the current teacher-effectiveness literature with that of mastery learning, beginning with two approaches to mastery learning developed in the Chicago area in the 1920s, and moving to Skinner's programmed instruction in the 1950s and 1960s. Ironically, Skinner developed his program because he was appalled by what was *not* happening in his daughter's fourth grade math class. Outgrowths of programmed instruction include models of individually prescribed instruction and computer-assisted instruction. The weakness of both of these methods, and of precision teaching

(Lindsley, 1971; 1984), which focuses on procedures for daily measurement of progress on target behaviors, is that they do not focus enough on the teaching act itself, the provision of quality instruction.

The mastery learning model (Block, 1971; Bloom, 1976, 1984) has been an attempt to address the instructional issues more specifically. It has included several components: the definition of objectives, the sequencing of objectives into learning units of about two weeks in length, the use of typical methods of instruction, and probes that provide feedback to the students. There are additional procedures to provide quality instruction, however, including: a clear and logical analysis of what is to be taught and its sequence; active student participation and practice; reinforcement for the students; and supplemental instruction if needed to reach mastery. "Correctives," or supplemental instruction, includes tutoring, reteaching, small-group sessions, and additional materials.

There have also been attempts to improve the effectiveness of the mastery-learning model. Several strategies have been demonstrated to improve the quality of the instruction. Leyton (1983) found that enhancement of prerequisite skills prior to teaching a unit was helpful. Testing prerequisites and preteaching prerequisite skills seem to be effective in teaching sequentially developed skills. In other studies, enhancing cues, increasing student participation, using a feedback-corrective procedure, and increased reinforcement levels all within a group setting, have led to improved results (Tenenbaum, 1982). Becker (1986), in reviewing the results of Bloom's mastery-learning model, concludes that it has been demonstrated to be effective.

Another method of direct instruction is that of *direct instruction (DI)*, (Becker, 1984) developed by Engelmann, Carnine, Becker and others. The method currently has been incorporated into over 43 commercially available programs in reading, language, spelling, and arithmetic. The research on DI is extensive and convincing (Becker, 1984). However, the programs themselves are not more widely adopted by schools and teachers for a variety of reasons, one of which relates to philosophical clashes between the high structure of DI and teachers' perceptions that it decreases their freedom, humanism, and creativity. As Benjamin (1981) states, the DI reading program:

> leaves nothing to chance. Every action by the teacher—verbal and nonverbal— is specifically outlined; every student response is similarly choreographed. Everywhere it is taught the same way: in small groups, with students and teachers face-to-face in touching range, and with only a flip chart, storybooks, or work sheets between them. (pp. 71-72)

Although much in DI is similar to the mastery models discussed above, in terms of focus on increasing engaged time with adults through teaching procedures and tight schedules, the unique focus of DI is probably the emphasis on the logical analysis of knowledge sets and teaching examples. Quality instruction, according to Becker (1985), "requires that the teacher knows what is being taught, how it ties in with related materials being (or to be) taught, how component skills can be put together into more complex problem-solving skills, how individual examples can be efficiently sequenced to teach a generalization" (p. 13-1).

Engelmann and Carnine (1982) provided a model of instruction which involves three separate analyses: analysis of behavior, analysis of communications, and analysis of knowledge systems. According to Becker, the analysis of behavior explores principles for teaching any task, including motivation and attention, reinforcement and feedback to students. The analysis of communications seeks a logical design of teaching sequences to transmit knowledge, in order to prevent misrules, overgeneralizations or undergeneralizations. It focuses on the specific discriminations to be taught, and how sets of stimuli are the same and how they are different. The third type of analysis is that of knowledge systems, the identification of "samenesses across apparently different pieces of knowledge" (p. 21).

Built into the various DI programs is careful attention to the three types of analyses, removing the burden from the teacher of developing an adequate instructional design. However, given that teachers often do not want to use the DI materials, it is helpful for the consultant to have an understanding of the instructional design structure of DI. Since much of what teachers in the early grades are required to teach is concept learning (shapes, colors, letters, nouns, comparatives), it is perhaps useful to focus on how Engelmann and Carnine (1982) approached the teaching of concepts.

For Engelmann (1969), a concept is defined by "the stimulus properties common to concept instances and not common to not-instances" (Becker, 1986, p. 185). Given that definition, in teaching a concept, it is necessary to use a procedure for discriminating the essential properties of, say, one color from the essential properties of other colors. A range of values for one color is demonstrated by examples, which become discriminative stimuli for the color being taught. The range of values of not-instances is also taught by the use of examples. Concept learning, in short, begins with a process of discriminating essential from nonessential properties through the use of examples. To provide the full range of examples needed for teaching most concepts, which requires multiple discriminations, the following must be provided:

1. There must be examples to provide discriminations between the relevant characteristics of positive and negative instances. For example, to learn the concept of blue, nonblue colors must be discriminated from blue ones.

2. Relevant from irrelevant characteristics must be discriminated within positive and negative instances. Colors need to be discriminated from other properties of objects such as shapes, materials, and spatial position. But even

within the negative instances, the color property must be discriminated from other properties to help the child determine that it is a negative, not simply an irrelevant characteristic.

3. When the relevant features of a concept have been discriminated from both relevant features of non-instances and from irrelevant features, the learner has mastered a general case and can respond correctly to other members of the general class not used in instruction.

On the basis of the kinds of discriminations needed to teach concepts, a basic paradigm has been created for teaching concepts:

1. It is impossible to teach a concept with a single example. Any instance of a concept must be an instance of many concepts, so a set of positive examples is needed.
2. All the positive examples must share the same quality that we want the learner to associate with the concept.
3. Since a group of concept instances can be instances of many concepts, a set of negative examples is also necessary. Negative examples need to be carefully chosen to rule out the irrelevant features of the positive examples.
4. It is possible to minimize the number of examples needed by using a common *setup* for the initial teaching of a concept, that is, the positive and negatives examples should share the greatest possible number of irrelevant features. The use of a similar object, different in only the critical feature of the concept, is an efficient way to produce this effect. In teaching colors, for example, using a red ball and a green ball, to show *not* instances of blue, demonstrated by a blue ball, is an example of how the *not*-examples are setup for initial teaching. The only thing changed in the *not*-example was the color.
5. To show the limits of a concept using the difference principle, juxtapose examples that are *minimally different* while giving them different labels (e.g., "orange," "not orange").
6. To show a range of positive features for a concept, sample that range using the sameness principle by juxtaposing positive examples that are as different as possible (within the context of the setup) while indicating that they are the same.
   Perhaps a clear example of how rules 5 and 6 operate is in the use of examples for the phonics rule that states that given an *e* on the end of a one-syllable, consonant-vowel-consonant word, the vowel says its name. To illustrate rule 6, widely different pairs would be used, such as "cope-kite" or "made-cute"; to illustrate rule 5, the sameness principle, closely matched pairs might include "cope-cop" or "cope-copy."

7. After teaching a concept, it is important to test with new examples to see if the concept has been learned.
8. The range of applications can be expanded by varying the setup to show what is irrelevant.

Becker (1986) indicated an 11-example sequence to teach and test most single-dimension basic concepts, after a setup is designed for presenting each of the 11 examples.

1. Begin with two different negative examples. Starting with negatives is not essential, but it is helpful in isolating the positive features early and reducing the chance of learning misrules.
2. Give three positive examples with a range of features, as follows:
   a. Example 3: A positive example, minimally different from (the negative) example 2.
   b. Example 4: A positive example.
   c. Example 5: A positive example minimally different from the next example, which is a negative one.
3. Show six random positive and negative examples, except that example 6 is a minimally different but negative example in contrast to example 5. These examples are presented in the form of questions to the student, to test concept acquisition ("Is this an X?").

After completing the 11 examples, the setup should be changed to vary the irrelevant features, and it is also recommended that, wherever possible, one should change positive examples directly into negative ones and vice versa. This principle of continuous conversion helps the child see how much change can occur without losing the essence of the concept. Figure 7-5 illustrates this teaching paradigm.

The use of this paradigm for teaching a concept helps us to reframe the problem of teaching the letter "m" that so disturbed Alex's teacher in chapter 1 under the heading "Providing Quality Instruction." A good exercise at this point is for the reader to treat the letter "m" as a concept, and to develop a teaching lesson for the letter "m" based on the principles described above and in Figure 7-6.

But it is not enough to understand how to teach a single concept. The letters that children are required to learn to decode are examples of a set made up of independent members; each and every member of the set must be taught individually. While the child may eventually get the idea of "letterness," each letter sound has to be taught separately. In other words, to learn to identify a sound is to learn a concept. To learn a set of related concepts, given that other sounds in the set define negative examples, requires multiple discrimination learning.

Example	Teacher Wording
1	Watch my hand, I'll tell you if it gets steeper. It didn't get steeper.
2	It didn't get steeper.
3	It got steeper.
4	It got steeper.
5	It got steeper.
6	Did it get steeper?
7	Did it get steeper?
8	Did it get steeper?
9	Did it get steeper?
10	Did it get steeper?
11	Did it get steeper?
12	Touch the line that is steeper.
13	Hold up a pencil so that it is steeper than this pencil.
14	Which hill is steeper? Hill A or Hill B?

FIGURE 7-5. An 11 step sequence for teaching a comparative concept. Source: From *Applied Psychology for Teachers: A Behavioral Approach* (p. 192) by W. C. Becker, 1986. Chicago, IL: Science Research Associates, Inc. Copyright 1986 by Science Research Associates, Inc. Reprinted by permission.

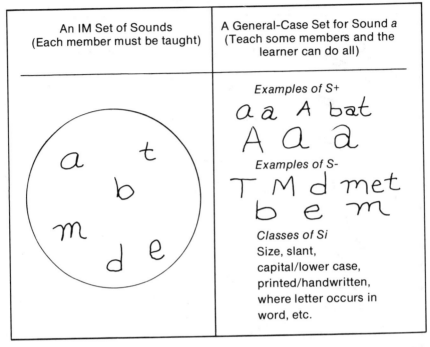

An IM Set of Sounds (Each member must be taught)	A General-Case Set for Sound *a* (Teach some members and the learner can do all)

FIGURE 7-6. Each member of an Independent Member (IM) set may be a general case. Source: From *Applied Psychology for Teachers: A Behavioral Approach* (p. 194) by W. C. Becker, 1986. Chicago, IL: Science Research Associates, Inc. Copyright 1986 by Science Research Associates, Inc. Reprinted by permission.

However, each concept the student learns is not totally isolated from other concepts. Much of what children need to learn in school is related to other skills, which is why we talk of a scope and sequence within subject matter. Addition must be discriminated from subtraction; the letter "d" from the letter "b"; the concept "up" from "down"; the concept "liberty" from "justice." The sameness within the concepts provides for the possibility of overgeneralization to inappropriate instances, so care must be taken in designing instruction to account for features common to two or more concepts.

Features that are common to more than one concept and that need to be discriminated from one another need to be carefully taught. Sometimes these common features provide a basis for forming higher-order concepts, so that all the lower-set instances are part of a higher-order class as well. The concepts "b" and "d" are both letters. In cases where the two concepts share a higher-order set, it is important to inform the student directly about how they are related to each other. In some cases, an instance of one concept can actually be an instance of another, in the way that dogs and cats are both animals.

Becker (1985) noted three cases in which errors are most likely to occur: (1) when many characteristics are shared in common by instances of two concepts; (2) when there are few differences between concept features; and (3) when there is little earlier discrimination training. Two ways to reduce the opportunity for errors are to exaggerate the difference between the two instances or to directly train the difference to be learned (here is where cues and prompts can be effective, such as coloring the sign for addition and subtraction differently in helping children take note of which procedure to use). If the teacher and consultant can analyze the samenesses and differences for each concept pair that causes confusion, the instructional process could be carefully designed to assist the learner in making the needed discriminations. When there are many differences, only a sampling of the difference may need to be taught; when there are few, each difference may need careful discrimination. The DI explanation of discrimination problems makes it easy to see why so many children confuse "b" and "d"; it is also clear what instructional intervention needs to be designed.

Many of the concepts that need to be taught to children are related. While good instruction usually proceeds by teaching one thing at a time, related concepts, such as letters or number facts, can best be taught through the process of cumulative programming. Cumulative programming is teaching two set members, and then adding in new members one by one to mastery level, until the complete set has been taught. Actually, this principle, which has been documented through research (Ferster & Hammer, 1966; Neef, Iwata, & Page, 1980) is a foundation for the sandwiching technique of Gickling and Havertape (1982). For example, Neef, Iwata, and Page found that interspersing known spelling items among unknown ones generated better acquisition and retention of the unknown items than when only unknowns were provided. In addition, the students preferred the method in which knowns and unknowns were interspersed.

Several advantages of cumulative programming have been identified. Easier items can be taught first; multiple feature concepts can be taught incrementally as new members are added and require new discriminations; students receive some right responses while working on new learning, so tend to prefer it; and highly similar concepts (defined as having many samenesses and few differences) such as "b" and "d" can be separated in time. As Becker (1986) states, "A common example of confusion in most of our learning histories is derived from the fact that stalactite and stalagmite were introduced in the same paragraph one day in ninth grade science. You know one goes up and one goes down, but which is which? (Or try: *abcissa* and *ordinate* or the symbols < and >) (p.198).

The DI emphasis on good instruction as the careful planning and sequencing of examples fits current cognitive theories. Simon (1985), in discussing the contribution of cognitive theory to school learning, suggested that good students learn from examples; they try to figure out how things work from careful examination of examples. His discussion of learning from examples suggests how much we could facilitate learning by the careful presentation of examples for learners to study.

Simon also focuses our attention on the need to teach children not only products, that is, the rules, but also on when to use them. The ability to recognize relevant cues in a situation, to call forth the appropriate rules and concepts, is an example of the meta-cognitive skills that are required for higher-order learning and use of knowledge. Combining Hiebert and Wearne's (1985) model of how students construct and execute decimal-computation procedures (see Tables 7-1 and 7-2 for the rule structure) as an example of Shulman's (1986) concept of pedagogical content knowledge, with the concept of teaching meta-cognitive skills, an approach to a method for teaching complex concepts such as decimal computations becomes more focused.

In fact, the emphasis in recent years has been on the active role of the learner in the teaching-learning act, suggesting that teaching effectiveness depends not only on what the learner knows, including prior knowledge, but also upon "what the learner thinks about during learning, such as the learner's active cognitive processing" (Weinstein & Mayer, 1986, p. 315). The importance of the processing issues is confronted in chapter 5, where assessment techniques are described to elicit the thought processes of the student. Weinstein and Mayer described several techniques that the student can be taught to use to facilitate the learning process. These techniques are referred to as learning strategies, and are defined as:

> behaviors and thoughts that a learner engages in during learning and that are intended to influence the learner's encoding process. Thus, the goal of any particular learning strategy may be to affect the learner's motivational or affective state, or the way in which the learner selects, acquires, organizes, or integrates new knowledge. (p. 315)

Weinstein and Mayer (1986) presented eight categories of learning strategies:

1. **Basic Rehearsal Strategies:** Rehearsal strategies, such as repeating the names of items in an ordered list, are useful for such tasks as remembering the order of the planets from the sun.
2. **Complex Rehearsal Strategies:** These strategies include copying, underlining or shadowing the materials presented, and are useful for tasks such as studying the causes of World War II.
3. **Basic Elaboration Strategies:** Forming a mental image or sentence relating items in a pair of items is an example of strategies useful in tasks such as forming a phrase or sentence to relate the name of a state and its major agricultural product.

4. **Complex Elaboration Strategies:** Paraphrasing, summarizing or describing how new information relates to existing knowledge are examples of this category, useful in common school tasks such as relating information about the structure of complex molecules to that presented earlier about the structure of simple molecules.

5. **Basic Organizational Strategies:** Such strategies as grouping or ordering of to-be-learned items from a list or reading section are useful in such tasks as being able to organize events leading up to the Declaration of Independence.

TABLE 7-1
Symbol Manipulation Rules Involved in Decimal Computation
(and Arithmetic Operations for Which They Are Taught)

Decision Point 1: Preparing Problem for Calculation

Class A. Inserting decimal points where needed.
    Rule 1. Insert a decimal point to the right of a whole number. (A, S, M, D)
Class B. Aligning numerals for calculation.
    Rule 1. Line up the decimal points. (A, S)
    Rule 2. Line up the numerals on the right. (M)
    Rule 3. Place the divisor to the left of the division sign and place the dividend underneath the sign. (D)
        Rule 3.1. Move the decimal point to the right of the last digit in the divisor and move the decimal point in the dividend a

Class C. Inserting zeros where needed.
    Rule 1. Insert zero in the right-most position(s). (A, S, D)
    Rule 2. Insert zero(s) between the repositioned decimal point and the right-most digit in the dividend. (D)

Decision Point 2: Calculating the Answer

Problem Type 1. Simple addition. (A)
    Problem Type 1.1. Addition with regrouping.
Problem Type 2. Simple subtraction. (S)
    Problem Type 2.1. Subtraction with regrouping.
Problem Type 3. Single-digit by single-digit multiplication. (M)
    Problem Type 3.1. Single-digit by multidigit multiplication.
        Problem Type 3.1.1. Single-digit by multidigit multiplication with zero.
        Problem Type 3.1.2. Multidigit by multidigit multiplication.
Problem Type 4. One-step division, no remainder. (D)
    Problem Type 4.1. One-step division, with remainder.
    Problem Type 4.2. Multistep division, no remainder.
        Problem Type 4.2.1. Multistep division, with remainder.

Note. From "A Model of Students' Decimal Computation Procedures" by J. Hiebert and D. Wearne, 1983, *Cognition and Instruction, 2*, p. 179. Copyright © 1985 by Lawrence Erlbaum Associates, Inc. Reprinted by permission of the publisher.

TABLE 7-2
Predictions of Most Frequent Procedural Flaws

Item	Expected Procedural Flaw	Expected Error Response
Addition		
4.6 + 2.3	Substitute the multiplication rule from Class A, Decision Point 3.	.69
5.3 + 2.42	Substitute the line up the numerals rule from Class B, Decision Point 1 and use the modified rule from Class A, Decision Point 3.	2.95 and 29.5
5.1 + .46	Substitute the line up the numerals rule from Class B, Decision Point 1 and use the modified rule from Class A, Decision Point 3.	.97 and 9.7
6 + .32	Fail to select a rule from Class A, Decision Point 1 and substitute the line up the numerals rule from Class B, Decision Point 1.	.38
4 + .3	Fair to select a rule from Class A, Decision Point 1 and substitute the line up the numerals rule from Class B, Decision Point 1.	.7
Subtraction		
.78 - .35	Substitute the multiplication rule from Class A, Decision Point 3.	.0043
.60 - .36	Substitute the multiplication rule from Class A, Decision Point 3.	.0024
.86 - .3	Substitute the line up the numerals rule from Class B, Decision Point 1 and use the modified rule from Class A, Decision Point 3.	.83 and 8.3
4.7 - .24	Substitute the line up the numerals rule from Class B, Decision Point 1 and use the modified rule from Class A, Decision Point 3.	.23 and 2.3
7 - .4	Fail to select a rule from Class A, Decision Point 1 and substitute the line up the numerals rule from Class B, Decision Point 1.	.3
Multiplication		
6 × .4	Use the modified rule from Class A, Decision Point 3.	.24
2 × 3.12	Use the modified rule from Class A, Decision Point 3.	.624
8 × .06	Use the modified rule from Class A, Decision Point 3.	.048
.34 × 2.1	Substitute the bring down the decimal rule (modified form) from Class A, Decision Point 3.	7.14 and 71.4
.4 × .2	Substitute the bring down the decimal rule (modified form) from Class A, Decision Point 3.	.8
.05 × .4	Substitute the bring down the decimal rule (modified form) from Class A, Decision Point 3.	.2 and 2

Division

2.1 + 3	(Model generates no prediction.)	
.24 + .03	Fail to apply Rule 3.1 in the rule sequence from Class B, Decision Point 1.	.08
.56 + 7	Fail to sample from Class B, Decision Point 3 and use the modified rule from Class A, Decision Point 3.	.8
.028 + .4	Fail to sample from Class B, Decision Point 3 and use the modified rule from Class A, Decision Point 3.	.7
42 + .6	Fail to sample from Class A, Decision Point 1 and use the modified rule from Class A, Decision Point 3.	.7
3 + .6	Reverse divisor and dividend.	.2

Note. From "A Model of Students' Decimal Computation Procedures" by J. Hiebert and D. Wearne, 1983, *Cognition and Instruction, 2*, p. 187. Copyright © 1985 by Lawrence Erlbaum Associates, Inc. Reprinted by permission of the publisher.

6. **Complex Organizational Strategies:** More complex tasks, such as outlining assigned chapters in a text, require being able to outline a passage or create a hierarchy.

7. **Comprehension Monitoring Strategies:** Comprehension monitoring includes checking for failures to comprehend, and is demonstrated in school tasks when the student uses self-questioning to check understanding of material in class or text.

8. **Affective and Motivational Strategies:** Included here are techniques such as relaxation when test-anxious or using thought-stopping to prevent thoughts of doing poorly from directing the learner's attention away from the material to be studied.

Increasingly the case is being made for direct instruction of students, particularly those who are less-skilled learners, in the acquisition of these learning strategies. As new assessment procedures are developed in the area of study skills, such as the LASSI (Weinstein, Zimmerman, & Palmer, 1987), it may become easier to find the specific areas of need for particular students in the domain of study skills, and to provide focused attention to developing these and other strategies.

DESIGNING AN INSTRUCTIONAL SEQUENCE

Each of the four types of modification (work setting, consequences, materials, and instructional procedures) should be considered in preparing an instructional plan for the child who has a demonstrated discrepancy between current and expected level of functioning. The framework within which these modifications comes, however, needs to be considered first. Archer and Edgar (1976) described three stages in learning a new skill or concept: initial acquisition, proficiency, and maintenance:

> During . . . initial acquisition, the child receives input on how to perform the desired behavior . . . gains some knowledge of the skill, its performance, and learns minimal usage of the skill. After the child has some knowledge of how to perform the desired skill, she moves to the second stage, in which she increases her proficiency . . . , [and] improves her accuracy and rate of performance. . . . The behavioral objective should include a criterion of mastery. . . . When the child reaches a desired level of proficiency, ongoing practice in the use of the skill is required for maintenance. . . . Some skills are maintained by the performance of higher-level skills (e.g., two-place multiplication maintains multiplication facts), while other skills need an organized system of review within the classroom. (p. 48).

They also stated that there are two types of classroom activities: direct teacher activities and independent child ones. The stage of initial acquisition is usually developed through direct teacher-child interaction, whereas proficiency and maintenance may be developed through independent activities structured by the teacher. During all stages, however, a process for feedback to correct errors must be built into the instruction.

The components of a good instructional sequence are clearly formulated (Archer & Edgar, 1976; Becker, 1986; Englert, 1984) and described in this chapter. One of the clearest discussions of good teaching, based on the models presented here, has been developed by Archer and Edgar (1976). After a careful curriculum-based assessment, the teacher decides what to teach. Having pinpointed the exact skill levels of the child, the next step is to "set clear long-range objectives, establish sequential steps leading to long-range objectives, and translate these steps into short-term objectives" (p. 34). The skills of task analysis and the various curriculum scope and sequences help the teacher to make the needed decisions here.

Before initiating instruction, the teacher structures and organizes the intervention by carefully selecting materials and tasks (curriculum modifications may be incorporated here); carefully using methods and procedures (thinking through the structure and logic of the instructional design); and arranging the environment to maximize the child's opportunity to engage in the desired behavior (considering the work setting and consequences of the child's behavior). In the initial acquisition stage, instructional input on the skill or concept is provided; in the second stage, supervised practice with feedback is structured.

In stage one, providing instructional input, the teacher needs to be sure that:

1. The child is attending to the instruction;

2. The child is given the opportunity to be involved actively with feedback provided;
3. Wherever possible, visual stimuli and verbal instruction are both provided;
4. The terms used by the teacher in instruction are within the child's vocabulary and are also kept as simple and consistent as possible;
5. The instruction itself is logically sequenced and carefully organized, following the rules described by Becker (1986) and others; when appropriate, the behavior is demonstrated for the child.

The second phase of initial acquisition is teacher-directed supervision of practice of the new skills. A high number of errors should not occur during this phase. There are a number of ways to ensure that practice will involve few errors and provide the learner with a successful experience. Prompts are used along with physical guidance as needed. There should be a plan to fade the prompts and cues as the student achieves proficiency. Corrective feedback on performance is required.

Independent work activities are structured after the learner has gained initial proficiency in order to provide drill and practice to increase accuracy and rate of performance. Seat work is designed to complement the instruction, not to provide busywork for the student or to teach the skill itself, and must focus on the same activity as the teacher-directed instruction. To maximize independence in seat work, it is helpful to use simple directions, standard formats that the student easily recognizes, and assignments that demand a response that the child can be held accountable for and that ensure success. Gickling and Havertape's (1982) sandwiching technique is a useful guideline in constructing drill and practice routine.

Throughout the instructional process, several features must be maintained. There must be corrective and performance feedback to the learner, provided frequently and as close to performance completion as possible. The contingent consequences following performance should be positive, and reinforcers appropriate to the pupil. Assessment should be ongoing, and a data-recording system planned that incorporates the short-term objective—the dimensions of the behavior to be measured—and decisions about how often to measure the behavior, how much to measure and record, a planned time to measure the behavior, and a recording system.

The instructional program is based on the best available data, but the consultant and teacher are aware that program modifications may be necessary. Using the data-management system, unsatisfactory progress can be observed early in the program. Questions then can be asked at each stage of the process. The basic questions to ask are:

1. Was the objective appropriate for the learner, that is, was the entry-level analysis correct? Were prerequisite entry-level skills in place for the student

for this objective? If not, revise the objective and plan to teach missing prerequisite skills.

2. Was the instructional sequence appropriate for the learner? Were the steps too large? Does the skill need to be sliced more thinly, that is, is it necessary to reduce the complexity or difficulty between steps in the instructional sequence? Would transition stories, for example, be useful here? Is the ratio of knowns to unknowns effective for this learner's rate of acquisition.

3. Are instructional procedures effective for this student? Were there enough opportunities for supervised practice before individual practice was begun? Was reinforcement delivered well and often enough? What additional resources need to be used to provide a more effective work setting for the child?

SUMMARY

The purpose of chapters 6 and 7 is to describe for the reader the components of quality instruction and to provide guidelines for modification of instruction to meet individual needs. Certainly not all that is known about good instruction is presented here, particularly for more-complex and higher-level instructional activities. However, the basis of what the research today has to offer to teaching basic skills is covered. Further, the attempt has been to demonstrate how the consultant and teacher can actually modify the four components that can be changed: the work setting, the delivery of consequences, the curriculum materials, and the instructional process. The total quality of the instructional activity received by the learner is dependent upon all four of the categories. Types of problems are categorized as "can't do" and "won't do" problems to provide guidance to the appropriate area to consider modifying.

The fields of cognitive psychology and instructional psychology are exploding. The information presented here provides only a modest beginning to a framework for program modification for students at academic risk. The need for educators, special-service providers, and school psychologists to continue to learn in this area and to encourage opportunities for them to directly utilize this information in classroom practice is critical.

The rules of instruction and classroom management are often not complex, although adopting them in the frenetic world of the classroom can be difficult. But if one spends much time in classrooms, the violation and/or nonexistence of many of the techniques described here would be found to be epidemic. Before we determine that children are psychologically or neurologically handicapped, it is necessary ethically that the instructional environment be examined and modified first. Adherence to quality instructional design can provide results that are often astounding.

Chapter 8

TEACHER ACCEPTANCE
OF CLASSROOM INTERVENTIONS

> *The consultant and the teacher both agreed that a very functional*
> *modification of that teacher's behavior had occurred. Four weeks*
> *later it had been extinguished. Why was obviously effective teacher*
> *behavior dropped from the teacher's repertorie? How shall such*
> *phenomena be studied?*
>
> —Berliner, 1985, p. 384

There is substantial evidence that a research base exists to improve the amount and quality of instruction, and that this can, in fact, result in more effective and efficient learning (Anderson et al., 1985; Walberg, 1984). The focus in this section thus far has been on that knowledge domain. However, before concluding this section of the book, it is necessary to examine another issue, that of teacher acceptance of instructional interventions. Many of the interventions described in the previous chapters are not widely used or known in the educational community, and it is therefore relevant to consider issues of educational diffusion in this context.

The process of innovation in schools has been described as "messy" and "rich," "full of coercion and shared struggle, indifference and heavy involvement, and uncertain results and real payoffs" (Huberman & Miles, 1984, p. 1). Two critical criteria might help us to understand how change in school processes such as the introduction of new classroom teaching techniques might come about. According to Checkland (1981), changes must be desirable from the perspective of those involved and must be "culturally feasible given the characteristics of the situation, the people in it, their shared experiences, and their prejudices" (p. 181). The difficulty in meeting these criteria for classroom innovations has been widely documented. Sarason

(1982) consistently described the complexity of the school as a social institution, examining why changes do not easily occur. Other researchers of the knowledge diffusion process, such as Rogers (1983), found a considerable time lag required for the widespread adoption of new educational ideas.

In attempting to disseminate the ideas of instructional consultation (IC), over and over the same issue has been raised: teachers will not accept having to do things differently. If the instructional interventions incorporated in IC are stuffed down the throats of the teachers, they are unlikely to be accepted and implemented any better than they have been through in-service training (Rosenfield & Rubinson, 1985). Acceptance of consultation itself has been called into question. Resistance here can be defined in terms of unwillingness by the consultee "to engage actively in a problem-solving process" (Piersel & Gutkin, 1983, p. 311). Piersel and Gutkin suggested that while school personnel may value the intended outcomes associated with consultation, there are often unfavorable reinforcement and even punishment contingencies associated with the use of consultation services. Some of these are discussed in chapter 2. There is a lack of empirical research to help understand the factors influencing the acceptability of the consultation process (Kratochwill & Van Someren, 1985).

But even if the consultation process is working well, there are some issues in intervention acceptability which seem to underlie potential teacher resistance to making adaptations in their practice to meet the needs of individual children experiencing learning problems (Witt, 1986). Because the process of consultation around children's learning often results in recommendations that necessitate changes in the ordinary and regular ways of doing things in schools, some additional information is presented in this chapter to alert the school consultant to potential roadblocks in teacher response to the kinds of interventions suggested here. These issues are particularly relevant to the area of change described in the previous chapters, changes in the ways teachers instruct and control their classrooms.

THE CULTURE OF THE SCHOOLS

In any organization, the likelihood of an idea or practice being successfully adopted depends, in part, on whether it is perceived as consistent with existing values, past experiences, and the needs of the organization (Rogers & Shoemaker, 1971). Griffen, Barnes, O'Neal, Edwards, Defino, and Hukill (1984) demonstrated that change is most successful when it is linked to ongoing processes and expectations in a school. There are a number of behavioral and programmatic regularities, that is, aspects of school culture, that need to be considered by the consultant who seeks to make changes in the ways things are done in schools.

According to Hood and Blackwell (1976), for example, school personnel have been found to examine the credibility of the source and the plausibility of a message in comparison to their own experiences. The implication is that teachers are most open to inputs based on experience, either their own or that of other teachers. As Huberman (1983) suggested, "an account by a teacher with children at the same level of how a discipline problem was successfully handled is likely to carry more weight than a half-day in-service workshop on the same topic" (p. 493).

As is emphasized over and over in this text, how ideas are presented and who presents them are exceedingly relevant to ideas' acceptance. In much of the innovation-diffusion literature, the powerful influence of social reference groups is documented (Costanzo, Archer, Aronson, & Pettigrew, 1986):

> As compared to nonperson sources of information, information transmitted via social diffusion is more likely to influence behavior. . . . Information received through interpersonal channels is more likely to be perceived, favorably evaluated, understood, and remembered. Also, because social reference groups tend to consist of similarly situated people, information communicated in this way is more likely to reach individuals who are structurally positioned to act. (p. 527)

For example, one of the major constructs presented here is that of instructional matching, the idea that material should be at the child's instructional level. When teachers have been presented with Harris' (1979) research indicating that the more comfortable the material is for the child, the more progress the child makes, they express surprise. When told that Harris found that the best reading gains were achieved by children who made fewer than three errors per hundred words in connected reading material, and the implications drawn for them for placing children in basal readers at their instructional level, they have often become distressed. They consistently comment that, if they followed that rule, they would be unable to "get through the curriculum." It is implausible to them to consider implementing instructional matching, given that it is not common practice, and they quickly label the practice of instructional matching as "unrealistic." As they filter the concept through their own experience, they tend to downplay the research on which it was based. Further, they worry about the effect of implementing such a practice on how the principal and the teacher in the next grade will view them.

The consultant who is aware of the curriculum-driven routines of the schools will not consider the teacher's behavior as simply resistance to research, but will expect the problem to arise as a culturally based response grounded in the teacher's experiences. If the consultant is not prepared to handle the teachers' concerns, teachers will not accept the concept of instructional matching. We have developed a number of strategies anticipating this concern, such as ensuring the support of the administrators and/or demonstrating how progress to higher levels will be enhanced by the use of instructional matching. But the additional strategy of working with high-status teachers in a school, who are interested in innovative practice, is also of value in introducing educational ideas that go against the traditional way of doing things.

ACCEPTABILITY OF INTERVENTIONS

As part of our increasing understanding of knowledge dissemination in schools, it has become apparent that we need to consider the acceptability of interventions. A growing area of research has focused on treatment acceptability (Kazdin, 1980a; 1980b; 1981). The notion that teachers may prefer different types of interventions is relatively new, but the lack of acceptability of interventions may, in fact, lead to their under-utilization or improper implementation (Witt, 1986; Witt & Elliott, 1985). While there is certainly a need to examine acceptability from the viewpoint of the legal and ethical concerns posed by some interventions, particularly aversive ones, a second reason is to increase the likelihood that "a treatment will be USED and will be implemented with integrity" (Witt & Elliott, 1985, p. 253).

Acceptability of treatment or intervention has been considered broadly, referring to "whether a treatment is appropriate for a given problem, whether it is fair, reasonable, or intrusive, and whether the treatment is consistent with conventional notions of what a treatment should be" (Witt & Elliott, 1985, p. 254). It incorporates judgments from consumers as to whether they *like* the intervention, that is, it is a subjective evaluation or perception of their satisfaction in using the intervention. This construct has been referred to as *social validity* (Wolf, 1978). Three levels for evaluation have been suggested, according to Witt and Elliott (1985): (1) the social significance and/or appropriateness of treatment goals: (2) the social appropriateness of the procedures used to implement the intervention (perception of preference, ease, effectiveness of the procedures); and (3) the social importance of the intended and possible unintended outcomes of treatment.

Although Witt and Elliott (1985) documented the difficulty in studying acceptability of interventions, they were able to draw conclusions, based on the research, about some of the conditions under which teachers are more likely to find an intervention acceptable. A factor that would on the face of it affect acceptability is that of the effectiveness of the treatment. In reviewing the research, Witt and Elliott presented conflicting evidence on this issue, concluding that "some interventions appear to get high marks for acceptability and usability *without* any demonstrable efficacy data" (p. 257). Our own experiences confirm this outcome; for example, in a visit to a pre-first grade in the fall of 1985, the teacher described her use of Frostig materials to train visual-perceptual motor skills to the children in her class. When a brief discussion of the research that documents the ineffectiveness of perceptual-motor training ensued, the teacher responded that she knew that but she saw enormous growth in the children, liked the materials, and would continue to use them. In spite of a decade of evidence to the contrary, perceptual-motor curriculum materials continue to be used in the schools.

But oddly enough, the reverse is also true. Berliner (1985) documented several instances in which teachers acknowledged the effectiveness of interventions and then elected to discontinue their use. Clearly, effectiveness is either a limited criterion or mitigated by other factors.

While the effectiveness of a particular intervention seems to be a relevant criterion for selecting an intervention, it is not always easy to predict whether a given intervention will be effective in any particular situation. Much of the empirical support for intervention effectiveness may be based on group-outcome measures, and in a specific case, the intervention may not work, may work minimally, or may even make the situation worse. There is a critical need for clinical replication studies, in which validated interventions are examined in different situations with different populations. In addition, something is often lost in the implementation, particularly since the actual conduct of the intervention is usually done by someone other than the consultant. There are no cookbooks to follow, and interventions sometimes require considerable skill to implement in the classroom. Since change requires effort and commitment on the part of teachers, confronting them with the need to view the intervention strategy as a hypothesis to try out, might not be very comforting, although it might be honest.

How willing teachers might be to accept a particular intervention can also be a function of the type of intervention. Most of the current research on acceptability has focused on behavioral interventions (Kazdin, 1980b; 1981). Also, although Witt, Elliott, and Martens have examined some of the issues from the perspective of the classroom teacher, they have focused on children with behavior problems rather than academic ones. In two studies (Witt, Elliott, & Martens, 1984; Witt, Martens, & Elliott, 1984), a significant effect was found for teachers rating as less acceptable interventions that required more of their time. These studies, and others, however, provide only general guidelines. As is true with respect to the effectiveness of treatments for individual children, individual teachers also differ in their willingness to engage in different types of interventions, and we have relatively little knowledge as yet to enable us to predict these relationships in advance.

Certainly the finding that there is a strong relationship between acceptability and the amount of time, effort, and resources expended in implementation (see Witt & Elliott, 1985, for a review of the literature) could be anticipated. As Witt and Elliott pointed out, many successful interventions were conducted as part of experimental projects with more resources than would be found in the typical neighborhood school. They raise the issue of cost-benefit-analysis types of research to determine if teachers would be more willing to expend effort if the intervention appeared to them to have a higher chance for success.

Having made the case that teachers seem unwilling to expend large amounts of time and effort on an intervention, there is also research (e.g., Algozzine, Ysseldyke, Christenson, & Thurlow, 1982; Gutkin, 1980; Gutkin, Singer, & Brown, 1980), which has demonstrated that teachers evidence a strong preference for involvement in interventions themselves. Given the recent literature indicating overreferral of mildly handicapped children by teachers for special education, these results are puzzling. As Witt and Elliott (1985), suggested, there seems to be a "need to further elucidate the conditions under which teachers handle behavior problems themselves or decide to refer a child to the principal, counselor, school psychologists, special-education teacher or other individual" (p. 263).

Further, although the literature on consultation suggests that teachers want school psychologists and other pupil-personnel staff to provide practical suggestions about ways to teach pupils experiencing difficulty in the classroom, as well as on the selection and use of instructional materials for special groups, it appears that teachers actually pose few questions for consultants about instruction (McKellar & Hartshorne, 1986). McKellar and Hartshorne investigated the types of instructional information desired by teachers in order to help them educate children who present problems in the classroom; they examined the frequency with which teachers request instructional versus noninstructional information. Table 8-1 presents the data from their preliminary study, indicating that instructional questions were sparse when compared to noninstructional questions about the etiology of the problem, discipline/management issues, and the emotional needs/values of students.

It is interesting to ask whether teachers turn to other than pupil-personnel staff for help in the area of instruction or whether they are unaware that there are other ways to handle instruction than those with which they are familiar. The author has been impressed, as a result of sitting in on child study team meetings in which teachers were referring children, with how little attention was paid to alternative teaching strategies compared with the internal dynamics of the child. Often members of the teams expressed belief that there was nothing else to be done with this child in the classroom, that the teacher had done all that was called for, an assumption that only with additional training on instruction did the teams begin to call into question.

A fourth factor considered by Witt and Elliott (1985) is the theoretical orientation of the intervention, including "what the intervention is called,

TABLE 8-1
Types of Questions Posed by Respondents

Questions Category	Percentage of Total 270 Questions Posed
Instructional	
Ability level	4.4
Content	0.7
Instructional activity	1.9
Materials	0.7
Methods	7.8
Prerequisites	0.7
Sequencing of instruction	0.4
Noninstructional	
Cause/nature of problem	13.0
Educational placement	4.8
Additional resources	5.2
Discipline/management	23.0
Emotional needs/values of student	14.1
Emotional needs of teacher	1.9
Parents/administration/community	8.5
Background information on student	7.8

Note: From McKellar & Hartshorne, 1986.

how it is described, and the theoretical foundations from which it is derived" (p. 263). Their review suggests that teachers do indeed seem to possess negative attitudes about some treatment approaches, with behavioral descriptions being viewed as less acceptable than humanistic or neutral ones. In a study by Witt, Moe, Gutkin, and Andrews (1984), pragmatic descriptions based on Dreikur's model of logical consequences were more acceptable to teachers than either behavioral or humanistic descriptions. However, they did find also that behavioral descriptions were most acceptable to newer teachers, suggesting perhaps that behavioral techniques have finally come to be part of teacher training. As a result of their review, Witt and Elliott (1985) concluded that it may be best to approach teachers from the perspective of the attitudes and values they hold rather than from the consultant's theoretical perspective. Drawing on Zeig's (1982) concept of utilization, in which interventions are phrased in the teacher's own language system, they suggest looking to the consultee's language for clues about how to verbalize intervention recommendations.

A similar perspective is developed in chapter 2, related to the building of the consultative relationship. There is a need to examine differences in underlying assumptions and perspectives (Colson & Coyne, 1978). Consultants are aware that they need to respond to the person as well as the referral issues (Caplan, 1970). The point that again needs to be stressed in this context is that the consultative alliance is not formed until the consultant can sense what life is like for the consultee, can view the problems "from a mutually shared inside while simultaneously keeping a sense of separateness and maintaining one's own frame of reference against which the other person's viewpoint and experience are contrasted" (Shectman, 1979, p. 787).

So long as consultants view the role only as one of bringing proven techniques and knowledge to problems in applied settings, issues of implementation and dissemination are largely unexplored. It is a given that our work as professionals is not value-free, and the first step is being explicit about our own belief systems as well as understanding and respecting the value systems of others (Bergin, 1980). To be effective as consultants, we need to explore how teachers conceptualize their problems and their decisions, and examine some of the assumptions that guide teacher behavior in the classroom (Rosenfield, 1985b).

Instructional consultation raises a number of such values issues. As Witt and Elliott (1985) stated, some teachers may be resistent to certain interventions because they do not view treatment of learning problems as within their role. Over and over again, child study team members, including teachers, special-education personnel, school psychologists and principals, have expressed that point of view to the author. They have indicated that home problems and internal deficits within the child have been the cause of the learning problems of the children referred to the child study teams. Resolution of the problem is seen in terms of family, referral and placement, and other interventions outside of the classroom.

There is evidence that people believe that solutions to problems are to be found on the same level as the origin of the problem; for example, "a problem with a biological origin must have a biological solution, or that if the variables producing the problem cannot be changed, then no solution is possible" (Brickmann, Rabinowitz, Karuza, Coates, Cohn, & Kidder, 1982, p. 369). Therefore, it should not be surprising that if the focus of both etiology and assessment is on family and child variables, teachers should feel relatively impotent in the solution process. As assumptions are explored with the staff of child study teams, it becomes clear that a pervasive feeling of helplessness to intervene is widespread among members, in part because of their own assumptions and assessment procedures. It is important for the consultant to take time to discuss the underlying assumptions, to avoid the "snare of assumed shared perceptions" (Munby, 1981), that the child study team members and the consultant derive equal significance to and identical meanings from the same situation.

In one case, a first grade child was referred by his teacher on the basis of poor handwriting and math skills (although he read well). The author was invited to visit the class one afternoon and had the opportunity to observe the teacher systematically following a highly structured (and clever) lesson plan from a teacher magazine on the construction of a Santa Claus face. Jay's classroom performance was clearly average compared to the rest of the class, and his product was a recognizable Santa. When the consultant pointed out the child's responsiveness to well-structured instruction in drawing the highly complex Santa Claus face, the team's response was that it was not up to the classroom teacher to provide individual instruction for children with problems (even though he had actually done the drawing in a whole class activity setting). Once the assumption had been made that he was impaired, it was difficult for the team to hear how to proceed with classroom instructional modification or even to fully acknowledge that the classroom teacher could have been successful with him. In fact, the classroom teacher's response to the child's drawing had been one of astonishment that he had done so well, rather than viewing the behavior as information that might be helpful to her in planning the child's instruction in handwriting.

Whereas much of the research on acceptability of school interventions in terms of theoretical orientation has been done with behavior problems, and indeed, with behavior-modification techniques, there is some hint of the importance of theoretical perspective on intervention acceptability in the academic sphere as well. Becker (1984) described a similar situation with respect to DISTAR programs of instruction in reading and mathematics:

> Like behavioral analysis and other innovations in education, the DI approach has often been attacked as being inconsistent with humanistic and other philosophies of education. From our experiences . . ., we knew that for 99 out of 100 teachers, the feelings of philosophic clash disappeared in 3 to 6 months as the teachers gained competence, and especially as they saw children learning who had failed with other methods. . . . About half of the teachers cited the dramatic changes in progress by their . . . students as the basis for change in attitude. (p. 51-52)

However, many teachers might not be willing to implement the program at all, so that the initial feeling of philosophic clash might not ever be worked through. Moreover, Berliner (1985) suggests that even success might not be enough to enable teachers to continue using interventions that work but that do not feel comfortable for one of a number of reasons. It is possible that other factors intervene, such as side effects or affective feelings experienced by the teachers such as those reported by Abidin (1975).

It is apparent that there are subtle factors that influence a teacher's willingness to implement a particular type of recommendation. Although much more research needs to be done in this area to pinpoint the interactions between particular types of interventions and the characteristics of teachers, the current state of the art suggests the importance of consultation skills in helping develop interventions that teachers will actually implement.

IMPLEMENTATION OF INTERVENTIONS

But even when the teacher verbally accepts or seems willing to try an intervention, an additional aspect needs to be considered. Rarely does an intervention get adopted whole by the teacher. An important aspect of acceptability is how much allowance there is for adaptation of the intervention by the classroom teacher. Classrooms and classes are perceived by teachers through their own lenses. Interventions are typically "modified according to the resources and demands of the setting in which they are applied . . . in a direction that makes them more acceptable to the users" (Witt and Elliott, 1985, p. 266). This phenomenon has been widely studied, and it is well-accepted that teachers will utilize innovations in the classroom in idiosyncratic ways (Doyle & Ponder, 1977-78). In fact, it is important not only to expect but encourage the individual practitioner to adapt the intervention to make it his or her own (Griffen, Barnes, O'Neal, Edwards, Defino, & Hukill, 1984).

The consultant, however, needs to ensure that the adaptation is one that has integrity with respect to the intervention itself. The issue of treatment integrity with respect (Yeaton, Greene, & Bailey, 1981), "the degree to which an intervention is implemented as intended" (Witt and Elliott, 1985, p. 266), has been considered in the program evaluation research literature, but less widely in consultation. We have observed, for example, in attempts to implement curriculum-based assessment techniques, reinvention by teachers, often in directions that led to the intervention becoming too difficult for the teacher to continue to use or in some way that actually violated an underlying assumption (Rosenfield & Rubinson, 1985).

In a recent consultation contact, a junior high school principal was discussing the paucity of intervention options his child study team recommended. He indicated that a fairly frequent intervention they suggested was contracting; when that failed, they did not know what else to recommend to the classroom teacher. And failure was fairly common! The consultant explored how contracting was being implemented. It was discovered at this point that the knowledge and skill basis for implementation of contracting by the staff was severely limited and that contracting probably was not being implemented with integrity. Several in-service options were then explored, including not only widening the number of interventions available to the child study team, but also training staff more intensely in the ones with which they were already familiar. In addition, the feedback process between the child study team and the teacher would be modified to include a discussion of implementation with the focus on problem solving rather than a feedback procedure in which the teacher reported whether or not the recommended intervention "worked."

In a related example, an elementary teacher had consulted her school prereferral team for help with a child with handwriting difficulty. As a result of the discussion, she had agreed with the recommendation to reduce the amount of written work he was expected to do each day (actually, that was only one of a number of recommendations; it would be interesting to explore in more detail why she decided to implement only that one), and she had attempted to do that. However, no one had checked back with her for several weeks to see how the implementation was going, and she had, during that time, become concerned because Ken was now finishing his work so early that he was getting into mischief. She was unsure what to do. Implementing this apparently simple recommendation had caused her a problem; the instruction to limit the amount of written work he was expected to do was too general, and she did not have the skills or underlying knowledge to know how to evaluate how much was too much, how much was too little, or what criteria to use to make that assessment. Instead of going back to the consultation team to discuss the implementation, she was on the verge of giving up the recommended intervention because "it didn't work" (in fact, he was now completing his work, but there were unfortunate side effects). She was also struggling with her own guilt about what she was doing ("It's okay for me to limit his work in first grade, but next year's teacher won't be so understanding; if I limit his written work, he won't be ready for the next grade").

In another example, a teacher had assured the team members that she knew how to do contracting, and indicated her willingness to set up a contract for work completion with Lenny. However, she reported back to the team that contracting did not work with him. An exploration of the actual process revealed a number of flaws in the contract itself, the most blatant of which was that the family had been involved with the reward for work completion and had failed to follow through with their part of the bargain. Because the teacher had given him the reinforcement she had promised, she felt that the child should have continued to perform the behavior. In addition, she demonstrated several problems in the conception of the contract itself, including delaying reward for several days and lack of clarity about what behavior she wanted. The difficult consultation problem raised by this case was how to provide help to someone who believed she did not need it-in the face of the teacher's belief that she could construct the contract without help from the available consultants, that she knew how to do it, and that in fact, the outcome was not related to the intervention but to the child's resistance to doing his work. The team initially had accepted at face value her claim that she knew how to develop contracts (the learning-disability-teacher-consultant on the team later told the author that the most difficult part for her in moving from a resource-room teacher to a teacher-consultant was discovering her colleagues' lack of skill). Recommendations without specifics, without discussion of underlying assumptions, and without ongoing consultation through the implementation process are apt to flounder.

This is not to deny that school-based consultants are busy people, and close follow-up of implementation is time-consuming. However, amazement is often expressed by new classroom consultants when they return to the scene to discover what actually was implemented compared to their assumption about what they and the teacher had "agreed" that the teacher would do. Tinkering with any intervention to adapt it to the specific teacher, child, and classroom setting is the norm, and both teacher and consultants ought to anticipate that two or three modifications of the general agreed-upon strategy might be needed before a useful plan is in place.

In working with teachers in classroom interventions, it has been this author's orientation to use the following pattern once the problem-identification phase has been completed:

1. Clarify the goal of the intervention.
2. Brainstorm together with the teacher the types of intervention strategies that might facilitate achieving the goal, bearing in mind the particular teacher, classroom, and child.
3. Help the teacher select an intervention strategy that makes sense to him or her and seems "do-able."
4. Work with the teacher to adapt the particular strategy to the child and situation, discussing implementation plans in detail.
5. Support the teacher's use of the strategy, including, where necessary, ensuring support of supervisors, and/or helping to find materials and other resources.
6. Monitor intervention implementation, often (daily) at first, even if by telephone, being certain to ask for a review of the specifics of how it is being done in the classroom or to conduct an observation. (In this stage it is important to maintain a relationship of collaboration, of two people working together, not of supervision.)
7. Ensure that evaluation data are being collected so that the effectiveness of the intervention is monitored.
8. Encourage and help plan modifications, as needed, of the intervention until it is clear that the child is making acceptable progress.
9. Structure an ongoing process to monitor the child on the intervention or maintain the growth and progress during termination of the intervention after the goal is obtained.

SUMMARY

Schools have been considered institutionalized organizations, according to Meyer and Scott, two organizational theorists (Perrow, 1985). As such, schools are structured in conformity to social and cultural expectations; the work processes are detached from the structure. Cultural values, symbols, and legitimacy determine behavior; work and output are merely assumed to be appropriate. In such an organization, changing worker(teacher) behavior presents special problems. Thus, consultant skill in helping teachers to accept interventions is an important aspect of the instructional consultation process. When the intervention includes a change in the behavior of teachers in the classroom in their interactions with learners(and most interventions, in truth, do) instead of directly changing the behavior of the child, effective consultation skills are needed.

The research on acceptability of interventions to teachers provides one source of knowledge for improving this process. Knowledge of perspectives and values provides an addition source of information. A process for monitoring implementation of the intervention is a third critical area. In many, if not all, cases, however, the strength of the underlying consultative alliance and the sense of support felt by the teacher as the process of change unfolds is perhaps the most critical variable of all.

Section IV

THE TERMINATION STAGE

In the last stage of consultation, the end game is played out. The single chapter that composes this section suggests how to conclude the consultation relationship in terms of both a written and an interpersonal format. For the school psychologist, however, particularly as an internal consultant, the consultation relationship should be a continuing one, even though on a particular case or project, the end stage may be reached.

Chapter 9

CONCLUDING CONSULTATION

So call the field to rest, and let's away
To part the glories of this happy day.
—Wm. Shakespeare, *Julius Caesar*

School psychologists and other educational consultants are busy people. Typically, our energy goes into the assessment and intervention stages of consultation, as it legitimately should. Carefully defining the problem, gathering the relevant assessment data, developing and implementing the intervention, all in a collaborative framework, are hard work. But as time goes on and the problem nears resolution (or not), it is not uncommon to begin to withdraw our energy and attention (Block, 1981), to move on to the next crisis or problem.

However, there is still business to be conducted, and the conclusion of the consultation process should be given careful attention. To some degree the nature of the ending depends upon how effective the consultation has been. According to Block (1981), a "clear crisp ending" is required. Further, he stated that "How you end will have an impact on whether the client calls you in again, regardless of the ups and downs of this project" (p. 193). Given that school psychologists are usually internal consultants, that is not a small issue.

TERMINATING AN UNSUCCESSFUL CONSULTATION

It is often the case that an unsuccessful consultation has a tendency to peter out, to just fade away, as consultant and consultee begin to avoid one another. Sometimes this happens early in the process, sometimes later, but missed appointments on either side usually suggest avoidance and a flawed consultation process.

Block (1981) suggested that the task of the consultant is to help consultees stay with their discomfort in the project despite their desire to retreat. At some point consultees begin to perceive that the focus of change is the consultee, that they are part of the problem and the solution. They may feel vulnerable, helpless to change. They may have difficulty giving up control of the situation. Implementing new behaviors may lead teachers to feel less expert in their classroom during the transition process. They may resent, no matter how delicately put, the negative feedback about their performance. Change, as has been discussed throughout, is a slow and often painful process, requiring energy, time, and commitment.

Block also makes it clear that the consultant is subject to the same flight fantasy when the project is not going well. Under those conditions, responsibility can be avoided by leaving and by blaming the consultee. It is important for the consultant to open a discussion about the consultation, to try to clear the air about where the problem is. An alternative strategy is for the consultant to obtain some supervision (peer or otherwise) to develop new skills or a new perspective in this or similar consultations.

If the consultant concludes that nothing can be done to improve the progress of this particular consultation project, it should be discussed openly. A clear decision needs to be made to terminate the consultation process. It may be desirable to try again at a later time. But one should not merely let the relationship fizzle out.

CONCLUDING A SUCCESSFUL CONSULTATION

Change in the school setting is difficult (Sarason, 1982). A successful intervention to meet a child's need is worth a celebration. The consultant must be sure to tell the teacher what he or she did to make it work, to "help the client get clear on what they (sic) did well" (Block, 1981, p. 194). Teachers need both informative feedback and reinforcement, to know that what he or she did is what made the difference.

Sometimes there is a tendency to maintain a relationship around a particular case with a teacher who is responsive to consultation efforts. Consultants, too, are responsive to reinforcement. But it is important both to leave the door open and to move on to other work.

How do we know when it is time to terminate a successful instructional consultation? The data should provide ongoing information that the intervention is working. A problem-solving process should be part of the consultation procedures, so that lack of progress under the intervention can be addressed without a loss of face by either consultant or consultee. But when the child is making satisfactory progress, as defined in advance, and the teacher is comfortable with both the progress and the intervention itself, it is time to move on to the next case. In one school system with a prereferral consultation model, the teacher and consultant both sign off on the case on the consultation log, signifying termination of the active phase of the case.

That is not to say that there should not be systematic follow-up to ascertain that the progress is being maintained. Further, a clear message to the teacher to contact the consultant if there is a problem is also part of the termination message. For consultants who have begun to manage their service delivery through the use of the computer, collecting, analyzing, and maintaining data are made easier. Also, the computer can be programmed to remind the consultant to check up on cases at periodic intervals (see Yoshida & LiPuma, 1985, for an example of how this is done).

COMMUNICATING THE RESULTS

The written record of a consultation process deserves special consideration. It should not be a surprise that the traditional psychological-report format makes little sense in the consultation model, if it makes much sense at all (see Ownby & Wallbrown, 1983, for a brief review of the research on teacher response to school psychologists' reports). First, instructional consultation departs considerably from the typical psychometric model of test and recommend, which fits the psychological report as we have come to recognize it. Moreover, the traditional report form is not directed at anyone, and consultation is clearly an interpersonal process. Those readers interested in a critique of the typical report form on its own terms are invited to read Batsche's (1983) analysis. However, the purpose here is to provide an alternative model that fits the consultation process.

A format that makes more sense for consultation is that of the memo or letter (Ross-Reynolds, 1985; Ross-Reynolds & Grimes, 1983). It is more personal and more likely to be read than formal reports (Ross-Reynolds & Grimes, 1983). The format of the memo or letter also lends itself to the major purpose of the consultation report: to provide a written record of the results of the interactions between the consultant(s) and consultee(s).

There should be no news in the report of a collaborative consultation. Rather, the report should clearly present a summary of the information gathered and the decisions made about intervention. The report itself should contain the following sections:

1. A sentence describing the purpose of the written communication, for example: I am writing this letter to summarize our joint efforts to improve Michael's reading skills.

2. A statement of the referral questions that the teacher and consultant have agreed to address; for example: After our two discussions about Christine's math difficulties, we established the following referral questions: (a) Does Christine understand the basic operations of addition and subtraction? and (b) How can we help Christine improve her recall of basic addition and subtraction facts?

3. For each referral question, relevant assessment data and recommendations should be presented. The consultant should provide the information in as clear a format as possible, using charts and graphs for clarity of presentation (see the computer-assisted instruction program developed by Thomas, 1983, for ways to improve the use of graphs for communicating results).

Only assessment data relevant to the referral questions are presented. There is no need to present material about the child or child's family that is not related to the specific referral questions. If the teacher is not concerned about the intellectual functioning of the child, there will be no intelligence-test report included (as presented earlier, there is no standard assessment battery considered routine in instructional consultation). Obviously also the information will be classroom based as much as possible.

In addition, all *recommendations* included are those that the teacher and consultant have *already agreed to implement* for the child. Each recommendation must be tied to a specific question that it is designed to address; also included must be how the recommendation is related to the assessment data, how it will be implemented, and who will implement it.

4. A plan for evaluation should be included, often as simple as the following: "We will meet again in two weeks to assess Christine's skills in recalling her facts from memory. In order to help us assess her progress, you have agreed to re-administer the 100 addition and 100 subtraction facts, under timed conditions, to see how many unknowns have now become knowns. At that time we can decide what changes in the intervention, if any, we might need to make."

5. A concluding statement is added, acknowledging the positive aspects of the working relationship and clarifying the ongoing availability of the consultant to the teacher if a problem arises in this situation or in another. For example: It has been a pleasure working with you to help Christine improve her math skills. While we have agreed to meet in two weeks, should any problems arise before then, please do not hesitate to contact me by leaving a note in my mailbox.

The written communication model presented here differs from the traditional report in several ways. First, it is personal, directed towards the other party in the consultation. Second, it is not a source of communication of the expert knowledge and advice of the consultant; rather it is a summary of the results of the collaborative efforts of the consultee and the consultant in their efforts to resolve the problem. All of the information has already been discussed and the recommendations are those that have been accepted by the consultee as reasonable for implementation. Third, it includes no overall evaluation, covering all aspects of the referred child, but is directed specifically to the referral concerns of the teacher. The appendix to this chapter contains several examples of written communications terminating the active stage of consultation efforts, selected to represent a variety of problems and age levels.

SUMMARY

There is a concluding stage to a consultation process, which should be completed in a planned way. To whatever degree the consultation has been successful (or not), the decision and process for ending the consultation should be a conscious one for all involved. The importance of this for internal consultants should be especially apparent.

For the written communication that provides a permanent record of the consultation experience, the consultant might consider a letter or memo format, in which the following major aspects are included: the purpose of the written communication; the agreed-upon referral questions; the results of the assessment procedures utilized to address the referral questions; the intervention recommendations decided upon by all involved; evaluation plans; and a concluding statement indicating openness of the consultant to further contact from the consultee. The written communication should contain only information directly related to the problem at hand. Ending the consultation process in a way that leaves the door open for further consultation interactions between the consultant and consultee is a major goal, especially for the internal consultant.

APPENDIX

Five reports are included in the appendix to this chapter, to illustrate several different issues, as well as provide examples of how written information is conveyed using the skills of instructional consultation and the format recommended in this chapter.

Report no. 1.   This letter was written at the conclusion of a consultation between a teacher and a school psychology student about a second grade child who was not showing any progress in reading. The school psychology student was functioning as an external consultant. The modifications in instruction involved curriculum modification, including placing the child at instructional level. An older student was used to tutor the child, providing an additional resource for the teacher to implement a distributed practice routine. A reward system was also developed for the child. The transcript of the initial interview for this case is presented in Appendix B. Note the two referral questions that were generated as a result of the interview with the teacher.

Report no. 2.   This letter was also written by a school psychology student functioning as an external consultant. In this case, handwriting problems of a second grade child were present, although the teacher did not have a scope and sequence in that area. Note the specificity in describing the CBA data as well as the interventions.

Report no. 3.   This report was written by a school psychologist who returned to this special education setting to conduct an instructional consultation. Although she had once been the school psychologist there, she was an external consultant when this consultation was completed. Note that the child in question had already been referred, labeled, and placed in a special-education program, but the school psychologist was able to provide valuable input into his instructional program.

Report no. 4.   This letter was written by an internal consultant, in the role of a learning-disability-teacher-consultant (she was also a school psychology student). It illustrates an instructional consultation that focused on a mathematics problem.

Report no 5.   The final report presented here is unique in that it grew out of an instructional consultation at the high school level. A resource-room teacher (who was also a school psychology student) worked collaboratively with a high school teacher to develop an instructional program to meet the needs of a low-functioning student, one whose parents had refused all attempts by the school to provide remedial or special education assistance.

Report No. 1

Dear Maureen,

I am writing this letter to summarize our joint collaborations in making Danny's reading experiences enjoyable (for both of you) and rewarding.

After our initial interview we decided to address the following referral questions:

Referral Questions

1. Why is Danny unable to consistently decode long and short vowel sounds?
2. Why is Danny unable to complete workbook assignments and other follow-up activities in reading (e.g., comprehension questions, fill-in, etc.)?

The Informal Reading Inventory/Phonic Analysis helped to answer and clarify these questions for us. As a result of the reading inventory, it was found that Danny, as you had mentioned in the initial interview, knows his beginning and ending sounds. However, Danny has not yet fully mastered phonetic rules. Consequently, he frequently guesses when identifying long and short vowel sounds. For example, in the word-recognition section of the inventory, he made the following errors: he read look for like, mad for made and life for live. This finding was also confirmed during the observation. Danny, even with assurance from you in decoding a word, found the task difficult as evidenced in the slow and tedious manner in which he approached the task.

The reason for Danny's difficulty in completing workbook assignments (referral question no. 2) became apparent as a result of the reading-inventory analysis. Danny is reading at frustration level. As a result of this, reading is not an enjoyable experience for Danny. As noted in the observation, Danny was off-task 66% of the time in comparison to a control child who was on-task 100% of the time.

Completing the workbook assignments, as well as other follow-up work pertaining to the reading lesson, requires the acquisition of specific prerequisite skills. These prerequisite skills include phonic and word-recognition skills. Danny's limited knowledge of phonic rules, along with his limited word-recognition skills at his current reading level, make it difficult for him to satisfactorily complete or comprehend his assignments. Thus, you get responses such as "We ate a strange for lunch."

Recommendations

Danny will begin at the Level 6 reader. He will be reading in the book "Across the Fence." However, we are going to control for difficulty. You and I will assess for knowns and unknowns in the first story. We will then prepare transitional stories and drill activities for the reading lesson. As we discussed earlier, the transitional stories (consisting of approximately 100 words) will be designed with a 15% margin of challenge. The sandwich technique will be utilized to introduce unknown words. Comprehension exercises will be designed from the content with the same margin of challenge—15%. Adjustments in story length will be made accordingly as Danny's skills develop.

In order to reinforce Danny's reading skills, a seventh grader will be working with him. The seventh grader will have an assigned time to come in. Danny and the seventh grader will make a word ring from the list of vocabulary words from the reader (which you constructed as a result of known/unknown assessment). Each day, Danny and the student will review the words on the ring. Once Danny is able to identify a word three times, it will receive a check. If Danny is not yet able to identify a word, it gets a slash. This activity will keep you abreast of known/unknowns and, therefore, will provide pertinent instructional information.

The seventh grader will also play instructional games utilizing games that you have already constructed. Since the games are related to the reader, they will not only reinforce Danny's current reading skills, but also provide opportunity to experience success. Danny, as a result of the new instructional strategies, will be familiar with the words and be more motivated to participate.

Phonetic analysis indicated that Danny needs to relearn phonetic rules, as well as the following consonant blends: scr, spl, sm, tw, and sk.

In order to accomplish this goal we designated a period of time that would be devoted to reteaching phonetic rules to Danny and two other students. However, we agreed this should be followed up by drill exercises. Again, we will utilize an upper class person to go over the drill exercises with the students. The drill will be controled for knowns and unknowns and will follow the sequential pattern of the curriculum. Drills will initially be constructed by you and me.

Danny will keep an index card file with phonic rules printed on them. There will be examples of each phonic rule included on the card. Danny will not be moved on until he has shown mastery of skills to a 95% level.

During reading, Danny will also be reinforced for any attempts at sounding out words. Consonant blends, as we discussed, will be taught in collaboration with the reading of vocabulary words. The seventh grade student will then reinforce this skill with instructional games.

As we discussed earlier, the seventh grade student will meet with you for approximately five minutes every morning. In this way, you and the student can review accomplishments as well as review the skill to be focused on for that day. A folder will be kept for Danny.

Danny has experienced much failure in reading. We discussed the importance of making this new instructional approach a rewarding experience for Danny, one that will make learning fun and make Danny feel good about learning.

In order to meet this objective, we have designed a system whereby Danny will be rewarded for satisfactory work. You had observed that Danny enjoys being a monitor. This was a big breakthrough for us since we were having difficulty coming up with appropriate reinforcers for Danny. Danny will now earn the privilege of being a monitor by completing eight pages of drill sheet at an 85% level. At that point he will earn a pass.

When the office is in need of a monitor, Danny will be allowed to go if he has earned a pass. This will serve two purposes; (1) It will make Danny feel good about learning; and (2) it will encourage Danny to complete his work accurately and neatly.

We are now in the process of implementing our instructional intervention. In order to note Danny's progress, we will be logging his accomplishments and progress as well as areas of concern. We will be making adjustments whenever necessary.

I'd like to thank you for your cooperation in this project. It has been a very rewarding experience.

Till our next appointment,

Lillian

Report No. 2

Dear Mrs. Sanders:

I am writing to summarize the results of my work with Jack in the areas of reading and writing. I realize that the decision as to whether or not Jack will continue in your room is still up in the air. Nevertheless, I hope that the information presented here will be helpful should he remain in your class as a second grader.

Our initial conversations on March 4 and 18 led to the development of the first referral question: What skill difficulty contributes to the poor appearance of Jack's written work? Subsequent assessment revealed that reading was also a problem area, resulting in the second question: Why does Jack have difficulty reading both aloud and silently?

Results from the handwriting assessment and analysis of writing samples indicate that Jack holds his pencil correctly, visually discriminates between basic strokes in letters, and visually identifies capital and lowercase letters in a sentence. Jack's ability to form letters when copying or writing from dictation is adequate, although the quality of his lowercase "e" can be improved. In addition, Jack at times confuses "b" and "d," or reverses "g" and "z." The main contributors to the poor appearance of his written work are his difficulties in maintaining accurate proportion between capital and lowercase letters in a sentence, and difficulties in spacing between letters and words. However, when these errors are pointed out to Jack in conjunction with strategies for developing the necessary skills, the quality of his handwriting significantly improves. In addition, Jack notices the change and is proud of his accomplishment.

Jack's reading difficulties result from a combination of factors, which became more evident as assessment progressed. As you suggested in our initial interview, his oral fluency is poor. This is partially due to his lack of knowledge of some vowel sounds, as well as most consonant blends and combinations (for a complete summary of his phonics skills and needs, please refer to the attached chart). However, an additional problem is his inability to blend sounds into words, including those sounds which are familiar to him. For example, although Jack was able to identify the word "all" and initial consonant sounds associated with the letters "j," "n," "p," "s," "z," he was unable to read any nonsense words produced by combining these consonants with the word (e.g., "jall").

During oral reading, these difficulties are manifested by frequent word omissions and substitutions. When substituting, Jack almost always uses initial consonant cues, as represented by his errors of saying "star" for street, "broom" for brother and "worked" for would. Other than employing this strategy, however, Jack generally does not attack unfamiliar words and instead attempts to derive passage meaning from pictures and words that he recognizes by sight. Word-attack difficulties limit his comprehension during both oral and silent reading and are the third factor in his poor reading performance.

Analysis of Jack's learning style suggests that he is most attentive when presented with material that he does not find frustrating. Observation reveals that when frustrated, he displays off-task behaviors that are not disruptive to others, but do detract from his ability to benefit from the instruction being provided. To avoid this, challenging material should account for approximately 15% of each assignment. This will allow him to successfully complete tasks and provide him with positive experiences across a variety of subject areas.

Jack is aware of his difficulties and responds well to situations in which individual help is available. You are accurate in referring to him as a child who "wants to learn." As a result, recommendations for modifying instruction in accordance with his needs and your existing classroom structure are outlined in the next section.

Recommendations

Because handwriting instruction is not part of your daily classroom schedule, modifications in Jack's writing assignments can be used to address the previously outlined needs. To maintain correct letter proportion, he should be instructed to make capital letters two lines tall and lowercase letters only one. Horizontal guidelines can be drawn initially as reminders, but replaced by verbal prompts once he masters the skill. To develop appropriate spacing, he should be instructed to leave enough room for one finger between words. Since I have already demonstrated and observed his ability to use this technique, verbal prompts should be sufficient as reminders prior to the start of written assignments.

For the purpose of reading instruction, Jack can begin at Preprimer 2 of the Houghton-Mifflin series. As the stories increase in difficulty, the number of unfamiliar words to which he is exposed should be controlled to avoid frustration. The student teacher assigned to your class can assist with this process by determining Jack's knowns and unknowns in relation to each story prior to its use in oral reading instruction. Once identified, unknown words can be combined in phrases with 2 to 3 knowns from the text and drilled until he can demonstrate recognition for 3 consecutive days (please refer to the attached sample drill sheet). Once Jack can recognize approximately 85% of the words in a story, transition into the text can be made. Although progress will be slow, these drill-and-practice procedures will allow Jack to read at a comfortable level and expand his sight vocabulary.

Jack requires individualized phonics training to increase his knowledge of vowel sounds, consonant combinations, and basic blending skills. Assignments in these areas from his present workbook can be continued. However, in response to your observation that he often has trouble identifying the workbook pictures, these pictures should be determined in advance and either identified for him or eliminated from the assignment.

To supplement the workbook in the area of blending, I have provided you with a series of phonics flash strips constructed from 28 frequently encountered sounds in your classroom reading material. These flash strips are illustrated below:

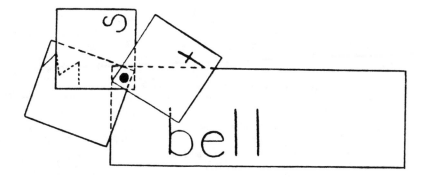

Level one builds upon Jack's knowledge of initial consonants to provide a model for breaking down and putting together component sounds in words. Level two provides similar practice using consonant blends and digraphs as the initial component sounds.

The advantage of these flash strips is their capacity to be used in a variety of settings (e.g., formal instructional periods, free time, homework assignments). Introduction to their use should involve demonstration of their purpose in forming similar words with different initial sounds. This can be modeled by verbally emphasizing component sounds and saying them at an increasingly faster rate until the word is recognizable. Once this process becomes familiar, Jack can use the strips individually or with another child to obtain verbal practice in blending the sounds he has mastered. Additional cards can easily be added to accommodate Jack's increasing sound/symbol vocabulary.

Since the combination of many sounds in these flash strips will form nonsense words, their use will also facilitate application of Jack's phonics knowledge to unfamiliar words. Word attack should be encouraged during textual reading as well as through the systematic use of positive reinforcement. When reading orally, he should be praised for attempts to attack unfamiliar words by identifying or blending component sounds. Reinforcement should occur regardless of whether he successfully pronounces the word, but should not be given in response to obvious guessing as this is one behavior we want to reduce. When he hesitates on a word, he should be prompted to sound it out and blend. Errors should be addressed by instructor modeling of the correct response.

My experiences in your class have been most enjoyable. Please feel free to contact me should you desire further assistance with any of the recommendations discussed here.

Sincerely,

Ilene

Attachment 1

Summary of Results from the Informal Phonics Inventory

Knowns	Unknowns
1. Can name letter a, c, e, f, g, h, i, j, k, l, m, n, o, p, q, r, s, t, u, v, w, x, y, z	Reverses letter names b-d
2. Can produce initial consonant sounds from visual stimuli: c, f, g, h, j, k, m, n, p, r, s, t, v, w, z	Confuses b-d; canot produce 1, q, y, x
3. Initial consonants through auditory recognition: b, c, d, f, g, h, j, k, l, m, n, p, r, s, t, v, w, z	q, x, y

4. Initial consonant blends and digraphs: sh, wh, sp, sn, sk	ch, th, st, sw, sl, bl, gl, fl, cl, pl, cr, pr, tr, br, dr, gr, fr
5. Can produce vowel sounds from visual stimuli: short a, e, i; long e, i, o, u	Short o, u; long a
6. Short vowel sounds through auditory recognition: a, e, i, o	Short u
7.	All vowel combinations
8.	All blending skills related to word recognition.

Attachment 2

Sample Reading Drill

Based upon Houghton-Mifflin Preprimer 3, story 1: The Biggest One in the Play

Anticipated Unknowns (should be verified by assessment)

1. play	9. teeth
2. surprise	10. lion
3. biggest	11. hide
4. work	12. helping
5. school	13. I'll
6. jump	14. apple
7. green	15. tree
8. frog	

Drill Content

1. come to a *play*	8. *teeth* like a *lion*
2. what a *surprise*	9. to *hide*
3. the *biggest* one	10. she is *helping*
4. come to *work*	11. *I'll* tell you
5. Come to *school*	12. a big *apple*
6. will not *jump*	13. a big *tree*
7. *green* like a *frog*	

Report No. 3

Dear Paula,

I am writing this letter to summarize our efforts to improve Carlos' reading skills.

After our initial interview on February 26th, we established the following referral questions.

1. Why does Carlos have difficulty putting the sounds of words together?
2. Why are his word-recognition skills inconsistent; that is, why can he read a word in the story correctly and not be able to read the same word later on in the story?
3. How can Carlos establish a more positive attitude toward reading?

The following is a detailed presentation of the results of Carlos's reading assessment. The first question to be answered is, why does he have difficulty putting words together when he knows the beginning, middle, and ending sounds? He almost always correctly reads the initial consonant of an unknown word. He often confuses b and d, g and q, p and q, and does not know the l and x sounds. The only initial blends he can read are br, sp, st, and pr. Usually, especially when prompted to do so, he will correctly read the ending consonant sound. He is not putting the word together because he does not know the vowel sounds. Not once on the Spache Supplementary Phonics Inventory was he able to demonstrate knowledge of long or short vowel sounds. To illustrate my point, here are some examples of his reading errors. He said book for bike, rids for rides, and gun for green. So you see that he generally gets the beginning and ending sounds, then guesses the middle vowel sound. When provided with the correct vowel sounds, he has no difficulty blending. With knowledge of the sounds contained in the word, he was able to successfully blend one-syllable real and nonsense words.

I will now address his inconsistent word recognition. As you so aptly pointed out in our initial interview, Carlos relies very heavily on both story and picture context when reading. In one of the reading lessons I observed, he often confused the words "Mother" and "Mary." And sometimes he read the words correctly. When the story read "Here is Mary," he could read "Mary" correctly because there was a picture of Mary directly underneath the sentence. In our work together he did this type of thing many times. This illustrates the point that he may read a word correctly when the context helps him out, but read the same word incorrectly when context clues are poor or not available to him. Further, encouraging him to utilize context clues during a reading lesson is not a useful strategy. He is a youngster who is so good at context reading that he generally does utilize all the context clues that exist. Therefore, encouraging further use of clues is useless because he has already utilized all the clues available to him. And as we saw, teacher encouragement to use context clues was the teacher activity that set off the most disruptive behavior, because he was being asked to do something he had already done.

Now we come to the third referral question, how can Carlos establish a more positive attitude toward reading? We need to break his cycle of failure by providing him with as successful a reading experience as possible. By setting him up for success, he will come to receive positive social and self reinforcement which will make reading a more positive experience. We have analyzed his learning style to determine under what conditions he can best achieve success. Carlos works best when he is provided with the objective of the lesson. For example, he needs to know, before teaching begins, that he is going to learn a certain sound, or is going to be asked to read a certain number of words. The objective provides a base from which he knows what to expect, and what is expected of him. For now, he can only handle a small amount of material that offers little challenge. This challenge must be in proportion to what he already knows. For example, he can successfully learn a new sound and read words with that sound when only 15% of the material is unknown to him. That is, in each lesson only 15% of the material should be new and previously unknown to the child. As he progresses in skill, more challenge can be offered, but the challenge must always be in proportion to his abilities. Also he requires extended practice in a skill, which can be achieved through frequent and short (perhaps 15 minutes of instruction) teaching sessions. The goal here is to present him with a small quantity of material and ensure relative success. Thus, he will learn in small increments, receive positive rewards, and eventually attain a more positive attitude toward reading.

At this point, I believe that I have addressed the three referral questions. In our work with Carlos we have ascertained more information that will be of value in developing a reading program for him. For instructional purposes, that is, the level at which new information can be provided, he should be placed on Preprimer Level 3 of the Harris-Clark reading series. I will soon discuss methods for adjusting this material for him.

When attempting to read silently, he meets too many unknowns to read without effort. Therefore, he becomes frustrated and tends to engage in disruptive behavior. In time, with continuous assessment and modification of the material for his instructional level, silent reading can be introduced.

Listening comprehension is excellent. He was able to answer main idea and detail questions up to Level 11 of the Harris-Clark series, and respond to inference and vocabulary questions at Level 10. This reflects the fact that through instruction which matches the child's abilities to the task demands, he can be raised to a fourth grade reading level. He enjoyed being read to, and was thrilled with his success as we proceeded from book to book while assessing listening comprehension.

The following are Carlos' known and unknown phonics skills:

Knowns	Unknowns
1. Can letter name: a,c,e,f,h,i,j,k,l,m,n,o, r,s,t,u,v,w,x,y,z	Reverses letter names: b-d,g-q,q-p
2. Initial consonant from visual stimuli: s,n,j,f,h,m,p,r,t,y,w,z,v	Confuses b-d,q-g,p-q
3. Consonant blends and digraph: br, sp, st, pr	cl, tr, ch, sh, gr, th, wh, pl, dr, ck, fl, bl, sm, sw, gl, st, sn, sk, fr, cr
4.	All long and short vowels
5.	All syllabication skills

Recommendations

Carlos will begin at the Level 3 reader. However, we are going to control for difficulty. You and I will assess knowns and unknowns, then prepare transitional stories and drill activities for the first story, "Who Rides." For now, the margin of challenge (challenge = hesitants + unknowns) for each transitional activity will be 15%. We will utilize the sandwich technique, by providing 2 or 3 knowns for each unknown. Transitional stories will be prepared from approximately 25 words of text. However, adjustments will be made as he progresses in skill, with the 15% unknown to 85% known ratio still maintained. After transitional activities, he should achieve almost 100% word recognition when placed on the basal reader. Comprehension questions for the reader will be presented orally and responses expressed orally, since this is the mode of expression he finds most comfortable. After completing transition activities and the story "Who Rides," you will proceed with the same assessment, transitional activities, basal-reader system for the remaining stories. Throughout this process we must keep in mind that progress may be slow, but it reflects his present rate of acquistion. What is most important is that we are providing him with a successful reading experience.

Carlos needs to overlearn material, which is accomplished through extended practice. New words, even after becoming "knowns," require consistent review. You will be responsible for placing all unknown words on 3 x 5 index cards. After the word becomes a "known" it will be given to him to place in a word box. Each afternoon Nancy, the class aide, will review these words with Carlos by presenting the cards one by one. If she gets a known response, the card will be given a √, a hesitant response will be given an o, and an unknown response will be given an x. Every time the word is reviewed, the status is checked again. Each word is presented until it gets 3 checks, then it is considered a "definite known" for the word pool for transitional stories and to illustrate his growth. Since he loves to compete with himself, the building of a pool of "definite knowns" will serve as reinforcing for him.

We need to encourage him to utilize word-analysis skills more. As these skills improve he will tend to use them more. For now, he needs to be prompted to blend and be positively reinforced for doing so. When he meets an unknown word and you believe that he does know the sounds, you will say, "Blend." If he does not know even one of the sounds, he should be supplied the word. Carlos responds well to social reinforcement. A simple "Good", or "Nice Work!" should be given after a blending attempt. Further, he should be discouraged from wild guessing. To accomplish this, reinforcement should be withheld when he guesses. When he comes upon an unknown word and guesses, he will be told, "You are guessing." Without reinforcement guessing should fade in time. If he utilizes word analysis, he will be given an appropriate reinforcer, whether he reads the word correctly or not. In this way recognition will become more consistent.

Carlos will begin an intensive individualized phonics program that concentrates on vowel sounds. One previously unknown sound will be taught at a time (see chart for unknowns). Lessons will be short, no more than 15 minutes. Again, he will never be exposed to more than 15% challenge. For now, vowels will be written in a color to differentiate them from consonants. As he becomes more proficient, the color can be faded. Carlos requires extended practice, so that much of the instructional material will have to be teacher-made. One sound should be taught until he has learned that sound, and then the sound should be overlearned through constant drill and practice. Whenever possible, words that Carlos is asked to read with the new sound should come from vocabulary within his basal reader. Again this will be a slow process of mini-lessons and drill. You will take responsibility for establishing the lessons and drill, but once the program is ongoing, Nancy will take over the drill component.

In June we will meet again to assess Carlos' skills as compared to the entry-level skills he possessed. We can readminister the Consonant Sounds and Vowels Sounds subtests from the Spache, and see how large his pile of "definite knowns" has grown.

Thank you for your cooperation and letting me come into your classroom. Be positive, and good luck.

Yours when needed,

Flo

Report No. 4

Dear Judy,

I am writing this letter to summarize our efforts to improve Beth's math skills.

After the second interview in which additional clarification occurred, the following referral questions were established:

1. Does Beth understand the basic concepts behind addition and subtraction?
2. Why does Beth continue to have difficulty recalling from memory basic addition and subtraction facts?

The results of the math assessment revealed the following information. The first area I will address deals with her mastery of basic math concepts. In order for us to understand whether or not she is mastering concepts in general and specifically those basic concepts considered necessary for achievement in the first years of school, I administered the Boehm Test of Basic Concepts. Her total score was 41-46, which places her in approximately the 70th percentile when compared with other second graders also in the low socioeconomic group. One of the concepts Beth missed measured quantitative knowledge. The concept involved equality and she was to put an X on the pictures that had an equal number of stars. She stated that she didn't know what equal meant and made an incorrect response. After the test was completed, I explained the meaning of equal and gave her a few examples to do to see if she then understood its meaning. She did all the extra examples correctly and seemed to have no problem with the concept.

I then began to probe further her knowledge of those math concepts necessary for understanding the processes of addition and subtraction. She had no difficulty matching sets in one-to-one correspondence. She seems to understand and can appropriately use the greater than and less than symbols. Terms such as most, least, few, largest, and smallest are parts of the language of sets that she understands. She demonstrated knowledge of addition and subtraction through the use of manipulatives. For example, when given 12 poker chips and asked to take away 6 chips, she was able to do so and give the correct answer. Problems were given in addition as well as subtraction and Beth had no difficulty with these tasks. Errors in operations were noted on samples of her written work as well as written assessment data. Frequently Beth would add when she was supposed to subtract. However, when she was made to focus on the incorrect responses she made, she immediately recognized that she performed the wrong operation. She may select addition over subtraction at times because she is more comfortable with the former operation. Her errors in operations seem to be more in the nature of performance rather than an inability to correctly interpret the plus and minus symbols.

The results of my assessment show that Beth does understand the basic concepts behind addition and subtraction. However, she seems at times to become confused about the language used and needs to have words carefully defined for her followed by clear examples. She also seems to be a youngster who is unsure of herself and needs to be given immediate feedback on her performance. Her uncertainty about her performance and her tendency at times to not focus carefully enough on a specific task, are contributing factors to the errors she makes.

I will now focus my attention on Beth's difficulty in recalling from memory basic addition and subtraction facts. Since she displayed knowledge of the algorithms in addition and subtraction involving 2 digits, with and without regrouping, I needed to go back to the basic addition and subtraction facts of sums 18 and less. I gave her 100 addition facts and 100 subtraction facts to compute on paper. She was instructed not to use her fingers or to count in her head. Any facts she did not know she was to leave unanswered. The results show that she knows all of her addition facts with sums of 6 or less, and the majority of the facts she didn't know involved sums of 14 or more. Of the 100 addition facts performed, she made errors on 13 of them. Subtraction facts proved to be much harder for her. She left unanswered 33, and answered 5 incorrectly. Of those 38 subtraction facts, 33 involved subtracting a one-digit number (0-9) from sums of 11 through 18. Only 5 involved subtracting from sums of 10 or less. It seems that her strategy of counting with her fingers never afforded her help in subtracting from sums of 11 or more. She never really got to learn these facts in order to incorporate them into her memory bank.

It seems that Beth is able to recall from memory most of her addition facts and some of her subtraction facts. She, however, at this point, appears to be overwhelmed by the many facts she does not know, especially in subtraction. Therefore these unknown facts much be retaught with only a few being introduced at one time.

Now that I have addressed the two referral questions, I would like to make some additional comments. It seems that Beth's math difficulties can be resolved with the appropriate instructional strategies and an awareness of her learning style. In working with Beth I found she responded very quickly to explanations followed by concrete examples applied to real life situations. This is especially true when concepts were presented to her. Although she still seems to be unsure of herself, nevertheless she is gaining confidence. Once she relaxes in a situation, she becomes a friendly and eager participant to learn. She responds very well to one-to-one instruction and positive reinforcement. She needs to be actively involved in the learning process in order to sustain her interest. Beth appears to have all the prerequisite skills needed to add and subtract. She is therefore ready to begin learning all the unknown facts and develop fluency in the known facts.

The following are Beth's unknown addition and subtraction facts.

Addition Facts—Sums 18 or Less

Unknowns

3 + 4, 3 + 9, 4 + 5, 5 + 6, 5 + 7, 5 + 9,
6 + 7, 6 + 8, 6 + 9, 7 + 8, 7 + 9, 8 + 9,
9 + 9.

Subtraction Facts—Sums 18 or Less

Unknowns

18 - 9, 17 - 9, 16 - 9, 16 - 8, 16 - 7,
15 - 9, 15 - 8, 15 - 7, 15 - 6, 14 - 9,
14 - 8, 14 - 7, 14 - 6, 14 - 5, 13 - 9,
13 - 8, 13 - 7, 13 - 6, 13 - 5, 13 - 4,
12 - 9, 12 - 8, 12 - 7, 12 - 6, 12 - 5,
12 - 4, 12 - 3, 11 - 8, 11 - 7, 11 - 6,
11 - 5, 11 - 4, 11 - 3, 10 - 8, 10 - 7,
10 - 6, 9 - 7, 8 - 5.

Recommendations

From the beginning we have agreed that you will involve Beth in the evaluation. She will help set the goals of instruction. She should have the goals of instruction clearly in her mind. You will take care to ensure that Beth knows where she is headed ("I'll be able to add and subtract from memory and get the right answers").

Beth needs to strengthen her self-image. You have provided a warm and supportive environment for her. Since she has met failure, it's very important for her to know that she is a valued person and that she is eventually capable of learning all of her addition and subtraction facts from memory and with automaticity. Continue providing Beth with reassurance.

Beth's instruction is to be structured in small steps. Drill the unknown facts through the use of flashcards, number-line, and manipulatives. In addition, have her simultaneously say and write each unknown addition fact being drilled that day. Facts will be written both horizontally and vertically. Following 15 minutes of drill give her a prepared practice sheet to do. No more than 15% of the problems should be unknown. These unknowns should be sandwiched between the knowns. Twenty facts comprising 17 knowns and 3 unknowns will be given in which she is required to write the answers from memory. Circle all the unknowns as a cue for her. Plus and minus signs will be emphasized and distinguished through color coding whenever both operations are presented in the same practice sheet. Eventually use color coding only periodically and gradually work towards phasing out color-coding cues entirely. An unknown fact must be presented and answered correctly three days in a row in order for it to become a definite known.

You will provide Beth with the means to observe her progress. Allow her to chart her progress daily. On a sheet of paper, list all the unknown facts that she is going to learn. When an unknown fact becomes a known fact (after 3 days of correct responding), Beth will place a star next to the learned fact. In the process of mastering these facts, each day when she answers an unknown fact correctly, she will enter a check mark in a column next to the corresponding fact. On the top of each column where check marks are being entered, you will have recorded the dates. Again as soon as a fact receives three check marks in a row, the fact then becomes a definite known fact and a star placed next to the fact.

You will see to it that she receives immediate feedback on drill and practice work. Provide her also with instructional materials that include self-checking devices. You will furnish Beth with flashcards for all the unknown facts. Include flashcards for known facts as well. On each flashcard the fact will be presented on both sides. On one side the answer will also be included. Beth will practice using them in the following way:

1. First look at the flashcard on the answer side (for example let's say 4 + 9 = 13. Read the whole thing aloud.
2. Then close your eyes and recite it several times.
3. Next go on to the next two or three cards doing the same thing. (Be sure you don't try to work on too many at one time).
4. Then turn the cards over to the side without the answers. Read the problem aloud and try to "hear" the answer. Then say it.
5. Turn the card over and check it. If you didn't get the answer fix it quickly by reading the whole thing, problem and answer, over several times.

You will give Beth short timed drills periodically to help speed up her response time. Facts included on a timed drill should only be those that she has mastered. Unknowns should never be included.

Whenever possible, Beth should be permitted to select a game or activity from materials which are available that will help reinforce math facts. Dominoes, cards, and dice are all effective concrete visual aids which can be used in games and sustain interest. Together we will plan activities and games for her, utilizing the aforementioned materials. Game activities and manipulatives can also be utilized to strengthen acquired concepts and explore new ones.

If I may I would like to make some additional comments about Beth. I found that in working with this youngster on numerous occasions, I gained some insight into her needs both academically and emotionally. I found that for Beth, a good support system was and is critical to her school success and self-esteem. I feel that she needs a lot of language-enrichment activities. She lacked knowledge of the meanings of many common words. It seems this is due primarily to the lack of exposure. She typifies the youngster who is missing basic language skills she is presumed to have. She brings home, loud and clear, the message of the Boehm. Basic knowledge of the meaning of certain words is essential for success in school. Beth presents herself in the beginning as a quiet and shy girl. However, once she relaxes, she enjoys talking, and she needs to be given an opportunity and even encouraged to verbalize her thoughts more often. I believe that with a good language-development program and exposure to a variety of enriching experiences, the learning process will become easier and more fruitful for Beth. If you like I will be more than glad to assist you in developing a good language program for Beth.

In the middle of June we will meet again to assess her skills in recalling her facts from memory. I will readminister the 100 addition and subtraction facts to see how many unknowns have now become knowns.

Thank you very much for your cooperative effort. I hope I have provided you with some useful information. It was a pleasure to work with such a dedicated and caring teacher. You will make a difference!

Sincerely yours,

Diana

Report No. 5

Dear Karen,

I am writing to you today in order to review our case regarding Randy, but first, I would like to thank you for allowing me to consult with you about her. We have accomplished a great deal over the past two months both in the area of understanding Randy and in the area of some techniques to help her achieve on a more independent basis.

When we initially began our work together, we had to define what it was we wanted to accomplish. At the onset, you felt that while you had been successful in dealing with Randy, in order to ensure her future success, she would have to learn how to become more independent of you.

Our first assumption about the difficulty Randy was experiencing was based upon her wearing thick glasses. We suspected that she might possibly be visually impaired in a serious way, given her appearance. Upon investigation, we learned that her eyesight with her glasses was corrected to 20/30. This would mean that with her glasses, she was not visually impaired in a serious way which would affect her work in class.

At this point, we decided to look at the skills she had and the ones she did not have. This, we decided, would give us a clearer picture as to why Randy was unable to work more independently in your class. We discovered that she did have some difficulties. These included:

1. Difficulty copying from far to nearpoint (blackboard to page)
2. Difficulty decoding some of the business terms used in the text
3. Difficulty copying numbers into columns
4. Difficulty completing the standard tests given for each unit which are published with the series
5. Difficulty doing any tasks requiring her to read information but very capable in ability to do the practical work in record keeping

As we could see, she was successful as long as you were working with her, but as soon as she was left on her own, it became too difficult for her to follow. The only thing it appeared that she was able to do adequately was the practical work in record keeping. We surmised that because she did not necessarily have to read in order to do the practical work, she was successful at it, even though copying numbers in the columns and words on lines did present some problems for her on occasion. In the long-run, however, we were aware of the fact that as the work became more difficult, she would be confronted with more problems. It was our task to see that she could accomplish the material in a manner which would ensure her success in the class.

In order to assist Randy in copying her numbers and words in the right places on the forms, you had her use a marker. This seemed almost immediately to correct the problem of her having to call upon you to make sure that she had copied correctly.

Her reading of the business terms and the problem of her not being able to pass any of the standard tests had to be approached in a different manner. I suggested that you present Randy with a list of the words utilized in each unit. As it turned out, a list was contained at the end of each unit in the chapter review. You had her learn these words at sight (sight words) so that she could become familiar with them. You found that she could connect meaning to many of the words without any trouble (e.g., sales receipt) but because she could not read them, she could not define them. The other words she did not know she would have to define by writing the definition from the glossary and then discussing with you so that you would be sure she knew them. The fact that she could look up the words in the glossary and copy them kept her doing more independent work, thus freeing you to work with others in the class. It also seemed to make her feel productive and not frustrated. She therefore did not have as many outbursts of loud talking and demanding type of behavior.

Modifying Randy's testing situation really meant having to make the most change. Since she was so successful at the practical work, we decided to have her prove that she knew that information by doing the practical parts of the test, and then we geared the more conceptual parts of the test toward the terms she had learned in the unit by having her define them through matching the correct term with its definition. Because she had used the glossary definitions and had gone over them with you, and because you used these definitions word for word on your test, she was able to recognize and read them with a fairly steady success rate.

Randy still has many obstacles to overcome while she tries to get through high school. Because both she and her family have refused any remedial help, she will need to learn through a modified curriculum approach. She is lucky to have had a teacher like you who was willing to help her in this manner. I am pleased that she will also be taking a course with you next year as well and I would be very happy to work with you in helping her again so that she may progress to an even better level.

Once again, thank you for working with me and I hope that we can continue in the fall.

Sincerely yours,

Joseph

Chapter 10

INSTRUCTIONAL CONSULTATION
A Final Word

Person who knows it all
has lot to learn
—Chinese fortune cookie

Over the past several years, increasingly insistent voices have been raised regarding the need to change how we should respond to children who are experiencing school learning problems. The dysfunctional special-education and regular educational systems have been described in detail (e.g., Anderson et al., 1985; National Commission on Excellence in Education, 1983; National Association of School Psychologists (NASP), 1985; Reynolds & Wang, 1983; Wang, Reynolds, & Walberg, 1986; Ysseldyke et al., 1984). The conflict in San Francisco over how to assess minority children for special-education placement has led that district to ban the use of intelligence tests for special-education classification and to an intense controversy over how to provide valid assessments which will determine instructional needs rather than IQ scores (Cordes, 1986).

One of the consistent themes in this litany has been the need for a transformation in the way services are delivered to children currently seen as "mildly handicapped," moving from categorization and labeling of these children to systems in which:

> instead, a child's situation would be identified as problematic only when he or she obviously was not learning or behaving in a manner that leads to personal success in the schools. The major identification procedures would be curriculum based and the remedies would likewise be in the curriculum realm, changing the instructional program and educational procedures to meet individual

217

needs. . . . This would mean more consultation to enhance mainstream school operations and less concentration on "referred" students who are on track for displacement to special classes and centers. . . . To create environments in which effective instruction and learning are the key concerns and activities of the school . . . means helping to apply all that is known about the improvement of instruction. (Ysseldyke et al., 1984, p.9)

Recognizing that it is not a benign act to label a child as handicapped, NASP also called, in very similar terms, for a transformation. The NASP position statement, "Advocacy for Appropriate Educational Services for All Children"(1985), also focuses on the need for schools to assume responsibility for a broader range of children in the mainstream, to provide instructional options and necessary support services within the general education system, to "evaluate the match between the learner and his or her educational environment, assessing the compatibility of curriculum and system as they interact with the child, rather than relying on the deficit-based model which places the blame for failure within the child" (p. 2). The advocacy paper also proposes alternative service-delivery models, ones that allow for increased support and retraining for all school personnel so that they can work effectively to provide services to a broader range of children with special needs within regular education.

What are the alternatives currently in place? Dawson (1986) captures the concern of many in school psychology in her comment that "while many school psychologists agree that "there must be a better way," we often have a hard time imagining other ways of doing things. Is it *really* possible to meet the needs of handicapped children without labeling them and without segregating them from their peers?" She goes on to describe a school setting based on the Adaptive Learning Environments Model (ALEM) (Wang, Gennari, & Waxman, 1985), in which the entire school functions on the basis of the principles that chapters 6 and 7 describe. Unfortunately, however, she describes the school psychologist in this system as continuing to perform a traditional evaluation role. She suggests that, with more time (the school psychologist is there only once a week to serve 1000 children), the role of the school psychologist could be broadened to include CBA and instructional consultation.

Instructional consultation, as it has been described here, is an alternative delivery system that is directed towards implementing these goals. It incorporates a broad research base in psychology and education, placing school psychologists and other educational specialists into a different stance regarding teachers and children with special needs. However, no claim is made that it will be easy to shift toward this consultation model. Making change is never easy, as has been stated over and over here and elsewhere. It is, in fact, no easier for school psychologists than it is for teachers to change their professional behavior. But it is time to begin to carry forth the transformation envisioned in the Blueprint for Training and Practice (Ysseldyke et al., 1984) and in the "Advocacy Paper" of NASP (1985). The model described in this book provides one alternative to current practice.

ISSUES IN IMPLEMENTATION
OF INSTRUCTIONAL CONSULTATION

Several questions remain regarding the implementation of an IC model. These include: (1) Are there legal and political issues that would facilitate or impede the use of this delivery system for services, given the highly legalistic structure of special education in today's schools? (2) How acceptable is instructional consultation to school psychologists, special educators, social workers, teachers, principals, and parents? (3) What training issues are involved? (4) What research supports this delivery system and what still needs to be done to develop an empirical base? Although only brief answers will be provided here, instructional consultants will need to develop clear responses to these questions if instructional consultation is not to become only another fad in the practice of school psychology and the life of the schools, or as one school psychologist put it, a mini skirt instead of a tweed suit.

Political and Legal Issues

First, there are legal questions. Does consultation violate any of the principles of P.L. 94-142? A resounding "No!" came from Galagan (1985), who, as Director of Legal Services, Advocacy Center for the Elderly and Disabled, and a lawyer has been extensively involved in special-education litigation. Writing for an issue of *Exceptional Children* devoted to curriculum-based assessment, he expounds on "the legal imperative for incorporating and implementing curriculum-based assessment measures in special-education evaluation systems" (p. 289) and concludes that there is "little, if any, evidence for the continued use of psychometric and projective instruments . . . that are of little instructional use" (p. 297). He presented case evidence to support his conclusions. For example,

> *Frederick v. Thomas* (419 F. Supp. 960 [E.D. Penn. 1976], aff'd 557F.2d 373 [CA 3 1977]) was one of the first cases to examine special-education evaluation practices.
> *Frederick v. Thomas* demonstrates in classic terms that ungoverned teacher-referral practices subject school systems to charges of . . . overidentification and misclassification of nonhandicapped students. . . . It also manifests the legal imperative for implementing viable prereferral screening procedures to isolate students who exhibit characteristics consonant with genuine handicapping conditions.

Curriculum-based assessment (CBA) techniques would provide effective screening data and engender more appropriate referrals. Initially their use would interdict the surreal view that if a student is referred there is an obvious reason to believe that he or she is handicapped and needs to be tested . . . (pp. 290-291).

Alpert and Trachtman (1980) also insisted that consultation prior to referral does not violate the intent of the special education laws and regulations, and that, in fact, PL 94-142 could be interpreted as a call for consulation services.

For those who need the specific changes in regulations or the imprint of the law itself to provide the mandate, that process seems also to be underway. Madeleine Wills (1986, November), the Assistant Secretary of Education for the Office of Special Education and Rehabilitation Services, set forth a federal initiative to challenge special educators "to use their knowledge and expertise to support regular education in educating children with learning problems" (p. 20). She made it clear that the basic issue for children with learning problems is not "finding something to call them so we can put money in a pot with a label on it" but rather "providing an educational program that will allow them to learn better" (p. 22).

At the state level, New Jersey (New Jersey State Department of Education, 1986), for example, is in the process of modifying its state regulations regarding the system for providing special education programs and services. The new plan would:

- Reduce the number of pupils who must be labeled "handicapped" in order to receive state-funded remedial programs by providing them with appropriate assistance through the general or regular educational programs offered by local school districts;
- Establish a school resource committee in each school building to assist pupils with educational difficulties by using the resources available within the general education program;
- Focus pupil evaluation procedures on instructional needs rather than on diagnostic categories or classifications;
- Emphasize the role of the child-study team in providing services to the general education population and programs;
- Increase both regular and special-education teacher staff competence through improved in-service and preservice. (pp. 1-2)

Clearly, well-developed instructional consultation skills will position the school psychologist to take part in a change that is being legally as well as professionally mandated.

Acceptability

A second question is whether school personnel accept IC as a service delivery model. In the discussion in chapter 8, the point is made that many of the issues around acceptability of instructional interventions in the classroom by teachers remain unresolved. There is a need for additional research to find the components of consultation that will most effectively allow for the classroom-based consultant to support change in the specific areas involved.

The issue of acceptability is not for teachers in regular education alone, however. Many school psychologists are resistant to moving into a new way of delivering their expertise. Comfort with testing and the traditional ways of delivering services is hard to abandon for the "messiness", as one school psychologist put it, of curriculum-based assessment. Special educators are equally reluctant to accept consultation rather than diagnosis and placement, and have asked whether the movement away from special-education placement means the diminishing of their field and, not least, the lessening of the number of jobs in special education. It is not enough to build a better mousetrap. It is equally important to help those involved in the change system become part of the new process.

Training

A third issue, related to that of acceptability, involves dissemination of the knowledge base underlying the model. Schon (1983) described the "unprecedented requirement for adaptability" that confronts the professional today: "Even if professional knowledge were to catch up with the new demands of professional practice, the improvement in professional performance would be transitory. The situations of practice are inherently unstable . . ." (p. 15).

But without their own in-depth understanding and comfort with curriculum-based assessment and effective classroom teaching and management techniques, it will be difficult for consultants to introduce new ideas into the consultation process. Special-education teachers, school psychologists, and others involved in providing assistance to classroom teachers, as well as the classroom teachers themselves, must receive preservice and in-service training in the knowledge base that exists.

That process is just beginning. How to have an impact on the training is a central issue beyond the scope of this book, but one that is central to the success of instructional consultation. It is difficult to find practice settings in which students can observe and practice instructional consultation under supervision. This problem is critical, especially given the recent research of Shapiro and Lentz (1985) on behavior-modification techniques, which points to the necessity for supervised practice. They found that:

those subjects who received direct supervision in given . . . procedures are much more likely to use the techniques than those who are exposed through course work or reading along. This suggests that graduate training in school psychology needs to place increased emphasis on applying behavioral techniques if they are to be available for use by school psychologists. . . . Because the relationship between supervision and use is so strong, school psychologists in training should be given direct supervision in as many techniques as possible to ensure adequate implementation of the range of procedures available as intervention strategies. (p. 334)

Many students receive little more than a course in consultation, and even less training in instructional psychology. Clearly, the transformation envisioned by the "Blueprint" document (Ysseldyke et al., 1984) will require extensive change in training programs. Perhaps postdoctoral work in instructional consultation or specialization in this model at the doctoral level may provide a short-term alternative. But a vision of the school psychologist as expert in the area of helping schools improve the academic performance of all children seems a valuable one to pursue for the future (Bardon, 1983).

Moreover, even those already trained continually need to update their knowledge and skills. The knowledge base presented in this text is only a small part of the total information on instruction and management. Shulman (1986), in examining the research on teaching that has accrued between the second *Handbook of Research on Teaching* and the third, states:

Findings have proliferated. Many have been replicated and extended. Policymakers and practitioners alike take the research seriously and apply its results to their activities. No contemporary field of applied social science research has attracted the range and diversity of disciplinary efforts in the pursuit of its question as has research on teaching. . . . The publication of this edition finds research on teaching in a state of admirable vigor and promising progress. . . . Research on teaching promises to lead to a deeper theoretical understanding of teaching, a continuing documentation of its many forms and functions, and the likelihood of more enlightened future approaches to the entire teaching enterprise. (p. 33)

The instructional consultant who has a firm grasp of the information presented in this book still has a wide field left to explore for possible strategies to assess and intervene to promote excellence, to help each child achieve closer to the maximum of which he or she is capable. Yet time and support for training are rarely available as part of the school's resources, and even more rarely do school-based professionals invest on their own in intensive life-long professional development.

Research

Another agenda is the need for research on instructional consultation, although the various components of the model are based on research already completed. For example, the issue of *Exceptional Children* in November 1985, provides some of the research foundations for CBA. Also, evaluation is easily built into examining the effectiveness of instructional consultation on individual cases, using single case-study methodology. However, more large scale research on the model as a whole has not been conducted. How effective is consultation for improving academic achievement of the consultee's client? Are there ways to improve the acceptability of instructional consultation as a specific innovation?

The effect of prereferral consultation services on student achievement outcomes has been demonstrated by Dickinson and Adcox (1984), who found that children could be helped to achieve behavioral and academic objectives in a relatively short period of time through a consultation program. A single case study comparing the traditional psycho-educational model with the instructional-consultation model is presented by Matalon (1987) in a case report on a fourth grade child who received services in reverse of the usual order. Liza was referred by her school (which did not have psychological services at that point) to a psycho-educational clinic for reading problems and received a traditional evaluation. The assessment resulted in a diagnosis of specific language disabilities, and two recommendations: (1) that the school and parents find a tutor to teach her reading utilizing the phonic approach, as her disability precluded a sight-word approach; and (2) that for reading practice she would take home the second grade-level book to read at home to her brother, as she had scored at the second grade on a standardized reading test. Because of a unique set of circumstances, the same school psychology student who did the initial assessment was later assigned to Liza's school for consultation services. She discovered that the school and parents did not find a tutor, and time and resource constraints had led to the second recommendation not being implemented. Moreover, the child was doing worse than before. Having learned she had a learning disability, she lost motivation and was unwilling to put forth any effort in or outside of the classroom.

The classroom teacher was interested in working with the psychologist in a collaborative consultation mode. The following excerpt is taken from the report of the psychologist to the teacher, and demonstrates the effectiveness of the instructional consultation in comparison to the more traditional model in which the child was labeled and a series of recommendations were sent to the teacher to implement without her input into the program or follow-up. Further, the use of the instructional consultation delivery system led to two other valuable outcomes. The teacher, having found value in the approach used in treating the reading problem asked for information about how to do CBA in math. Second, as the report shows, another child in the class who was experiencing a reading problem was involved with Liza in the reading program. By developing an in-class instructional intervention, more than one child benefited from the services of the school psychologist.

These are the procedures we undertook to apply CBA to Liza's academic program:

In order for Liza to learn on her instructional level, we had to assess her entry reading level. We knew that the third grade book was too hard for her. Thus, I assessed her instructional level by creating an informal reading inventory with the 1st, 2nd, and 3rd grade readers. The results showed that her entry level was at the 2nd grade reader.

The following program was established and implemented: You took each story of the reader (level 2.2), starting with the first story, and copied the words on 3 x 5 index cards. You presented these cards to Liza one by one in order to assess Known, Hesitants, and Unknowns, during the time you spend with her reading group (which includes only Liza and Carlos, who have the same reading level and would both be part of the CBA academic program).

This information you passed to the volunteer, whom you taught to prepare drill exercises. The volunteer prepared these exercises using a margin of challenge of 20% Unknown and Hesitant words with the "sandwich" technique. That means that in her lessons Liza was going to have, for example, 2 words that she cannot read together with 8 words she knows how to read, and that these Unknown words are going to be presented in between Known words. Further practice on these words was done at the end of the day, when Liza was shown the flashcards one by one. If she knew the word the card was marked with a K, if she was hesitant the card was marked with an H, and if she did not know the word the card was marked with a U. Every time a word is reviewed, the status is checked again. This practice was administered by one of Liza's peers (a perfect match!). Once all the words in the story were known, the actual reading of the story was done with you during the reading-group time.

Although setting up this program required careful planning in order to structure it into the classroom schedule, and some parts of it were done as trial-and-error (you remember that one volunteer was not appropriate, and the second volunteer, although very good, was not communicating with you on her progress), we started seeing concrete results very soon. In our last telephone conversation you told me that you started the *4th* story of the 2nd grade reader! This progress of Liza in a month or so was not achieved during a whole academic year or more (remember that she has been failing to read at the 3rd grade reading level since 3rd grade). At this point we know that CBA is the right academic program for Liza—she is progressing in her reading with big steps! Matalon, (1986)

Along with outcome studies, there is a need for studies of the process of instructional consultation. Research is now ongoing to study the communication interactions between consultant and teachers in referral interviews, comparing team interviews with those of individual consultants (e.g., Hanson, Kuralt, & Rosenfield, 1987).

Much still needs to be done with respect to examining aptitude-treatment interaction effects of classroom-based interventions with different types of learners (e.g., Schmidt, 1985), as well as the problems teachers face in providing individualized instruction. Doyle (1985) raised some of these questions:

> The central question in adaptive instruction shifts from "How can instruction be made more adaptable?" to "When is adaptation necessary and what are its consequences?" This latter question would seem to be important for the development of knowledge about adapting instruction and for understanding what happens when programs of adaptive instruction are implemented in schools. (p. 101)

Implementing individualized or adaptive programs is difficult and expensive. For example, Doyle (1985) presented the case that "variations in the time students need to learn are quite problematic for teachers under classroom conditions" (p. 94), and may in some cases be more than an individual teacher can accommodate. We need more research on how to facilitate this process. Opportunities for research on this model are plentiful, and should provide an agenda for field-based research for years to come if the practice of IC is to have a sound empirical base.

CONCLUSION

Much that is written in this book describes the need for change in the schools. The focus, in particular, has been on the need for teachers to change their knowledge, skills, and attitudes about children with learning problems, to broaden both their willingness and their skills with respect to a wider range of learning styles and abilities. But the need for change is not limited to teachers, who are the consultees in instructional consultation. The professional undertaking the role of the consultant is often taking on a new role as well. It requires courage, energy, and commitment to move away from traditional roles, whether it is the testing kit or the self-contained resource room, and into the classroom and the consultant role. Support needs to be provided to the new consultant as well as to the consultee, by peers, trainers, supervisors, and principals.

Instructional consultation is one way to move into a new role with respect to schooling and mildly handicapped children. It is a delivery system that provides more personnel in the schools working towards improved academic performance of students. Consulting in the schools requires both skill in the steps and stages of consultation and knowledge of instruction and learning. Implementing that delivery system presents a challenge for our profession.

Appendix **A**

COMMUNICATION SKILLS

EXERCISE 1: PRACTICING INTERVIEW RESPONSES

Respond to the following statements. Refer back to the text if you are uncertain what is being requested. Share your responses with a colleague for validation.

The Initial Interview: Communication Strategies*

Practicing Communication Responses

1. You begin with a statement about the purpose of the initial interview. The teacher has referred a 10-year-old third grade student to you. She has indicated that her concern is about his academic progress. Write your opening statement:

2. Fill in your response to the teacher in the place indicated, using the type of response requested; if no specific response type is requested, select the most appropriate category:

    T: Okay, first of all, you know that I am the Resource Room teacher, so I only see John for one hour at a time each day.
    C: Yes.

---

*From Rosenfield et al. (1985)

227

T: The biggest problem that I can see is that there just doesn't seem to be any carryover from what goes on in here and what takes place in the regular classroom. Of course, the classroom work is really the main determinant of what happens to John in terms of passing or failing.

C: (Paraphrase)

T: Yes, that's a major problem. I've been working with John for two years now. Last year, we spent practically the whole year working on the short vowel sounds, which I thought had been completed. But then, when John came back this year, and I gave him a review, he didn't know them again. When he is back in the classroom, and reading out of a different book in there, he does not know the sounds.

C: (Clarifying Question)

In this interview, a teacher has referred a six-year-old first grader with behavior and learning problems. This segment is about five minutes into the interview.

T: And in a way, even though he's only six, he seems a lot more immature than the other children, in a comparison based on the class.

C:

T: Well . . . he's umm, he's so small he's like a baby, when at times he behaves like a baby. When he doesn't get my attention right away, he pouts, and puts his head down. Just behavior like that. Whereas a lot of the other children do want my attention immediately, but they realize there are certain circumstances where there's only one of me. Whereas he doesn't seem to realize that fact.

C: (Perception Check)

In this interview, the school psychologist is conducting a referral interview with the teacher of a second grader whose learning problems the teacher calls "insurmountable":

T: Okay. First, he has trouble with vowel sounds—he can't see that the sound for "a" is *a* and so on. He has a problem with phonics.

C:

T: Well, he has trouble analyzing a word, breaking them up; he has trouble hearing the differences in sounds like *ah* and *eh*. He really doesn't know the sounds. He's like a kid coming brand new into school. He has no decoding skills, if you know what I mean. He can't say what the letters say: he can't do "y," "z," and "v," for example.

C:

T: Well . . . yes. He knows the difference between the sound of "b" and "d." Also he doesn't reverse those two like some kids would. Now I checked his records and he does have slight earaches on occasion—apparently nothing serious—but it's obvious his problem goes beyond that. I checked his WISC-R; I forget his exact scores but he was of average intelligence. His verbal score was lower than his performance score—I did notice that.

C: (Offering Information)

EXERCISE 2: EXAMINING YOUR COMMUNICATION SKILLS

Directions:

1. Make a tape recording of an initial referral interview.
2. Using record sheet (Table A-1), rate each of your responses in one of the categories and mark a tally for each response in the appropriate box. Convert the tallies to percentages.

3. After recording your responses, ask yourself the following questions:

  a. Did I use too many questions, shifting from one area to another without obtaining all of the information needed?

  b. How often did I use paraphrasing and perception checking? In retrospect, did I miss important opportunities to use those categories of responses?

  c. Did I clarify unclear responses? Where else might I have used clarifying responses?

  d. Are there goals I want to set for myself in improving my use of communication skills?

4. Set small goals for yourself, like increasing the number of clarifying responses. You can re-cycle the process, taping additional interviews, until you are satisfied that you are actually using good communication strategies. Periodically taping an interview and analyzing it to determine whether your skills are being maintained at a high level are also recommended.

TABLE A-1
Record Sheet

	Tally	Total	%
1. Requesting Clarification			
2. Paraphrasing			
3. Perception Checking			
4. Active Listening			
5. Asking Focused, Relevant Questions			
6. Offering Information			
7. Examining Child's Work			
8. Asking Irrelevant Questions			
9. Other			

REFERRAL INTERVIEW
TRANSCRIPT

EXERCISE 1:   PRACTICING INTERVIEW RESPONSES

The following transcript is that of an initial referral interview. It presents an opportunity for the reader to analyze both the communication skills used and the content.

1. **Using the format in chapter 3 in the section on Communication, analyze the skills used. Write in your own responses where you think they would improve the interview.**
2. **Generate two referral questions that you think the information provided would support. What additional assessment data would you plan to collect?**

You can check out your conclusions against those of the consultant by turning to the appendix in chapter 9, on report writing, where the outcome of this case, in terms of the final report, is provided in Report no. 1.

AN INITIAL INTERVIEW TRANSCRIPT

Child's Name: Danny   Grade: Second
Date of Interview: 02/03/85

SP: I want to talk to you about Danny and the academic behaviors he has that concern you most in the classroom. Try to focus on when they occur, how often, and what influences them. If we work together we may be able to accomplish this in 20 to 30 minutes. We will be looking at the curriculum, what you are asking the student to do, what the child can do, and where he is failing to do it. So then, tell me about Danny.

T: Well, Danny is great break dancer. He's not too bad in math. Sentence writing he's not too good in, neither is his grammar. Reading is his worst problem. His comprehension and phonic skills are very poor. Some days he knows it . . .

SP: Tell me more about his reading problem.

T: Well, in phonics, for example, some days he could put all three sounds together, other days he knows the sounds and he can't put them together. He doesn't try.

SP: What sounds does Danny get frequently?

T: He knows the beginning and ending sounds. He gets confused with the blends.

SP: What about the vowels?

T: He doesn't know the long and short vowels all the time. He's shaky on the "r" controlled vowel sounds . . . but then he can get one of the hardest phonetic rules.

SP: Which one is that?

T: The rule for adding "ing." Like "top-topping" and "save-saving." But then when it came to how do you pronounce "g" after "e," I'll ask him, and he says, "I don't know."

SP: What do you do when Danny doesn't know a word?

T: We go through the whole thing—beginning sound, vowels, and ending. I tell him to look at the sentence. I ask if there are any clues that could help him.

SP: What does he do then?

T: He doesn't do anything! Sometimes I tell him the word, or the other students in the group say the word.

SP: Umhmm. Reading must be a frustrating situation for him and for you.

T: He doesn't like it.

SP: It must be pretty hard for him. How many students are in his reading group?

T: Danny is in the lowest reading group. There are six kids in the group. We started with the last book of the first grade series. He was left back in the first grade, you would think he'd remember. I have his workbook. We went over these pages, he didn't fix one answer when we went over it. So I told him to do it by himself. He fixes the answers one at a time. He comes up to my desk each time. I tell him he is not finished. I tell him again, look at the ones that are wrong and fix all of them. This is after I've pinpointed what is wrong. Then, Danny moseys on back to his seat and does the same thing.

SP: It's good that you repeat the directions to him. What does he do when you are correcting the workbook pages?

T: He stares around. He has no discipline and a very poor attention span.

SP: Could you explain that to me—poor attention span?

T: I call his name and he pays no attention. He stares out of the window. One day, I just told him that he no longer had to do any work. I sat him in the back. When the kids would give out papers, they would ask, "Should we give Danny one?" I would just say, "I don't know, does he want to do any work?" He got upset and started to do work, but that didn't last.

SP: Sometimes it's difficult to reach a child and we try all sorts of things.

T: I just don't know what's going on with him. Some days he can do most of the work, and other days he's just out of it. His family life doesn't help.

SP: It's a trying situation. You mentioned earlier that he has problems in writing. Can you tell me something about his writing?

T: The things he puts down in sentences do not make any sense. (Shows his notebook.) Here's an example:
"I have end cans of soda."
"I ate a strange for lunch."

He pays no attention to his fill-ins. I read the sentences. All they have to do is remember the word! He doesn't take time to figure things out. He has no motivation. In Englisn today we had past tense. All you had to do is read the sentence and fill in the correct word. He gets five wrong, corrects one and says, "I'm finished." Then I tell him to read his answers. He says, "Oh, no, no," and fixes his answers.

SP: Are they correct when he fixes them again?

T: Sometimes.

SP: I'd like to go over the information you've told me so far. Danny's reading shows he does not know all the sounds, but he's often able to get beginning and ending sounds. Vowels and blends are difficult for him. He knows some phonetic rules. In reading he sometimes cannot put all the sounds together to make a word. Then you or the children help him out and he continues reading?

T: Yes, till he gets stuck again.

SP: Reading doesn't seem to flow right now for him. And in his written language, he often fills in the incorrect word and has to correct it many times before getting it right.

T: Yes, well, some days. Other times he does just fine.

SP: I forgot to ask about his comprehension skills during reading. Would you tell me something about his skills in reading comprehension?

T: Well, he's not too good in making inferences. If you say, "Why did this happen?" orally he can answer the questions. But if you put it on the board, forget it. He dislikes any boardwork. I would really like to see him making connections, putting sounds together, putting thoughts behind his sentences. I'd like to know he's making connections. So is this a good case?

SP: Yes, of course it is. If we work together, I'm sure we'll come up with some ideas to help him.

T: I sure hope so. I'm afraid he'll be left back again, and then he'll end up being referred. I'd really like to help him.

SP: As I said before, if we work together, we can come up with some strategies that may help him. I'd like to look at his reading books if that's possible. Which series are you using?

T: Ginn.

(At this point, the psychologist looked at the reading text, workbook, and notebook. She asked to borrow one of his completed reading workbooks, after noticing that most of the pages had lots of *X*s on them. She and the teacher agreed that the psychologist would call in a few days to make another appointment.)

Appendix C

PART I

STEPS IN CONDUCTING
DIRECT ACADEMIC ASSESSMENT[1]

1. Determining Desired Academic Progress

The first step is to determine the rate at which typical students master the scope and sequence of a given curriculum. That becomes the criterion measure for desired progress. Three alternatives are suggested for determining criteria for desired progress. The most straightforward method for determining what is expected for typical students in a particular classroom is to ask the teacher. Usually, teachers can specify minimum expectations for average performance in their classroom curricula. A list of the sequenced objectives and approximate completion dates for each needs to be generated (e.g., see Fig. C-1).

If teachers are unable or unwilling to specify these expectations, there may be school-district criteria for minimum progress. A third way is to establish district or school norms for the curriculum based on actual performance of the children (Shinn, 1985).

After the data are obtained, a graph is constructed. The abscissa is divided into equal time units. The ordinate displays that sequence of materials or objectives for the children according to the time in which the average student is expected to master each unit. A diagonal line is drawn, from left to right, to represent average progress through that period of time in the curriculum at

---

[1](This section is largely based on the model of Deno & Mirkin, 1977)

239

issue. Figure C-2 demonstrates how average performance on phonics in one school system might be graphed, based on the scope and sequence in Figure C-1. We now have, based on this example, a picture of the expected time it takes for average pupils to progress through the four-year reading phonics curriculum.

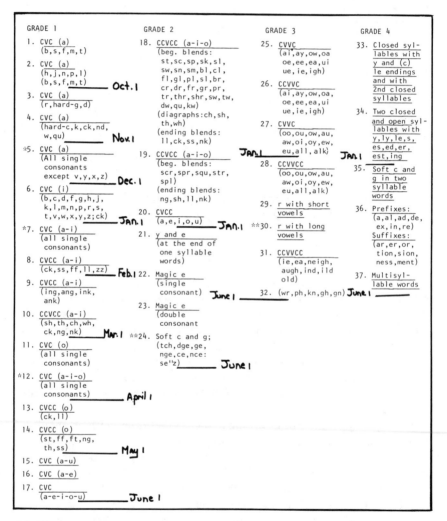

FIGURE C-1. Expected Progress for Average Students in Phonics. From "Phonetically Regular Words for Use in Teaching and Testing Both Reading and Spelling" by B. Gallistel and E. K. Ellis, 1970, *Reading and Spelling Categories,* Minneapolis, MN: Department of Psycho-educational Studies, University of Minnesota. Adapted by S. L. Deno and P. K. Mirkin in *Data-Based Program Modification: A Manual,* p. 79. Reprinted by permission.

STUDENT: *Average*
SCHOOL: *River Run*
CURRICULUM: *Phonics*

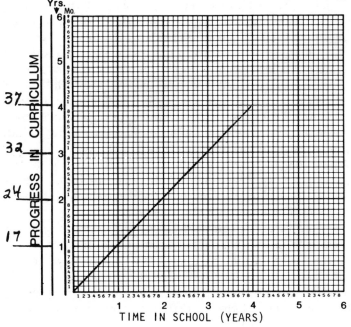

FIGURE C-2. Progress Graph for Average Students for 4-Year Phonics Sequence. River Run School. From *Data-Based Program Modification: A Manual* (p. 80) by Stanley Deno and Phyliss Mirkin, 1977 by the Leadership Training Institute/Special Education, University of Minnesota. Reprinted by permission.

2. Determining Actual Progress of Target Student

Against the measure of desired, or typical progress, the referred student's mastery level is charted. To do so, an informal classroom inventory is constructed and used to assess the pupil's progress in the curriculum area in question. The procedure can be used for any academic subject.

In reading, the examiner could, for example, choose three or more selections at random from each third of each book in the basal series. Comprehension questions are written for each selection, and the comprehension questions should reflect the types of questions asked at that grade level for assessment of comprehension. Procedures for conducting informal reading inventories can be utilized (see, e.g., Moran, 1978, pp. 41-71, any remedial reading text, or chapter 5); sometimes the basal reading series includes an informal reading inventory. Deno and Mirkin (1977) suggest using Starlin and Starlin's (1974) guidelines for establishing reading levels (these are somewhat different from the ones provided by Gickling & Havertape, 1982), which are presented in Table 5-1 in chapter 5.

Math skill progress could be assessed in a similar way, based on math series used. However, it is also possible to use a progress measure based on a skills sequence, since math is usually taught from that perspective. To begin, the examiner should prepare three sets of at least 25 problems in each skill-sequence category, each set containing five problems from the target category and one from each preceding category. The child is presented with three sets of problems from the category that represents the level in which the child would be if he or she were making average progress. The data collected are the total number of correct and incorrect digits written for each minute. (Each mark the child makes is counted, including the mark made to indicate carrying. Recording each movement/minute, based on the work of precision teachers, is done to decrease the risk of treating all problems as of equal complexity and length. Given that problems differ in length of time needed for completion due to variations in number of required operations and digits in the answer, this method is seen as more accurate.)

For each set of problems, the correct and incorrect number of responses are ordered from high to low, and medians constructed. It is the median measure of correct/incorrect rate per minute that represents progress in math. These median rates are then compared to criteria established for mastery, frustration, and instructional levels. While local norms probably need to be established, Table C-1 presents the criteria developed in one school system.

TABLE C-1
Normative Data for CBA in Reading by Grade Level

Medians: Grades 1-3		
Frustration Level	Instructional Level	Mastery Level
0-9 digits/min.	10-19 digits/min.	20 or more digits/min.
correct and/or	correct and/or	correct and
8 or more digits/min.	3-7 digits/min.	2 or fewer digits/min.
incorrect	incorrect	incorrect

Medians: Grades 4 and Above		
Frustration Level	Instructional Level	Mastery Level
0-19 digits/min.	20-39 digits/min.	40 or more digits/min.
correct and/or	correct and/or	correct and
8 or more digits/min.	3-7 digits/min.	2 or fewer digits/min.
incorrect	incorrect	incorrect

Note. From Deno and Mirkin (1977) pp. 89-90.

In each case, after mastery levels for target and average students have been established, they are plotted on the progress graph. There is now a clear picture of how the child would progress over time, compared to his or her peers, if there were no intervention.

3. Determining Desired Academic Performance for Target Student

Performance measures provide information on the child's mastery of a particular task. Again, level of task mastery is related to median student performance in that school or class. The focus is no longer on the child's place in the scope and sequence, but on evaluating baseline and change in the child's level of mastery of a particular skill.

The first step is selection of the task itself on which mastery is to be established. While the task must lend itself to being counted reliably, it must also be an objective that the student must learn in order to succeed in the curriculum. No matter which area the task is in (number of math problems computed correctly/span of time; number of letters spelled correctly in sequence/ minute; or number of letters written/ minute), the desired performance is based on classroom skills that are to be mastered in order for the child to make adequate progress through the school curriculum.

Again, norms must be established to determine what desired performance for the skill could be. A random group of 8 to 10 students should be selected, based on the teacher's evaluation of the students as average in performance of this skill. A timed sample of performance of these students on the objective of interest is then obtained. The data are summarized and arranged so that a median can be obtained to serve as the measure of desired performance *for that task in that classroom*. The performance should be graphed.

4. Determining Actual Performance of Target Student

Once the criterion for performance has been established in step 3, the target child's functioning on the task is assessed using the same procedure. Frequency and accuracy are recorded on at least three samples of performance, using three different sets of materials. Again, the data are recorded, and a median score determined. The results are plotted on the same graph as the desired performance level, so that a visual picture of the discrepancy between the child's performance and the performance of his or her average classmates can be assessed.

5. Computing Discrepancy Ratios

The final step, should this be desired for making decisions about whether to intervene or to make a determination about placement eligibility (see Deno & Mirkin, 1977, for further discussion of the use of this method for determining special education eligibility), is to compute a discrepancy ratio between desired and actual level. To determine the rate at which the student is making progress compared to other children in the school in mastering the curriculum, divide the larger of the progress levels by the smaller. For example, if the desired mastery level for beginning third grade is completion of Book G, or 18 months of progress, and the child is only reading on page 60 in Book C, which represents 4 months of progress, the equation would be:

$$\frac{18 \text{ months of progress}}{4 \text{ months of progress}} = 4.5X$$

The child in this case is progressing at a rate 4.5X less than desired for average pupils of his or her age and grade. In the time it takes the child to master one month of work, his peers are mastering four and one-half months of work.

The same equation is computed for performance. Again, the larger performance level is divided by the small one. If the median score of children in the referred child's grade is 20 math facts/minute, and the referred child's performance is 10 facts/minute, the ratio is 2.0X; that is, the child writes answers to math facts at a rate 2X less than average for his age and grade. A discrepancy ratio worksheet is used to organize the data, and the question of whether there is a discrepancy between desired and actual performance can be answered using the data. The decision then needs to be made about where intervention should be started.

PART II

Note: The formats on pages 246-259 were designed by Mary Lou Wojtusik, a learning-disabilities-resource-room teacher-consultant in the New Britain, Connecticut, School System. They were developed for use in the prereferral-intervention phase. They have been reprinted here with her permission.

ADDITION

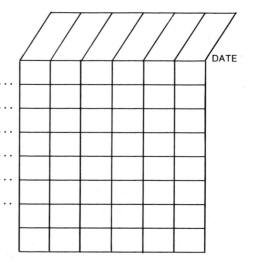

FACTS UP TO 10: No trading

1 dig.[1] + 0 ....

1 dig. + 1 dig. ....

1 dig. + 1 dig. + 1 dig. ....

2 dig. + 1 dig. ....

2 dig. + 2 dig. ....

3 dig. + 3 dig. ....

Facts memorized to:

FACTS 10 TO 18: With trading

2 dig. + 0 ....

1 dig. + 1 dig. ....

1 dig. + 1 dig. + 1 dig. ....

2 dig. + 1 dig. ....

2 dig. + 2 dig. ....

3 dig. + 3 dig. trading in ones .....

3 dig. + 3 dig. trading in tens ......

3 dig. + 3 dig. trading in ones, tens

Facts memorized to:

CORRECT +   ERROR O

_____

[1]dig. = digit

246

SUBTRACTION

FACTS TO 10: No trading

						DATE

1 dig. - 1 dig. ....

1 dig. - 0 ....

2 dig. - 1 dig. ....

2 dig. - 2 dig. ....

3 dig. - 3 dig. ....

Facts memorized to:

FACTS 10 TO 18: With trading

						DATE

2 dig. - 0 ....

2 dig. - 1 dig. ....

2 dig. - 2 dig. ....

3 dig. - 3 dig. trading in ones place

3 dig. - 3 dig. trading in tens, ones
3 dig. (0 in ones) - 3 dig. trading
   in ones ....
3 dig. (0 in tens) - 3 dig. trading
   in tens ....
3 dig. (0 in ones, tens) - 3 dig.
   trading ....

Facts memorized to:

CORRECT +   ERROR O

MULTIPLICATION

						/DATE

1 dig. x 1 dig. ....

1 dig. x 0 ....

1 dig. x 1 ....

2 dig. x 1 dig. no trading ....

2 dig. x 1 dig. trading in ones .....

3 dig. x 1 dig. trading in ones .....

3 dig. x 1 dig. trading in tens ......

3 dig. x 1 dig. trading in tens, ones

2 dig. x 2 dig. no trading ....

2 dig. x 2 dig. trading in ones .....

3 dig. x 2 dig. trading in tens, ones

Tables memorized:

CORRECT   +   ERROR   O

DIVISION

						DATE
1 dig. ÷ 1 dig. no remainder						
1 dig. ÷ 0						
0 ÷ 1 dig.						
2 dig. ÷ 1 dig. no remainder						
1 dig. ÷ 1 dig. with remainder						
2 dig. ÷ 1 dig. with remainder						
3 dig. ÷ 1 dig. no remainder						
3 dig. ÷ 1 dig. with remainder						
3 dig. ÷ 2 dig. no remainder						
3 dig. ÷ 2 dig. with remainder						
4 dig. ÷ 3 dig.						
Tables memorized:						

CORRECT   +   ERROR   O

ALPHABET CHECKLIST

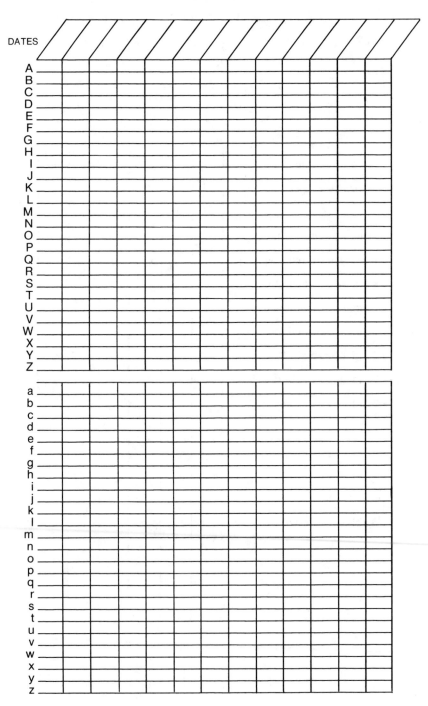

DATES

A
B
C
D
E
F
G
H
I
J
K
L
M
N
O
P
Q
R
S
T
U
V
W
X
Y
Z

a
b
c
d
e
f
g
h
i
j
k
l
m
n
o
p
q
r
s
t
u
v
w
x
y
z

CORRECT +   ERROR O

CONSONANT SOUNDS CHECKLIST

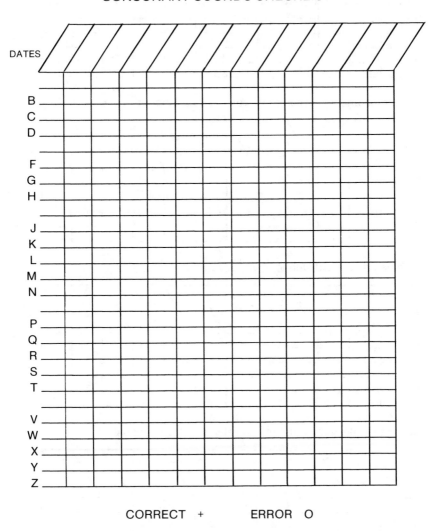

DATES

B
C
D

F
G
H

J
K
L
M
N

P
Q
R
S
T

V
W
X
Y
Z

CORRECT +   ERROR O

LONG VOWEL CHECKLIST

NAME _____

Child can give vowel sound in isolation:

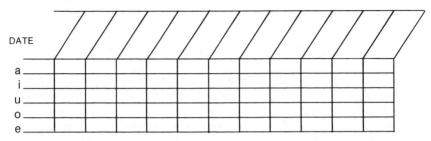

Child can name vowel sound in word said by teacher:

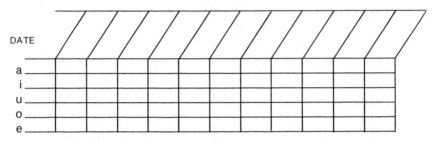

Child can read word with long vowel sound:

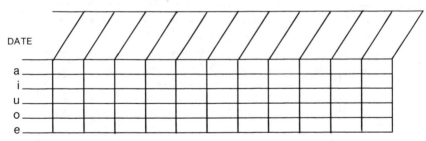

Child can write word with long vowel sound from dictation:

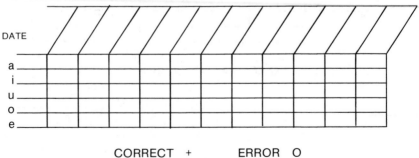

CORRECT +   ERROR O

SHORT VOWEL CHECKLIST   NAME _____

Child can give vowel sound in isolation:

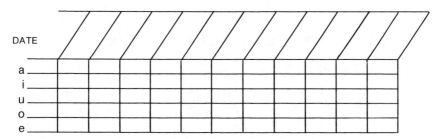

Child can name vowel sound in word said by teacher:

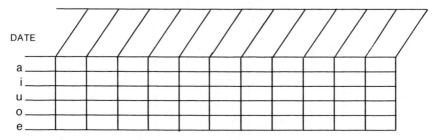

Child can read word with short vowel sound:

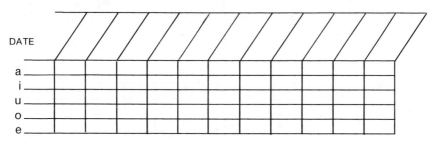

Child can write word with short vowel sound from dictation:

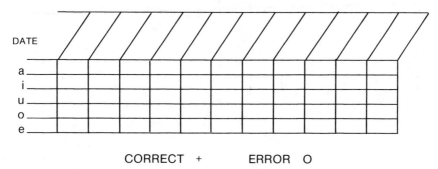

CORRECT +   ERROR O

CONSONANT DIGRAPHS CHECKLIST   NAME _____

Can give sound in isolation when teacher flashed digraph:

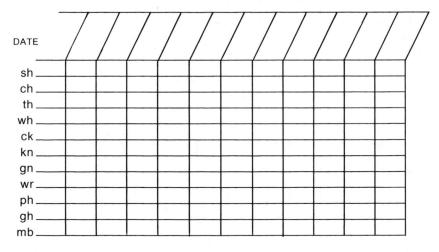

DATE

sh
ch
th
wh
ck
kn
gn
wr
ph
gh
mb

Can name digraph in word said by teacher:

DATE

sh
ch
th
wh
ck
kn
gn
wr
ph
gh
mb

Can read word with digraph:

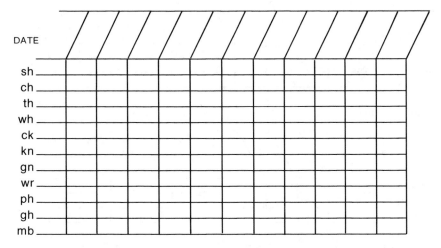

DATE

sh
ch
th
wh
ck
kn
gn
wr
ph
gh
mb

Can write word with digraph (dictation):

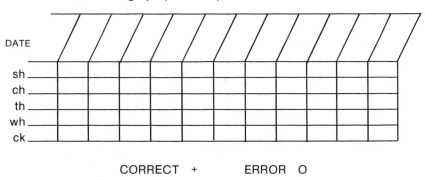

DATE

sh
ch
th
wh
ck

CORRECT +   ERROR O

BLENDS CHECKLIST

NAME _____

Can name blend at beginning of word stated by teacher:

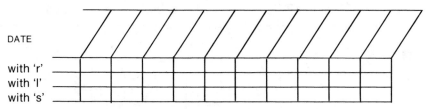

DATE

with 'r' _____
with 'l' _____
with 's' _____

Can state a word beginning with blend flashed by teacher:

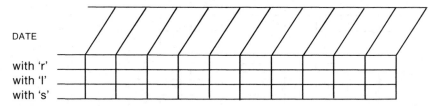

DATE

with 'r' _____
with 'l' _____
with 's' _____

Can read SV/LV words with blends:

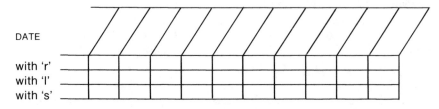

DATE

with 'r' _____
with 'l' _____
with 's' _____

Can write SV/LV words with blends:

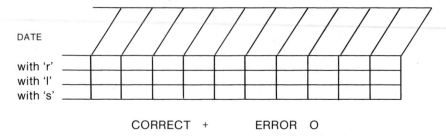

DATE

with 'r' _____
with 'l' _____
with 's' _____

CORRECT   +   ERROR   O

GINN WORDS CHECKLIST

"Fish and Not Fish"
Level 3

WORDS										DATE
eat									
fish									
*dolphin									
see									
big									
will									
*whale									
mom									
what									
this									
*shark									
where									
does									
like									
water									
grandma									
make									
do									
can't									
have									
mix									
now									
looks									
put									
need									
clay									
bake									
bread									
has									
then									
*dough									
hen									
who									
pig									
did									
cut									
help									

CORRECT +   ERROR O

*Enrichment

GINN LEVEL 3	"Fish and Not Fish"
eat	can't
fish	have
dolphin	mix
see	now
big	looks
will	put
whale	need
mom	clay
what	bake
this	bread
shark	has
where	then
does	dough
like	hen
water	who
grandma	pig
make	did
do	cut
	help

WORDLIST: NUEVA CARTILLA FONETICA

WORDS												DATE
tapa												
pito												
pato												
nota												
toma												
puse												
ese												
tomate												
tia												
asa												
esa												
tete												
tito												
lima												
mula												
lata												
sala												
pelo												
mala												
una												

CORRECT +   ERROR O

WORDS											DATE
a											
o											
e											
i											
u											
ma											
mi											
mu											
me											
mo											
pa											
po											
pe											
pi											
pu											
to											
te											
ti											
tu											
ta											

CORRECT   +   ERROR   O

Note: The following assessment tools were reprinted from: Teaching children with learning handicaps in the regular classroom, 1985, September, edited by Dr. Stan F. Shaw and Dr. Beth Kurker-Stewart, and developed for the Connecticut State Dept. of Education, Bureau of Special Education and Pupil Personnel Services, through a grant (Project no. 253-211-962-04-07) to the EASTCONN Regional Service Center.

Check consistent or frequent errors only.

Put initials of child next to errors that he or she consistently makes.

____ 1. Consonant sounds used incorrectly (specified letters missed) _____

____ 2. Vowel sounds not known (specify as above) _____

____ 3. Sounds omitted at beginning of words _____

____ 4. Sounds added at beginning of words (e.g., a blend given when single consonant required) _____

____ 5. Omission of middle sounds _____

____ 6. Omission of middle syllables _____

____ 7. Extraneous letters added _____

____ 8. Extraneous syllables added _____

____ 9. Missequencing of sounds or syllables (transposals like *from* to *form*) _____

____ 10. Reverals of whole words _____

____ 11. Endings omitted _____

____ 12. Incorrect endings substituted (*ing* for *en* or for *ed*) _____

____ 13. Auditory confusion of *m/n* or *th/f/v* or *b/p* or other similar sounds _____

____ 14. Spelling phonetic with poor visual recall of word appearance _____

____ 15. Spelling laborious, letter by letter _____

____ 16. Revisualization of very common sight words poor (e.g., *one, night, said*) _____

____ 17. Spells, erases, tries again, etc. to no avail _____

____ 18. Reversals of letter shapes *b/d* or *p/q* or *u/n* or *m/w* (specify)
_____

____ 19. Spelling so bizarre that it bears no resemblance to original; even pupil cannot read his own frequently _____

Observe also (additional hazards to problem spellers):

____ 20. Mixing of upper and lower case letters _____

____ 21. Inability to recall how to form either case for some letters
_____

____ 22. Spatial placement on line erratic _____

____ 23. Spacing between letters and words erratic _____

____ 24. Poor writing and letter formation, immature eye-hand coordination _____

____ 25. Temporal disorientation: slowness in learning time, general scheduling, grasping the sequence of events in the day and those usually known to his contemporaries _____

____ 26. Difficulty in concept formation; not able to generalize and transfer readily, to abstract "the rules and the tools" _____
_____

_____ Adds unneeded letters (e.g., dresses)

_____ Omits needed letters (hom for home)

_____ Reflects mispronunciations (pin for pen)

_____ Reflects dialectical speech patterns (Cuber for Cuba)

_____ Reverses whole words (eno for one)

_____ Reverses vowels (braed for bread)

_____ Reverses consonant order (lback for black)

_____ Reverses consonant or vowel directionality (brithday for birthday

_____ Reverses syllables (telho for hotel)

_____ phonetically spells words or parts which are not phonetic (Cawt for caught)

_____ Associates wrong sound with a given set of letters (u learned as ou in you)

_____ Used "Neographisms," such as letters without discernible relationship with dictated word

_____ Combination patterns of above

Adapted from Edgington, R. (1970). "But he spelled them right this morning!" *Academic Therapy, 3,* 59.

The following forms, developed by Shirley Berman, school psychologist in New Britain, CT, are used in the peer tutoring system that is part of a prerefferal intervention program.

Common Deficiencies in Penmanship

Defect	Example of Errors
1. Too much slant	a. Writing arm too near body
	b. Thumb too stiff
	c. Point of nib too far from fingers
	d. Paper in wrong direction
	e. Stroke in wrong direction
2. Writing too straight	a. Arm too far from body
	b. Fingers too near nib
	c. Index finger alone guiding pen
	d. Incorrect position of paper
3. Writing too heavy	a. Pressing index finger too heavily
	b. Using wrong type of pen
	c. Penholder too small in diameter
4. Writing too light	a. Pen held too obliquely or to straight
	b. Eyelet of pen turned to side
	c. Penholder too large in diameter
5. Writing too angular	a. Thumb too stiff
	b. Penholder too lightly held
	c. Movement too slow
6. Writing too irregular	a. Movement lacks freedom
	b. Movement of hand too slow
	c. Pen gripping
	d. Incorrect or uncomfortable position
7. Spacing too wide	a. Pen progresses too fast to right
	b. Excessive, sweeping lateral movement

Note. From Educational Assessment of Learning Problems by G. Wallace and S.C. Larsen, 1978, Allyn & Bacon, Inc.: Boston. Reprinted by permission.

Student Helper's Homeroom Teacher _____						
Student Helper	In Use? (pencil, please)		Available Days & Hours	PPT Member Involved	Non-PPT Member Involved	Assigned to:	
	Yes	No				Student(s)	Teacher

| Student _____ & Teacher _____ | Tutor _____ & Teacher _____ |

Schedule: Day _____ Time: from _____ to _____ Place _____
                        _____   from _____ to _____
                        _____   from _____ to _____ Materials _____

STUDENT OBJECTIVE:

Date	Activity & Progress	Date	Activity & Progress

The following form is used for monitoring cases in the Connecticut early intervention project.

Case Monitoring Form:

NAME _____   DOB: _____   GRADE _____

TEACHER _____   SCHOOL _____

PROBLEM AREA _____   STAFF ASSIGNED _____

Date	Objective(s)	Baseline Data and/or Interventions	Review Date	Student Response and Evaluation of Progress

If problem is resolved, please record signatures.

_____   _____   _____
Referring Person   Case Coordinator   Date

(Completed by Case Coordinator with teacher)

cc: Building Principal
    District Coordinator of Special Education
    Teacher

Case Monitoring Form:

NAME ___Cary Hind_____ DOB: __9/27/77__ GRADE __4_____

TEACHER ___Pat Row_____ SCHOOL ___North_____

PROBLEM AREA ___Reading_____ STAFF ASSIGNED ___KC & PR_____

Date	Objective(s)	Baseline Data and/or Interventions	Review Date	Student Response and Evaluation of Progress
2/1/87	Determine instructional level in reading	CBA in Holt reading series: Level 6: 98% Level 7: 92% (Baseline) Level 8: 83% Level 9: 78%	2/8/87	
2/8/87	Cary will be able to read vocabulary in levels 7-9 with 95% accuracy	Individual and group instruction by classroom teacher; peer tutoring and individual practice using flash cards; games, home-work assignments, writing/composing phrases and sentences using reading vocabulary. Use of ratio of 80% knowns to 20% unknowns in all drill work.	3/18/87	Mastery reached: Level 7: 99% Level 8: 97% Level 9: 98%
3/18/87	Cary will continue working using intervention technique, with monthly monitoring		4/18/87	

If problem is resolved, please record signatures.

_____   _____   _____

Referring Person   Case Coordinator   Date

(Completed by Case Coordinator with teacher)

cc: Building Principal
    District Coordinator of Special Education
    Teacher

REFERENCES

Abidin, Jr., R. R. (1975). Negative effects of behavioral consultation: "I know I ought to, but it hurts too much." *Journal of School Psychology, 13*, 51-57.

Alberto, P. A., & Troutman, A. C. (1982). *Applied behavior analysis for teachers*. Columbus, OH: Charles E. Merrill.

Alessi, G., & Kaye, J. H. (1983). *Behavioral assessment for school psychologists*. Kent, OH: National Association of School Psychologists.

Algozzine, B., Ysseldyke, J. E., & Christenson, S. (1983). An analysis of the incidence of special class placement: The masses are burgeoning. *Journal of Special Education, 17*, 141-147.

Algozzine, B., Ysseldyke, J. E., & Christenson, S., & Thurlow, M. (1982). *Teachers' intervention choices for children exhibiting different behaviors in school*. Minneapolis: University of Minnesota, Institute for Research on Learning Disabilities.

Alper, T. G., & White, O. R. (1971). The behavior description referral form: A tool for the school psychologist in the elementary school. *Journal of School Psychology, 9*, 177-181.

Alpert, J. L., & Associates. (1982). *Psychological consultation in educational settings*. San Francisco: Jossey-Bass Publishers.

Alpert, J. L., & Meyers, J. (1983). *Training in consultation*. Springfield, IL: Charles C. Thomas.

Alpert, J. L., & Trachtman, G. M. (1980). School psychological consultation in the eighties. *School Psychology Review, 9*, 234-238.

Amabile, T., & Stubbs, M. (Eds.). (1982). *Psychological research in the classroom*. New York: Pergamon Press.

Anderson, L. M. (1981, April). *Student responses to seatwork: Implications for the study of student's cognitive processing*. Paper presented at AERA, Los Angeles.

Anderson, R. C., Hiebert, E. H., Scott, J. A., & Wilkinson, I. A. G. (1985). *Becoming a nation of readers: The report of the commission on reading*. Champaign, IL: The Center for the Study of Reading.

Anderson, T. H., & Armbruster, B. B. (1986). Readable textbooks, or, selecting a textbook is not like buying a pair of shoes. In J. Orasanu (Ed.), *Reading comprehension: From research to practice* (pp. 151-162). Hillsdale, NJ: Lawrence Erlbaum Associates.

Archer, A., & Edgar, E. (1976). Teaching academic skills to mildly handicapped children. In S. Lowenbraun & J. Q. Affleck (Eds.), *Teaching mildly handicapped children in regular classes*. Columbus, OH: Charles E. Merrill.

Aronson, E. (1978). *The jigsaw classroom*. Beverly Hills, CA: Sage.

Bardon, J. (1983). Psychology applied to education: A specialty in search of an identity. *American Psychologist, 38*, 185-196.

Batsche, G. (1984). *Referral-oriented, consultative approach to assessment/decision-making*. Des Moines, IA: Iowa Department of Public Instruction.

Batsche, G. (1983). The referral oriented, consultative assessment report writing model. In J. Grimes (Ed.), *Communicating psychological information in writing* (pp. 26-43). Des Moines, IA: Iowa Department of Public Instruction.

Becker, W. (1984, March). *Direct instruction: A twenty year review*. Paper prepared for the XVI Annual Banff International Conference on Behavioral Science.

Becker, W. (1986). *Applied psychology for teachers: A behavioral cognitive approach*. Chicago: SRA.

Benjamin, R. (1981). *Making schools work*. New York: Continuum.

Bennett, N., Desforges, C., Cockburn, A., & Wilkinson, B. (1984). *The quality of pupil learning experiences*. London: Lawrence Erlbaum Associates.

Bents, R., Lakin, K. C., & Reynolds, M. (1980). *Class management*. Unpublished paper.

Bergan, J. R. (1977). *Behavioral consultation*. Columbus, OH: Charles E. Merrill.

Bergan, J. R. (1980). The structural analysis of behavior: An alternative to the learning-hierarchy model. *Review of Educational Research, 50*, 625-646.

Bergan, J. R., & Jeska, P. (1980). An examination of prerequisite relations, positive transfer among learning tasks, and variations in instruction for a seriation hierarchy. *Contemporary Educational Psychology, 5*, 203-215.

Bergan, J. R., & Schnaps, A. (1983). A model for instructional consultation. In J. Alpert & J. Meyers (Eds.), *Training in consultation* (pp. 104-119). Springfield, IL: Charles C. Thomas.

Bergan, J. R., Stone, C. A., & Feld, J. K. (1984). Rule replacement in the development of basic number skills. *Journal of Educational Psychology, 76*, 289-299.

Bergan, J. R., Towstopiat, O., Cancelli, A. A., & Karp, C. (1982). Replacement and component rules in hierarchically ordered mathematics rule learning tasks. *Journal of Educational Psychology, 74*, 39-50.

Bergin, A. (1980). Psychotherapy and religious values. *Journal of Consulting and Clinical Psychology, 48*, 95-105.

Berkowitz, M. I. (1975). *A primer on school mental health consultation.* Springfield, IL: Charles C. Thomas.

Berliner, D. C. (1985). The clinical educational psychologist: Scientist and practitioner. In J. Bergan (Ed.), *School psychology in contemporary society: An introduction* (pp. 378-393). Columbus, OH: Charles E. Merrill.

Bersoff, D., & Grieger, R. M. (1971). An interview model for the psychosituational assessment of children's behavior. *American Journal of Orthopsychiatry, 41*, 483-493.

Biklen, D. P. (1985). Mainstreaming: From compliance to quality. *Journal of Learning Disabilities, 18*, 58-61.

Block, J. H. (1971). *Mastery learning.* New York: Holt, Rinehart & Winston.

Block, P. (1981). *Flawless consulting.* Austin, TX: Learning Concepts.

Bloom, B. S. (1976). *Human characteristics and school learning.* New York: McGraw Hill.

Bloom, B. S. (1984). The 2 sigma problem: The search for methods of group instruction as effective as one-to-one tutoring. *Educational Research, 13*, 4-16.

Bloom, B. S., Englehart, M. D., Furst, E. J., Hill, W. H., & Krathwohl, D. R. (1956). *Taxonomy of educational objectives: Handbook I, Cognitive domain.* New York: Longman.

Bloome, D., & Green, J. (1985). Looking at reading instruction: Sociolinguistic and ethnographic approaches. In C. N. Hedley & A. N. Baratta (Eds.), *Context of reading* (pp. 167-184). Norwood, NJ: Ablex Publishing Corporation.

Boehm, A. (1986). *Boehm test of basic concepts-Revised.* San Antonio, TX: The Psychological Corporation.

Boehm, A. E., & Weinberg, R. A. (1977). *The classroom observer: A guide for developing observation skills.* New York: Teachers College Press.

Bohlmeyer, E. M., & Burke, J. P. (1987). Selecting cooperative learning techniques: A consultative strategy guide, *School Psychology Review, 16*, 36-49.

Brickman, P., Rabinowitz, V. C., Karuza, Jr., J., Coates, D., Cohn, E., & Kidder, L. (1982). Models of helping and coping. *American Psychologist, 37*, 368-384.

Brillant, J. (1986). Parenting style and children's sutained instrinsic motivation subsequent to receiving extrinsic rewards. Unpublished doctoral dissertation, Fordham University, New York.

Brofenbrenner, U. (1976). The experimental ecology of education. *Teachers College Record, 78*, 157-204.

Brown, V., Hammill, D., & Wiederholt, T. J. (1978). *The test of reading comprehension.* Austin, TX: Pro-Ed.

Burton, R. (1982). Diagnosing bugs in simple procedural skills. In D. Sleeman & J. Brown (Eds.), *Intelligent tutoring systems* (pp. 157-183). New York: Academic Press.

Cancelli, A. A., Bergan, J. R., & Jones, S. (1982). Psychometric and instructional validation approaches in the hierarchical sequencing of learning tasks. *Journal of School Psychology, 20*, 232-243.

Caplan, G. (1970). *The theory and practice of mental health consultation.* New York: Basic Books.

Chall, J. (1983). Literacy: Trends and explanations. *Educational Researcher, 12*, 3-8.

Chandy, J. (1974, August). *The effects of an in-service orientation on teacher perception and use of the mental health consultant.* Paper presented at the annual meeting of the American Psychological Association, New Orleans.

Checkland, P. (1981). *Systems thinking, systems practice.* Chichester, England: Wiley.

College Board (1986). *DRP handbook.* New York: Author.

College Board (1985). *Readability report* (7th Ed.). New York: Author.

Colson, D., & Coyne, L. (1978). Variation in staff thinking on a psychiatric unit. *Bulletin of the Menninger Clinic, 42*, 414-422.

Conoley, J. C., & Conoley, C. (1982). *School consultation: A guide to practice and training.* New York: Pergamon Press.

Cordes, C. (1986, April). Assessment in San Francisco. *Monitor, 17*, 16-17.

Costanzo, M., Archer, D., Aronson, E., & Pettigrew, T. (1986). Energy conservation behavior: The difficult path from information to action. *American Psychologist, 41*, 521-528.

Cronbach, L. J. (1975). Beyond the two disciplines of scientific psychology. *American Psychologist, 30*, 116-127.

Dardig, J., & Heward, W. (1984). *Sign here* (2nd Ed.). Bridgewater, NJ: Fournies & Associates.

Dawson, P. (1986). Alternative service delivery: From vision to reality. *Communique, 14 (7-8)*, 1, 7.

Deno, S. (1985). Curriculum-based measurement: The emerging alternative. *Exceptional Children, 52*, 219-232.

Deno, S., Marston, D., & Mirkin, P. K. (1982). Valid measurement procedures for continuous evaluation of written expression. *Exceptional Children, 48*, 368-371.

Deno, S., & Mirkin, P. (1977). *Data-based program modification: A manual.* Reston, VA: Council for Exceptional Children.

Deno, S. L., Mirkin, P. K., & Chiang, B. (1982). Identifying valid measures of reading. *Exceptional Children, 49*, 36-45.

Deno, S. L., Mirkin, P. K., Lowry, L., & Kuehnle, K. (1980). *Relationships among simple measures of spelling and performance on standardized achievement tests* (Research Report No. 21). Minneapolis: University of Minnesota, Institute for Research on Learning Disabilities. (ERIC Document Reproduction Service No. ED 197 508).

DePaulo, B. M., & Fisher, J. D. (1980). The costs of asking for help. *Basic and Applied Social Psychology, 1*, 23-35.

DHEW (1977, December 29). *Assistance to states for education of handicapped children: Procedures for evaluating specific learning disabilities. Part III.* Federal Register.

Dickinson, D. J., & Adcox, S. (1984). Program evaluation of a school consultation program. *Psychology in the Schools, 21*, 336-342.

Dillon, J. T. (1979). Defects of questioning as an interview technique. *Psychology in the Schools, 16*, 575-580.

Donaldson, M. (1978). *Children's minds.* New York: W. W. Norton & Company.

Doyle, W. (1979). Making managerial decisions in classrooms. In D. L. Duke, (Ed.), *Classroom management* (pp. 42-74). Chicago: University of Chicago Press.

Doyle, W. (1985). The knowledge base for adaptive instruction: A perspective from classroom research. In M. C. Wang & H. J. Walberg (Eds.), *Adapting instruction to individual differences* (pp. 91-102). Berkeley, CA: McCutchan Publishing Corporation.

Doyle, W., & Ponder, G. A. (1977-78). The practicality ethic in teacher decision-making. *Interchange, 8*, 1-12.

Dunn, R., & Dunn, K. (1972). *Practical approaches to individualizing instruction.* West Nyack, NY: Parker Publishing Company.

Durkin, D. (1978-79). What classroom observations reveal about reading comprehension instruction. *Reading Research Quarterly, 15*, 481-533.

Edington, R. (1970). But he spelled it right this morning. *Academic Therapy, 3*, 58-59.

Egan, G. (1986). *The skilled helper* (3rd ed.). Monterey, CA: Brooks/Cole.

Elkind, D. (1976). Child development in educational settings. *Educational Psychologist, 12,* 49-58.

Emmer, E. T., Evertson, C. M., Sanford, J. P., Clements, B. S., & Worsham, M. E. (1984). *Classroom management for secondary teachers.* Englewood Cliffs, NJ: Prentice-Hall.

Englert, C. S. (1984, October). Measuring teacher effectiveness from the teacher's point of view. *Focus on Exceptional Children.* Denver: Love Publishing Company.

Engelmann, S. (1969). *Conceptual learning.* San Rafael, CA: Dimensions Publishing Company.

Engelmann, S., & Carnine, D. (1982) *Theory of instruction.* New York: Irvington Publishers.

Evertson, C. (1976). *Learning from teaching.* Boston: Allyn & Bacon.

Evertson, C. M., Emmer, E. T., Clements, B. S., Sanford, J. P., & Worsham, M. E. (1984). *Classroom management for elementary teachers.* Englewood Cliffs, NJ: Prentice-Hall.

Farr, R., Carey, R., & Tone, B. (1986). Recent theory and research into the reading process: Implications for reading assessment. In J. Orasanu (Ed.), *Reading comprehension: From research to practice* (pp. 135-149). Hillsdale, NJ: Lawrence Erlbaum Associates.

Ferster, C. B., & Hammer, C. E., Jr. (1966). Synthesizing the components of arithmetic behavior. In W. K. Honig (Ed.), *Operant behavior: Areas of research and application* (pp. 634-676). New York: Appleton-Century-Crofts.

Feuerstein, R. (1979). *The dynamic assessment of retarded performers.* Baltimore: University Park Press.

Floden, R. E. (1985). The role of rhetoric in changing teachers' beliefs. *Teaching and teacher education, 1,* 19-32.

Ford, L., & Rosenfield, S. (1980). An intervention in a "special" class. *School Psychology Digest, 9,* 99-103.

Gagné, R., & Briggs, L. (1979). *Principles of instructional design* (2nd Ed.). New York: Holt, Rinehart & Winston.

Gagné, R., & Dick, W. (1983). Instructional psychology. *Annual Review of Psychology, 34,* 261-295.

Galagan, J. E. (1985). Psychoeducational testing: Turn out the lights, the party's over. *Exceptional Children, 52,* 288-298.

Germann, G., & Tindal, G. (1985). An application of curriculum-based assessment: The use of direct and repeated measurement. *Exceptional Children, 52,* 244-265.

Gettinger, M. (1984). Individual differences in time needed for learning: A review of literature. *Educational Psychologist, 19,* 15-29.

Gickling, E., & Havertape, J. (1982). *Curriculum-based assessment* (self-study format, C. Righi & F. Rubinson, Eds.). Minneapolis: National School Psychology Inservice Training Network.

Glaser, R. (1985a). Foreword. In R. C. Anderson, E. H. Hiebert, J. A. Scott, & I. A. G. Wilkinson. *Becoming a nation of readers* (v-viii). Champaign, Il: The Center for the Study of Reading.

Glaser, R. (1985b, October). *The integration of instruction and testing.* Paper presented at the ETS Invitational Conference on the Redesign of Testing for the 21st Century, New York.

Goodwin, D. L., & Coates, T. J. (1977). The teacher-pupil interaction scale: An empirical method for analyzing the interactive effects of teacher and pupil behavior. *Journal of School Psychology, 15,* 51-59.

Goodwin, W. L., & Driscoll, L. A. (1980). *Handbook for measurement and evaluation in early childhood education.* San Francisco: Jossey-Bass.

Gordon, E. W., DeStefano, L., & Shipman, S. (1985). Characteristics of learning persons and the adaptation of learning environments. In M. C. Wang & H. J. Walberg (Eds.). *Adapting instruction to individual differences* (pp, 44-65). Berkeley, CA: McCutchan Publishing Corporation.

Graden, J. L., Casey, A., & Christenson, S. L. (1985). Implementing a prereferral intervention system: Part I. The model. *Exceptional Children, 51*, 377-384.

Griffen, G. A., Barnes, S., O'Neal, S., Edwards, S. A., Defino, M. D., & Hukill, H. (1984). *Changing teacher practice: Executive summary of an experimental study.* Austin: University of Texas, Research and Development Center for Teacher Education.

Grimes, J. (Ed.). (1985). *School psychology innovations: Resources for inservice training.* Des Moines: Iowa Department of Public Instruction.

Grimes, L. (1981). Error analysis and error correction procedures. *Teaching Exceptional Children, 14*, 17-20.

Gutkin, T. B. (1980). Teacher perceptions of consultation services provided by school psychologists. *Professional Psychology, 11*, 637-642.

Gutkin, T. B., Singer, J. H., & Brown, R. (1980). Teacher reactions to school-based consultation services: A multivariate analysis. *Journal of School Psychology, 18*, 126-134.

Hanson, J., Kuralt, S., & Rosenfield, S. (1987, March). A comparison of communication strategies used in problem referral interviews by child study teams and individual consultants. Paper presented at meeting of The National Association of School Psychologists, New Orleans.

Haring, N., & Gentry, N. D. (1976). Direct and individualized instructional procedures. In N. Haring & R. Schiefelbusch (Eds.). *Teaching special children* (pp. 72-111). New York: McGraw-Hill.

Harris, A. J. (1979). The effective teacher of reading, revisited. *The Reading Teacher, 33*, 135-140.

Hartmann, D. P. (1984). Assessment strategies. In D. H. Barlow & M. Hersen (Eds.). *Single case experimental design: Strategies for studying behavior change* (2nd ed., pp. 107-139). New York: Pergamon Press.

Hartmann, D. P. (Ed.). (1982). *Using observers to study behavior.* San Francisco: Jossey-Bass.

Hasselbring, T. S. (1984). Computer-based assessment of special-needs students. *Special Services in the Schools, 1*, 7-19.

Hasselbring, T. (1983). *Computerized test of reading comprehension* (computer program). Nashville, TN: Expert Systems Software.

Hasselbring, T., & Kinzer, C. (1984). *Computerized cloze procedure* (Computer program). Nashville, TN: Expert Systems Software.

Haupt, E. J., Van Kirk, V. J., & Terraciano, T. (1975). An inexpensive fading procedure to decrease errors and increase retention of number facts. In E. Ramp & G. Semb (Eds.), *Behavior analysis: Areas of research and application* (pp. 225-232). Englewood Cliffs, NJ: Prentice-Hall.

Hiebert, J., & Wearne, D. (1985). A model of students' decimal computation procedures. *Cognition and Instruction, 2*, 175-205.

Homme, L. (1970). *How to use contingency contracting in the classroom.* Champaign, IL: Research Press.

Hood, P. & Blackwell, I. (1976). *The educational information market study.* San Francisco: Far West Laboratory for Educational Research and Development.

Huberman, M. (1983). Recipes for busy kitchens: A situational analysis of routine knowledge use in schools. *Knowledge: Creation, Diffusion, Utilization, 4*, 478-510.

Huberman, M., & Miles, M. (1984). *Innovation up close.* New York: Plenum Press.

Idol-Maestas, L. (1983). *Special educator's consultation handbook.* Rockville, MD: Aspen Systems Corporation.

Jencks, J., Smith, M., Acland, H., Bane, M. J., Cohen, D., Gintis, H., Heyns, B., & Michelson, S. (1972). *Inequality: A reassessment of family and schooling in America.* New York: Basic Books.

Jenkins, J. R., & Pany, D. (1978). Standardized achievement tests: How useful for special education? *Exceptional Children, 44*, 448-453.

Johnson, D. W., & Johnson, R. T. (1975). *Learning together and alone*. Englewood Cliffs, NJ: Prentice-Hall.

Karniol, R., & Ross, M. (1977). The effect of performance-relevant and performance-irrelevant rewards on children's intrinsic motivation. *Child Development, 48*, 482-487.

Kazdin, A. E. (1981). Acceptability of child treatment techniques: The influence of treatment efficacy and adverse side effects. *Behavior Therapy, 12*, 493-506.

Kazdin, A. E. (1980a). Acceptability of alternative treatments for deviant child behavior. *Journal of Applied Behavior Analysis, 13*, 259-273.

Kazdin, A. E. (1980b). Acceptability of time-out from reinforcement procedures for disruptive child behavior. *Behavior Therapy, 11*, 329-344.

Kendall, P. C., Padawer, W., Zupan, B., & Braswell, L. (1985). Developing self-control in children: The manual. In P. Kendall & L. Braswell (Eds.), *Cognitive-behavioral therapy for impulsive children*. New York: Guilford Press.

Kennedy, M. (1983). Working knowledge. *Knowledge: Creation, Diffusion, Utilization, 5*, 193-211.

Kerr, M. M., & Strain, P. S. (1978). Use of precision planning techniques by teacher trainees with behaviorally disordered pupils. *Monographs in Behavior Disorders*.

Kounin, J. (1970). *Discipline and group management in classrooms*. New York: Holt, Rinehart & Winston.

Krathwohl, D. R., Bloom, B. S., & Masia, B. B. (1964). *Taxonomy of educational objectives. Handbook II: Affective domain*. New York: McKay.

Kratochwill, T. R., & Severson, R. A. (1977). Process assessment: An examination of reinforcer effectiveness and predictive validity. *Journal of School Psychology, 15*, 293-300.

Kratochwill, T. R., & Van Someren, K. R. (1985). Barriers to treatment success in behavioral consultation: Current limitations and future directions. *Journal of School Psychology, 23*, 225-239.

Langer, J. A. (1983). How readers construct meaning: An analysis of reader performance on standardized test items. In R. Freedle (Ed.), *Cognitive and linguistic analysis of test performance*. Norwood, NJ: Ablex.

Leventhal, B., & McCarron, R. (1985). *Writing transition stories for a basal reading series*. Unpublished paper.

Leyton, F. S. (1983). *The extent to which group instructions supplemented by mastery of the initial cognitive prerequisites approximate the learning effectiveness of 1-to-1 tutorial methods*. Unpublished doctoral dissertation, University of Chicago.

Lidz, C. S. (1981). *Improving assessment of school children*. San Francisco: Jossey-Bass.

Lindsley, O. R. (1971). Precision teaching in perspective: An interview with Ogden R. Lindsley. *Teaching Exceptional Children, 3*, 114-119.

Lindsley, O. R. (1984, March). *The history of precision teaching*. Paper presented at the XVI Annual Banff International Conference on Behavioral Science, Banff, Alberta.

Littlejohn, S. W. (1978). *Theories of human communication*. Columbus, OH: Charles E. Merrill.

Luft, J. (1969). *Of human interaction*. Palo Alto, CA: National Press Books.

Lytle, S. (1982). *Exploring comprehension style: A study of twelfth-grade readers' transactions with text*. Unpublished doctoral dissertation, University of Pennsylvania.

Mager, R. F. (1962). *Preparing instructional objectives*. Palo Alto, CA: Fearon.

Marston, D., & Magnusson, D. (1985). Implementing curriculum-based measurement in special and regular education settings. *Exceptional Children, 52*, 266-276.

Matalon, T. (1987, March). A case study comparing psycho-educational assessment and instructional consultation. Paper presented at meeting of National Association of School Psychologists, New Orleans.

McCloyd, V. C. (1979). The effects of extrinsic rewards of differential value on high and low intrinsic interest. *Child Development, 50*, 1010-1019.

McKellar, N., & Hartshorne, T. S. (1986, April). *Information desired by teachers in instructional consultation.* Paper presented at the meeting of the National Association of School Psychologists, Hollywood, FL.

McDermott, R. P., & Hood, L. (1982). Institutionalized psychology and the ethnography of schooling. In P. Gilmore & A. A. Glatthorn (Eds.), *Children in and out of school: Ethnography and education* (pp. 232-249). Washington, D.C.: Center for Applied Linguistics.

Messick, S. (1984). Assessment in context: Appraising student performance in relation to instructional quality. *Educational Research, 13,* 3-8.

Meyers, J. (1985, August). *Diagnoses diagnosed: 1985.* Paper presented at the Meeting of the American Psychological Association, Los Angeles.

Meyers, J., & Alpert, J. (1983). So that's what happened to consultation training. In J. Alpert & J. Meyers (Eds.), *Training in consultation* (pp. 221-231). Springfield, IL: Charles C. Thomas.

Meyers, J., Parsons, R. D., & Martin, R. (1979). *Mental health consultation in the schools: A comprehensive guide for psychologists, social workers, psychiatrists, counselors, educators, and other human services professionals.* San Francisco: Jossey-Bass.

Moran, M. R. (1978). *Assessment of the exceptional learner in the regular classroom.* Denver: Love Publishing Company.

Morris, R. J. (1985). *Behavior modification with exceptional children.* Glenview, IL: Scott, Foresman, & Company.

Moyer, J. R., & Dardig, J. C. (1978). Practical task analysis for special educators. *Teaching Exceptional Children, 11,* 16-18.

Munby, H. (1981, December). *The place of teachers' beliefs in research on teacher thinking and decision making and an alternative methodology.* (Report No. 9042). Austin, TX: Research and Development Center for Teacher Education.

National Association of School Psychologists. (1985, April). *Advocacy for appropriate educational services for all children: A position statement.* Author.

National Commission on Excellence in Education. (1983). *A nation at risk: The imperative for educational reform.* Washington, DC: U.S. Government Printing Office.

Neef, N. A., Iwata, B. A., & Page, T. J. (1980). The effects of interspersal training versus high-density reinforcement on spelling acquisition and retention. *Journal of Applied Behavior Analysis, 13,* 153-158.

New Jersey State Department of Education. (1986, January). *A plan to revise special education in New Jersey.* Trenton, NJ: Author.

Ownby, R. L., & Wallbrown, F. H. (1983). Evaluating school psychological reports, Part I: A procedure for systematic feedback. *Psychology in the Schools, 20,* 41-45.

Paine, S. C., Radicchi, J., Rosellini, L. C., Deutchman, L., & Darch, C. B. (1983). *Structuring your classroom for academic success.* Champaign, IL: Research Press.

Parsons, R. D., & Meyers, J. (1984). *Developing consultation skills.* San Francisco: Jossey-Bass Publishers.

Paskewicz, C. (1984, April). *When behavioral consultation fails.* Paper presented at the Meeting of the National Association of School Psychologists, Philadelphia.

Perrow, C. (1985). Review essay: Overboard with myth and symbols. *American Journal of Sociology, 91,* 151-155.

Peterson, P. L., Swing, S. R., Stark, K. D., & Wass, G. A. (1984). Students' cognitions and time on task during mathematics instruction. *American Educational Research Journal, 21,* 487-515.

Piersal, W., & Gutkin, T. (1983). Resistance to school-based consultation: A behavioral analysis of the problem. *Psychology in the Schools, 20,* 311-320.

Reschly, D. J., & Genshaft, J. (1986, April). *Preliminary report: Survey of NASP leadership and practitioner members on selected issues.* Unpublished paper.

Resnick, L. B. (1981). Instructional psychology. *Annual Review of Psychology, 32,* 659-704.

Reynolds, M. C., & Wang, M. (1983). Restructuring special school programs: A position paper. *Policy Studies Review, 2,* 189-212.

Rogers, E. (1983). *Diffusion of innovations* (3rd ed.). New York: Free Press.

Rogers, E., & Shoemaker, F. (1977). *Communication of innovation: A cross-cultural approach.* New York: Free Press.

Rosenfield, S. (1984, August). *Instructional Consultation.* Paper presented at American Psychological Association, Toronto.

Rosenfield, S. (1985a). Management of instruction. In J. Ysseldyke, (Ed.), *School psychology: State of the art* (pp. 97-104). Minneapolis: National School Psychology Inservice Training Network.

Rosenfield, S. (1985b). Teacher acceptance of behavioral principles. *Teacher education and special education, 8,* 153-158.

Rosenfield, S. (1985c, August). *Classroom intervention.* Paper presented at Meeting of the American Psychological Association, Los Angeles.

Rosenfield, S., & Rubinson, F. (1985). Introducing curriculum-based assessment through consultation. *Exceptional Children, 52,* 282-287.

Rosenfield, S., Rubinson, F., Righi, C., LiPuma, J., & Yoshida, R. (1985). Interviewing: Communication strategies. In J. Grimes (Ed.), *School psychology innovations: Resources for inservice training.* Des Moines, IA: Iowa Department of Public Instruction.

Rosenshine, B. V. (1976). Classroom instruction. In N. Gage (Ed.), *The psychology of teaching methods.* Seventy-fifth Yearbook of the National Society for the Study of Education. Chicago: University of Chicago Press.

Rosenshine, B. V. (1980). How time is spent in elementary classrooms. In C. Denham & A. Lieberman (Eds.), *Time to learn* (pp. 107-126). Washington, DC: National Institute of Education.

Rosenshine, B., & Stevens, R. (1986). Teaching functions. In M. C. Wittrock (Ed.), *Handbook of research on teaching* (3rd ed., pp. 376-386). New York: MacMillan.

Ross-Reynolds, G. (1985). Report writing. In J. Grimes (Ed.), *School psychology innovations: Resources for inservice training.* Des Moines: Iowa Department of Public Instruction.

Ross-Reynolds, G., & Grimes, J. (1983). Three counter proposals to the traditional psychological report. In J. Grimes (Ed.). *Communicating psychological information in writing* (pp. 10-25). Des Moines: Iowa Department of Public Instruction.

Rubin, L. (1982). Instructional strategies. In H. J. Walberg (Ed.). *Improving educational standards and productivity: The research basis for policy* (pp. 161-176). Berkeley, CA: McCutchan Publishing Corporation.

Russell, R., & Ginsburg, H. (1984). Cognitive analysis of children's mathematics difficulties. *Cognition and Instruction, 1,* 217-244.

Sarason, S. (1982). *The culture of the school and the problem of change* (2nd ed.). Boston: Allyn & Bacon.

Sarason, S. (1985). *Caring and compassion in clinical practice.* San Francisco: Jossey-Bass.

Sarason, S. B., Levine, M., Goldenberg, I. I., Cherlin, D. L., & Bennett, E. M. (1960). *Psychology in community settings: Clinical, educational, vocational, social aspects.* New York: Wiley.

Saudargas, R. A., & Creed-Murrah, V. (1981). *Student/teacher observation code.* Knoxville, TN: University of Tennessee, Department of Psychology.

Schmidt, M. (1985). *A comparison of fading, anticipation, and overlearning procedures on retention of computation facts in handicapped children.* Unpublished doctoral dissertation, Fordham University, New York.

Schmuck, R. (1985). Learning to cooperate, cooperating to learn: Basic concepts. In R. Slavin, S. Sharan, S. Kagan, R. Hertz-Lazarowitz, C. Webb, & R. Schmuck (Eds.), *Learning to Cooperate, cooperating to learn* (pp. 1-4). New York: Plenum Press.

Schon, D. A. (1983). *The reflective practitioner.* New York: Basic books.

Schowengerdt, R. V., Fine, M. J., & Poggio, J. P. (1976). An examination of some bases of teacher satisfaction with school psychological services. *Psychology in the Schools, 13*, 269-275.

Shapiro, E. S., & Lentz, F. E. (1985). A survey of school psychologists' use of behavior modification procedures. *Journal of School Psychology, 23*, 327-336.

Shapiro, E. S., & Lentz, F. E. (1986). Behavioral assessment of academic behavior. In T. R. Kratochwill (Ed.), *Advances in school psychology, vol. 5*. (pp. 87-140). Hillsdale, NJ: Lawrence Erlbaum Associates.

Sharan, S., & Sharan, Y. (1976). *Small-group teaching*. Englewood Cliffs, NJ: Educational Technology Publications.

Shaw, S. F., & Kurker-Stewart, B. (1985). *Teaching children with learning handicaps in the regular classroom*. (Project No. 253-211-962-04-07). Hartford: Connecticut State Department of Education.

Shectman, F. (1979). Problems in communicating psychological understanding: Why won't they listen to me? *American Psychologist, 34*, 781-790.

Shinn, M. R. (1985, August). *Curriculum-based assessment practices for school psychologists: The development and use of local norms in special education decision-making*. Paper presented at Meeting of the American Psychological Association, Los Angeles.

Shulman, L. S. (1986a). Paradigms and research programs in the study of teaching: A conandbook of research on teaching (3rd ed., pp. 3-36). New York: MacMillan.

Shulman, L. S. (1986b). Those who understand: Knowledge growth in teaching. *Educational Researcher, 15*, 4-14.

Silverstein, S. (1974). *Where the sidewalk ends*. New York: Harper & Row.

Simon, H. (1985, August)/ *Contributions of cognitive theory to school learning*. Paper presented at the Meeting of the American Psychological Association, Los Angeles.

Slavin, R. E. (1985). An introduction to cooperative learning research. In R. Slavin et al. (Eds.), *Learning to cooperate, cooperating to learn* (pp. 5-15). New York: Plenum Press.

Slavin, R. E. (1980). *Using student team learning* (rev. ed.). Baltimore, MD: Center for Social Organization of Schools, John Hopkins University.

Slavin, R., Sharan, S., Kagan, S., Hertz-Lazarowitz, R., Webb, C., & Schmuck, R. (1985). *Learning to cooperate, cooperating to learn*. New York: Plenum Press.

Sloane, H. N., Buckholdt, D. R., Jensen, W., & Crandell, J. (1979). *Structured teaching*. Champaign, IL: Research Press.

Starlin, C., & Starlin, A. (1974). *Guides for continuous decision making*. Bemidji, MN: Unique Curriculums Unlimited.

Steely, D., & Engelmann, S. (1979). *Impementation of basic reading in grades 4-6*. Eugene, OR: Engelmann-Becker Corporation.

Stubbs, M. (1982). Conversation II: Issues in the Application of Research Results. In T. M. Amabile & M. L. Stubbs (Eds.), *Psychological research in the classroom* (pp. 21-35). New York: Pergamon Press.

Tenenbaum, G. (1982). *A method of group instruction which is as effective as one-to-one tutorial instruction*. Unpublished doctoral dissertation, University of Chicago, Chicago.

Tessler, R. C., & Schwartz, S. H. (1972). Help seeking, self-esteem, and achievement motivation: An attributional analysis. *Journal of Personality and Social Psychology, 21*, 318-326.

Thomas, A. (1985). Graphing. In J. Grimes (Ed.), *School psychology innovations: Resources for inservice training*. Des Moines: Iowa Department of Public Instruction.

Tindal, G., Wesson, C., Deno, S. L., Germann, G., & Mirkin, P. K. (1985). The Pine County model for special education delivery: A data-based system. In T. Kratochwill (Ed.), *Advances in school psychology, 4* (pp. 223-250). Hillsdale, NJ: Lawrence Erlbaum Associates.

Tolstoy, L. (1967). On teaching the rudiments. *Tolstoy on education*. (L. Weiner, Trans.). Chicago: University of Chicago Press. (Original work published 1862).

Tombari, M., & Bergan, J. (1978). Consultant cues and teacher verbalization, judgments, and expectancies concerning children's adjustment problems. *Journal of School Psychology, 3*, 212-219.

Tucker, J. A. (1985). Curriculum-based assessment: An introduction. *Exceptional Children, 52*, 199-204.

Valentine, M. (in press). *Discipline problems in the school: A practical guide.* Austin, TX: Rivercity Publishing Company.

Van Houten, R. (1979). The performance feedback system: Generalization of effects across time. *Child Behavior Therapy, 1*, 219-236.

Van Houten, R. (1980). *Learning through feedback: A systematic approach for improving academic performance.* New York: Human Sciences Press.

Walberg, H. J. (1984). Improving the productivity of America's schools. *Educational Leadership, 41*, 19-30.

Walberg, H. J. (1985). Instructional theories and research evidence. In M. C. Wang & H. J. Walberg (Eds.), *Adapting instruction to individual differences* (pp. 3-23). Berkeley, CA: McCutchan Publishing Corporation.

Wang, M. C., Gennari, P., & Waxman, H. C. (1985). The adaptive learning environments. In M. C. Wang & H. J. Walberg (Eds.), *Adapting instruction to individual differences* (pp. 191-235). Berkeley, CA: McCutchan Publishing Corporation.

Wang, M. C., Reynolds, M. C., & Walberg, H. J. (1986). Rethinking special education. Educational Leadership, *43*, 26-31.

Wang, M. C., & Walberg, H. J. (Eds.). (1985). *Adapting instruction to individual differences.* Berkeley, CA: McCutchan Publishing Corporation.

Weinstein, C. E., & Mayer, R. E. (1986). The teaching of learning strategies. In M. C. Wittrock (Ed.), *Handbook of research on teaching* (3rd ed., pp. 315-327). New York: MacMillan.

Weinstein, C. E., Zimmermann, S. A., & Palmer, D. R. (in press). Assessing learning strategies: The design and development of the LASSI. In C. E. Weinstein, E. T. Goetz, & P. A. Alexander (Eds.), *Learning and study strategies: Issues in assessment, instruction, and evaluation.* New York: Academic Press.

Weybright, F., & Avigad, R. (1984). A preventive model for SBST. *Clinical Scope, 1*, 3.

Will, M. (1986). Educating students with learning problems. A shared responsiblity. Washington, DC: U.S. Department of Education.

Winnett, R. A., & Winkler, R. C. (1972). Current behavior modification in the classroom: Be still, be quiet, be docile. *Journal of Applied Behavior Analysis, 5*, 499-504.

Witt, J. C. (1986). Teachers' resistance to the use of school-based interventions. *Journal of School Psychology, 24*, 37-44.

Witt, J. C., & Elliott, S. N. (1985). Acceptability of Classroom Intervention Strategies. In T. Kratochwill (Ed.), *Advances in school psychology, Vol. 4* (pp. 251-288). Hillsdale, NJ: Lawrence Erlbaum Associates.

Witt, J. C., & Elliott, S. N. (1983). Assessment in behavioral consultation: The initial interview. *School Psychology Review, 12*, 42-49.

Witt, J. C., Elliott, S. N., & Martens, B. K. (1984). Acceptability of behavioral interventions used in classrooms: The influence of teacher time, severity of behavior problem, and type of intervention. *Behavioral Disorders, 10*, 95-104.

Witt, J. C., Martens, B. K., & Elliott, S. N. (1984). Factors affecting teachers' judgments of the acceptability of behavioral interventions: Time involvement, behavior problem severity, and type of intervention. *Behavior Therapy, 15*, 204-209.

Witt, J. C., Moe, G., Gutkin, T. B., & Andrews, L. (1984). The effect of saying the same thing in different ways: The problem of language and jargon in school-based consultation. *Journal of School Psychology, 22*, 361-367.

Wolf, M. M. (1978). Social validity: The case of subjective measurement or how applied behavior analysis is finding its heart. *Journal of Applied Behavior Analysis, 11*, 203-214.

Woodward, A. (1986). Over-programmed materials: Taking the teacher out of teaching. *American Educator, 10*, 26-31.

Yeaton. W. H., Greene, B. F., & Bailey, J. (1981). Behavioral community psychology strategies and tactics for teaching community skills to children and adolescents. In A. E. Kazdin, & B. B. Lahey (Eds.), *Advances in Clinical Child Psychology* (vol. 4, pp. 244-288). New York: Plenum Press.

Yoshida, R., & LiPuma, J. (1985). Case management. In C. Maher (Ed.), *Professional self-management: Techniques for special services providers* (pp. 201-215). Baltimore: Paul H. Brookes.

Ysseldyke, J. E., & Christenson, S. L. (1986). *The instructional environment scale*. Austin, TX: Pro-Ed.

Ysseldyke, J. E., and Others. (1984). *School psychology: A blueprint for training and practice*. Minneapolis: National School Psychology Inservice Training Network.

Ysseldyke, J. E., Thurlow, M., Graden, J., Wesson, C., Algozzine, B., & Deno, S. (1983). Generalizations from five years of research on assessment and decision making: The University of Minnesota Institute. *Exceptional Education Quarterly, 4*, 75-93.

Zeig, J. K. (Ed.). (1982). *Eriksonian approaches to hypnosis and psychotherapy*. New York: Brunner/Mazel.

AUTHOR INDEX

SUBJECT INDEX